NARRATIVE AND NUMBERS

NARRATIVE

AND

NUMBERS

THE VALUE OF STORIES IN BUSINESS

ASWATH DAMODARAN

Columbia Business School
Publishing

Columbia University Press
Publishers Since 1893
New York   Chichester, West Sussex
cup.columbia.edu
Copyright © 2017 Aswath Damodaran
All rights reserved

Library of Congress Cataloging-in-Publication Data
Names: Damodaran, Aswath, author.
Title: Narrative and numbers : the value of stories in business /
Aswath Damodaran.
Description: New York : Columbia University Press, [2017] | Includes index.
Identifiers: LCCN 2016037437 | ISBN 978-0-231-18048-1 (cloth : alk. paper) |
ISBN 978-0-231-54274-6 (e-book)
Subjects: LCSH: Narrative inquiry (Research method) |
Business communication. | Feedback (Psychology) | Corporations—Valuation.
Classification: LCC H61.295 .D36 2017 | DDC 659.2—dc23
LC record available at https://lccn.loc.gov/2016037437

Columbia University Press books are printed on permanent
and durable acid-free paper.
Printed in the United States of America

Cover design: Diane Luger
Cover image: © Dollar Photo Club/Jalees & Smith

CONTENTS

PREFACE

As early as middle school, the world divides us into storytellers and number crunchers, and once divided, we stay in our preferred habitats. The numbers people seek out numbers classes in school, go on to numbers disciplines in college (engineering, physical sciences, accounting), and over time lose their capacity for storytelling. The storytellers populate the social science classes in school and then burnish their skills by becoming history, literature, philosophy, and psychology majors. Each group learns to both fear and be suspicious of the other, and by the time they come into my valuation class as MBA students, that suspicion has deepened into a divide that seems unbridgeable. You have two tribes, each one speaking its own language and each convinced that it has a monopoly on the truth and that the other side is the one that is wrong.

I must confess that I am more a numbers person than a storyteller and that when I first started teaching valuation, I catered almost entirely to those of my ilk. As I have wrestled with valuation questions, one of the most important lessons I have learned is that a valuation that is not backed up by a story is both soulless and untrustworthy and that we remember stories better than spreadsheets. While it did not come naturally to me, I started to animate my valuations with stories, and I have rediscovered the storytelling side that I had suppressed since sixth grade. While I am still instinctively a left-brainer, I have in a sense rediscovered my right brain. It is this experience of tying stories to numbers (or vice versa) that I have tried to bring into this book.

On a personal note, this is my first book written in the first-person singular. While you might find the repeated use of "I" and "my" off-putting and perhaps an indication of an outsized ego, I realized as I was writing about my valuations of individual companies that the stories that I was telling about those companies were my stories, reflecting not only what I thought about them and their managers but also my reading of the landscape. Thus, I will describe my attempts to tell stories about Alibaba in 2013, Amazon and Uber in 2014, and Ferrari in 2015, and to convert these stories into valuations. Rather than use the royal "we" and force you, as readers, to adopt my stories, I felt it would be much more honest (and more fun) to let you pick apart my stories and disagree with them. In fact, you can put this book to best use by taking my story about a company, say Uber, thinking about what parts of my story you disagree with, coming up with your story, and then valuing that company based on your story. A related peril of laying bare my narratives on real companies is that the real world will deliver surprises that will make each of my narratives wrong, sometimes horrendously so, over time. Rather be scared of that prospect, I welcome it, since it will allow me to revisit my stories and improve and enrich them.

I will try to wear many hats in this book. I will, of course, spend a great deal of time looking at companies as an investor from the outside and valuing them, since that is the role that I most frequently play. I will sometimes play the role of an entrepreneur or founder trying to convince investors, customers, and potential employees of the viability and value of a new business. Since I have not founded or built any multibillion-dollar companies, you may not find me convincing, but there is perhaps something of value that I can offer. In the last few chapters, I will even look at the connection between storytelling and number crunching through the eyes of top managers of publicly traded companies, with the admission again that I have not been a CEO of a company in my lifetime.

If I accomplish my objectives, a number cruncher reading this book should be able to use my template to build a narrative to back his or her valuation of a company and a storyteller should just as easily be able to take a story, no matter how creative, and convert it into numbers. More generally, I hope that the book becomes a bridge between the two tribes (storytellers and number crunchers), giving them a common language and making them both better at what they do.

NARRATIVE AND NUMBERS

1

A Tale of Two Tribes

What comes more naturally to you, storytelling or number crunching? It is a question that I start my valuation classes with, and for most of us the answer usually comes easily, because in this age of specialization, we are forced to choose between telling stories and working with numbers early in our lives, and once that choice is made, we spend years not only increasing our skills in that chosen area but also ignoring the other. If you buy into the common wisdom of the left brain governing logic and numbers and the right brain controlling intuition, imagination, and creativity, we are using only half our brains in our daily lives. I think that we can become better at using our brains, if we can start working on the side that we have let lie dormant for so long.

A Simple Test

I know it is early in the book to be doing a valuation, but let's assume that I showed you a valuation of Ferrari, the legendary luxury auto company, at the time of its initial public offering. Let's assume that this valuation takes the form of a spreadsheet with forecasted revenues, operating income, and cash flows and that the key assumptions are presented as numbers. I tell you that I expect Ferrari's revenues to grow 4 percent a year for the next five years, before dropping down to the growth rate of the economy; that the pretax operating margin will be 18.2 percent; and that the company will be able to generate €1.42 in revenues for every €1 it invests in the business. If you are not a numbers person, you are probably already lost, and even if you are, it is unlikely that you will remember the numbers for long.

Consider an alternative. I could tell you that I see Ferrari as a maker of luxury automobiles that can charge astronomically high prices for its cars and earn huge profit margins because it keeps its cars scarce and available only to an exclusive club of the very wealthy. That story is more likely to be remembered, but without specifics, it tells you little about how much you should be willing to pay for the company.

There is a third option, where I tie the low revenue growth (4 percent) to Ferrari's need to maintain its exclusivity, with that same exclusivity allowing it to generate its huge profit margins and maintain stable earnings over time, since those who buy Ferraris are so wealthy they are unaffected by the ebbs and flows of the economy that affect other automakers. By tying my numbers to a story about the company, I not only ground my numbers but also provide a forum for you to offer your own story for Ferrari, which will then yield a different set of numbers and a different value for the company. That, in a nutshell, is the endgame for this book.

The Allure of Storytelling

For centuries, knowledge was passed on from generation to generation through stories, told and retold, perhaps gathering new twists, as they tend to do, with each retelling. There is a reason that stories have such a hold over us. Stories not only help us connect with others but, as research indicates, they are far more likely to be remembered than numbers, perhaps because they trigger chemical reactions and electrical impulses that numbers do not.

Much as we love stories, though, most of us are also aware of their weaknesses. For the storytellers, it is easy to wander into fantasyland, where the line between good stories and fairy tales gets crossed. That may not be a problem if you are a novelist, but it can be a recipe for disaster if you are building a business. For those listening to stories, the danger is a different one. Since stories tend to appeal to the emotions rather than to reason, they also play on our irrationalities, leading us to do things that do not make sense but feel good, at least when we do them. In fact, as con men through the ages have discovered, nothing sells better than a good story.

There is a great deal we can learn by looking at the allure of stories and how they are sometimes used to further both good causes and bad ones. It is amazing that, given the diversity of storytelling, you find patterns in stories; great stories share commonalities, structures that get used over and over. It is also true that while some people are better storytellers than others, the craft of storytelling can be taught and learned.

As a novice to storytelling, there are three thoughts that come to mind as I look at the long and well-researched history of storytelling. The first, and most humbling, is the realization that much of what is offered as good business storytelling practice has been known for centuries, perhaps going back to primitive times. The second is that good storytelling can make a huge difference in the success of a business, especially early in its life. To be a successful business, not only do you have to build a better mousetrap, but you have to tell a compelling story about why that mousetrap will conquer the business world to investors (to raise capital), to customers (to induce purchases), and to employees (to get them to work for you). The third is that storytelling in business comes with more constraints than storytelling in novels, since you are measured not just on creativity but on being able to deliver on your promises. The real world is very much a part of your story, and much as you would like to control it, you cannot.

The Power of Numbers

For much of our history, our use of numbers was constrained by two factors: collecting and saving large amounts of data was labor-intensive and analyzing the data was difficult and expensive. With computerized databases and computational tools becoming available to the masses, the data world is getting "flatter" and more democratic, allowing us all to play number-crunching games that we could never have tried a few decades ago.

As we enter an age when numbers are gathered in cyberspace and everyone can access and analyze them, we are also seeing them displace storytelling in unexpected places. In *Moneyball*, Michael Lewis, a master storyteller who finds a way to animate even the driest business stories, tells the tale of Billy Beane, the general manager for the Oakland Athletics, a professional baseball team.[1] Beane abandoned the old tradition of listening to baseball scouts telling which young pitchers and hitters had the most potential and replaced those stories with statistics based on what worked on the field. His success has had an impact on other sports, giving birth to sabermetrics, a number-driven discipline for sports management that has adherents in almost every sport.

So why are we drawn to numbers? In a world of uncertainty, numbers offer us a sense of precision and objectivity and provide a counterweight to storytelling. That precision is often illusory, and there are uncountable ways in which bias can find its way into numbers. Notwithstanding those limitations, in investing and finance, as in many other disciplines, the number crunchers or "quants" have essentially used the power of numbers to both inform and intimidate. The crisis of 2008 was a cautionary note to those who would let common sense be overwhelmed by complex mathematical models.

Two real-world developments, huge databases that can be accessed instantaneously and powerful tools to work with that data, have tilted the balance in almost every endeavor, but particularly so in financial markets, toward numbers. These developments have come with a cost, which is that the problem that you face in investing now is not that you don't have enough data but that you have too much, often pulling you in different directions. One of the ironic consequences of this data overload is that, as behavioral economists have established conclusively, our decision making has become even more simplistic and irrational because we have all this data at our disposal. Another irony is that as numbers come to dominate so many business discussions, people are trusting them less, not more, and falling back on stories.

To use numbers well in decision making, you have to manage the data, and there are three aspects to data management. The first is that you follow simple rules in collecting data, including judgments on how much data and over what time period, and look for ways to avoid or at least minimize the biases that can find their way into that data. The second is to use basic statistics to make sense of large and contradictory data and statistical tools to fight data overload. You may be one of those people who remembers your statistics class from college fondly and puts it to good use when you have lots of numbers in front of you, but if so, you are more the exception than the rule. For too many of us, sadly, statistics is the forgotten discipline, making us vulnerable to data manipulation. Finally, you have to come up with interesting and innovative ways of presenting the data to make them understandable to those who might not grasp the statistical nuances. For those of you who are natural storytellers, this may represent a bit of a climb, but it will be time well spent.

It is easy to understand the draw of big data when companies like Amazon, Netflix, and Google use the information they accumulate about their customers not only to fine-tune their marketing but to alter their product offerings. At the same time, you have to recognize both the limits and the dangers of data-driven analysis, in which biases are hidden behind layers of numbers, imprecision is masked by precise-looking estimates, and decision makers let models make choices for them on what to do and when to do it.

Valuation as a Bridge

So let's see where we stand. We relate to and remember stories better than we do numbers, but storytelling can lead us into fantasyland quickly, a problem when investing. Numbers allow us to be disciplined in our assessments, but without stories behind them, they become weapons of intimidation and bias rather than discipline. The solution is simple. You need to bring both stories and numbers into play in investing and business, and valuation is the bridge between the two, as shown in figure 1.1.

In effect, valuation allows each side to draw on the other, forcing storytellers to see the parts of their stories that are improbable or implausible, and to fix them, and number crunchers to recognize when their numbers generate a story line that does not make sense or is not credible.

How can you adapt and control storytelling in the context of valuing businesses and making investments? You begin by understanding the company you are valuing, looking at its history, the business it operates in, and the competition, both current and potential, it may face. You then have to introduce discipline into your storytelling by subjecting your story to what I call the *3P test*, starting with the question of whether your story is *possible*, a minimal test that most stories should meet; moving on to whether it is *plausible*, a tougher test to overcome; and closing with whether it is *probable*, the most stringent of the tests. Not all stories that are possible are plausible, and among all plausible stories, only a few are probable. Until this point,

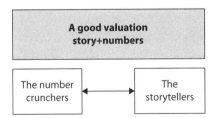

Figure 1.1
Valuation as a bridge between numbers and stories.

you are primarily on the storyteller's turf, but you now have to follow up by explicitly linking your tested story to numbers that determine value, that is, the value drivers of a business. Even the most qualitative stories about corporate culture, management quality, brand name, and strategic imperatives can and should be connected to value inputs. It is those value inputs that should become the numbers in models and spreadsheets that lead to the value assessments on which you base your decisions. There is one final step in this process, and it is one that most of us find challenging. If you tell good stories, it is natural to get attached to them and to view any questioning of those stories as an affront. While it is good to be able to defend your stories against challenges, it is also important to keep the feedback loop open, listening to comments, questions, and critiques and using them to modify, adapt, or change your story lines. Being told that you are wrong is never easy, but listening to those who disagree with you the most will make your stories stronger and better. This sequence is pictured in figure 1.2.

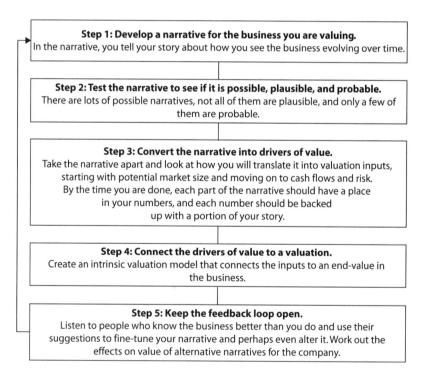

Figure 1.2
The story-to-numbers process.

This process is structured and may just be a reflection of my linear thinking and natural instincts as a number cruncher. It has worked for me and I will use it to take you through my valuations of both young, high-growth companies like Uber and mature businesses like Vale. If you are a natural storyteller, you may find this sequence to be not just rigid but also a crimp on your creativity. If so, I would strongly recommend that you develop your own sequence for getting from story to numbers.

Change Is a Constant

While every valuation starts with a story about a company, and the numbers flow from that story, the story itself will change over time. Some of this change will be the result of macroeconomic shifts, as interest rates, inflation, and the economy map out their own paths. Some will be the result of competitive dynamics, as new competitors enter, old competitors modify their strategies, and some competitors drop out of the market the company is targeting. Some story shifts can be traced to changes in management, both in terms of personnel and tactics. The bottom line is that it is hubris in storytelling (and the number crunching that emerges from it) to assume that the story you tell will remain immune from the real world.

I will classify narrative alterations into three groups: *narrative breaks*, in which real-life events decimate or end a story; *narrative changes*, in which actions or outcomes lead you to alter the story that you are telling in fundamental ways; and *narrative shifts*, in which occurrences on the ground don't change the basic story but do alter some of its details in good or bad ways. So what are the causes of narrative alterations? The first is news stories about the company, some emanating from the company and some from outsiders (regulators, analysts, journalists) who track the company. Thus, every earnings report from a company, to me, is an occasion for me to reexamine my story for that company and tweak it or change it significantly, depending on the content. Management retirements (forced or voluntary), corporate scandals, and activist investors buying shares in the company can all lead to narrative reassessments. An acquisition announcement, a stock buyback, or increasing or ceasing to pay dividends can also fundamentally change how you look at a company. The second cause is macroeconomic stories, wherein changes in interest rates, inflation, commodity prices, or even political upheavals can lead you to change the way you think about an individual company's prospects and value.

If you are an investor who likes stability in your stories (and in value), you will be uncomfortable making the changes the real world thrusts upon you, and you can react in one of two ways. The first is to restrict your investing to companies with established business models in stable markets, where your story does not change over time, and that is the path that many old-time value investors have chosen to take, pointing to the history of success that others who have taken this path have had in the past. The other is to learn to live with the discomfort of change and to accept that not only is it unavoidable but that the biggest business and investment opportunities exist in those environments where there is the most change. One reason that I am increasingly attracted to the storytelling aspect of valuation is because I have chosen the second path. In the process, I have learned that you cannot value companies prone to change using just equations and models; you also need a narrative that you can go back to when the numbers are in flux.

The Corporate Life Cycle

A construct I find useful in understanding businesses is that of the corporate life cycle. Businesses age, much like individuals, with big differences across companies in the aging process. I present my vision of the life of a business in figure 1.3.

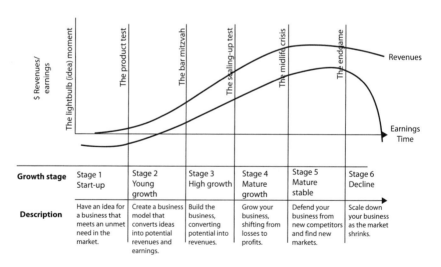

Growth stage	Stage 1 Start-up	Stage 2 Young growth	Stage 3 High growth	Stage 4 Mature growth	Stage 5 Mature stable	Stage 6 Decline
Description	Have an idea for a business that meets an unmet need in the market.	Create a business model that converts ideas into potential revenues and earnings.	Build the business, converting potential into revenues.	Grow your business, shifting from losses to profits.	Defend your business from new competitors and find new markets.	Scale down your business as the market shrinks.

Figure 1.3
The corporate life cycle.

What connection does this have with stories and numbers? Early in the life cycle, when a business is young, unformed, and has little history, its value is driven primarily by narrative, with wide differences across investors and over time. As a company ages and develops a history, the numbers start to play a bigger role in value, and the differences across investors and over time start to narrow. Using the story/number framework, I look at how the process changes over the life cycle of a firm, from start-up to liquidation.

While I will frame the book around investing and valuation, the connection between stories and numbers is just as important, if not more so, for those on the other side of the process—the founders and managers of businesses. Understanding why stories matter more at some stages of a business and numbers speak more loudly at others is critical not only for attracting investors but for managing these businesses. I hope to use this insight to look for the characteristics you would need in top managers at each stage in the process and why a great manager at one phase of the life cycle may very quickly find himself or herself out of his or her depth in a different phase.

Conclusion

Much as I would like to tell you that the rest of the book will be a breeze for you, the nature of this book makes that promise impossible to fulfill. If, as I noted earlier, my objective is to get both poets and quants to read this book, with the hope that the poets will find a way to bring numbers into their storytelling and the quants will develop a skill for telling stories that back up their numbers, each group will find one half of this book easy (because it plays to their strengths) and the other half to be more of a grind (because it is challenging the weak sides of their brains). I hope that you will both persevere and work through your struggles, and I can only offer my own experience as a guide.

I am a natural number cruncher and storytelling has never come easily to me. For most of my early years, teaching and doing valuation, I skimped on the storytelling and jumped into valuation models quickly. The first time I tried to incorporate storytelling into my valuation, the result was stilted and unconvincing (even to me), but I forced myself to keep working on my storytelling side. I will never be a Gabriel García Márquez or a Charles Dickens, but I do feel more comfortable telling tales about businesses and connecting them to valuations now. Since you will be reading some of these tales in this book, you can be the judge!

2

Tell Me a Story

We all love stories; we relate to them and we remember them. From the beginnings of recorded history, stories have been used to inform, to convince, to convert, and to sell, and it is no surprise therefore that businesses have taken to storytelling. In this chapter I look at how storytelling has been central to learning, why stories continue to have so much power over us, and why the need for storytelling has actually increased in the information age. If the first part of this chapter is about the good side of storytelling, the last part is about the dangers of runaway storytelling and how the emotional appeal of stories can lead to bad decisions.

Storytelling Through History

Stories have been with us since the very beginning of time. In 1940 a group of children in France came upon cave paintings of animals and a human being that can be traced back more than 33,000 years (to between 15,000 B.C.E. and 13,000 B.C.E.). The first printed stories, which tell the story of a Sumerian king, Gilgamesh, are from 700 B.C.E. and were recorded on stone pillars, but there is also evidence that the Egyptians wrote stories almost 3,500 years ago on papyrus. There is evidence of storytelling in every ancient civilization.

Illustrative of the staying power of these ancient stories are two classics, Homer's *Odyssey* and Aesop's fables. Homer is believed to have spun his yarn for the ages in 1200 B.C.E., predating the creation of a written Ionic Greek language by almost 500 years. Aesop lived around 550 B.C.E., and his stories were not recorded until almost 200 years after his death. Ancient religions in almost every part of the world have spread their messages through stories, whether they be the Bible, the Koran, or the Bhagavad Gita. Through much of this time, these stories were passed on from generation to generation in oral form, but in a testimonial to their power, the core of these stories stayed remarkably intact.

With the invention of the printing press, stories acquired both bigger audiences and staying power, as they took book form and traveled across many lands. That in turn allowed for the creation and nurturing of universities and formal education, though only a small proportion of people were able to read and write. These "learned" people still used the power of the spoken word to pass stories on to the unlettered. Literature majors around the world *read* Shakespeare, but it is worth remembering that his plays were written to be *performed* at the Globe Theater. The bottom line is that it is not just that the history of humanity and the history of storytelling that are entwined, but that without storytelling to carry it through time, we might not know our own history.

The Power of Stories

So what is it that gives stories their staying power? It is a question researchers have tried to answer, not only to understand the allure of stories but also in the hope of using these findings to help people tell better and more memorable stories.

Stories Connect

A well-told story connects with listeners in a way that numbers never can. The reasons for the connection are varied across both stories and listeners, and the extent of the connection can vary in intensity. In recent years scientists have turned their attention to why and are finding that the connections may be hardwired into our brains as chemical and electrical impulses.

Let's start with the chemical explanation. Paul Zak, a neuroeconomist at Claremont Graduate University, identified a neurochemical called oxytocin, a molecule in the hypothalamus of the human brain.[1] He argues that oxytocin, whose synthesis and release is associated with trust and caring, is created and released when a person listens to a powerful story (or narrative) and that this release can lead to changes in the listener's postnarrative behavior. In addition, during stressful moments in stories, the brain releases cortisol, allowing the listener to focus. Other research also finds that happy endings trigger the limbic portion of the brain, its reward center, to release dopamine, a trigger for hope and optimism.

Greg Stephens, Lauren Silbert, and Uri Hasson have a fascinating study of how electrical impulses in the brain seem to respond to storytelling in what they term "neural coupling."[2] In particular, they report on an experiment in which a young woman tells a story to twelve subjects, and the brain waves of both the storyteller and the listeners are recorded. They note two phenomena as the story is told. The first is that the brain waves of the storyteller and listeners synchronize, with the same parts of the brain lighting up for both, although there is a time lag on the part of the listeners (as they process the story). To test whether it is the story itself that made the difference, the story was told in Russian (which none of the listeners understood), and the brain wave activity ceased, thus illustrating that it is the story (and understanding it) that seems to make the connection. The second and more intriguing finding is that during some parts of the story, the listeners' brain impulses precede those of the storyteller, suggesting that involved listeners start predicting the next steps in the story. Overall, as the synchronization in brain waves between the storyteller and those listening to the story increases, communication becomes more effective.

There is one final aspect of storytelling that is worth emphasizing. Peter Guber, in his book *Tell to Win*, notes that when listeners are absorbed in a story, they become more willing to accept arguments uncritically, that is, to drop their guard.[3] Melanie Green and Tim Brock, two psychologists, argue that in these fictionalized worlds, listeners change the way they process information and that highly absorbed listeners are thus less likely to detect inaccuracies and inconsistencies in stories than are less involved listeners.[4] That allows storytellers more license to develop story lines that otherwise would have been challenged, but as we will note later in this chapter, this is a mixed blessing in business storytelling, since it is abused by con men and fraudsters.

The bottom line is that storytelling can draw in listeners and get them to act in ways that they would not have acted had they been presented with just the facts. As an added bonus, if you can get listeners to become absorbed in your stories, they are more willing to accept your assumptions and perspective, and thus your conclusions.

Stories Get Remembered

I have been teaching for more than three decades and am lucky enough to still run into students from decades past who reminisce fondly (at least in front of me) about my classes. It is astonishing how often and how well they remember the little anecdotes and stories I have scattered through my classes over time, though the details of the classes and the numbers have long been lost in the fog of their memories.

I am not unique in this experience, as studies indicate the staying power of stories. Stories get remembered much better and for longer periods than numbers. In one study, subjects were read stories and expository texts and their memory was tested later.[5] Even though the content was the same, the stories were remembered about 50 percent more than the expository passages. As to why some stories get remembered more than others, researchers hypothesize that it is causal connections within the story that make them more memorable, especially if subjects have to work to make inferences and see the connections. Thus, when subjects are given different versions of the same paragraph to read, they are less likely to remember the paragraph if the causal relationship is either too obvious or very weak, but are more likely to remember it if the causality is understated but requires some work on the part of subjects to connect.

If there is a lesson I have learned from these studies for storytellers, it is that stories work best if they not only involve listeners but require them to think on their own and make their own connections. Those connections may very well have been the ones I wanted them to make in the first place, but it is not only more effective but also more memorable if listeners make them, rather than having them force fed. As with so much else in life, when it comes to storytelling, I have discovered that less is more.

Stories Spur Action

Not only do stories allow for emotional connections between storytellers and listeners and get remembered more vividly and for longer periods, they can elicit listeners to act. As part of his research on storytelling, Paul Zak also looked at whether the increase in oxytocin, the neurochemical that he identifies as the one released during stories, was associated with actions after the stories had been told. In one experiment, in which subjects were asked to watch public service announcement videos produced by the British government, the increase in oxytocin resulting from watching the videos was measured and higher increases were associated with bigger donations to the charities mentioned in the videos.

The studies also found that some stories evoked bigger increases in neurochemicals and thus elicited more actions than others. For instance, narratives with dramatic arcs to them resulted in more responses than flat narratives, as did stories that caused viewers to become more engaged with the story characters.

The Special Case of Business Stories

If stories allow for stronger connections, are remembered longer, and spur action, it should come as no surprise that businesses have used storytelling to advance their interests with different constituent groups. With potential investors, the storytelling is designed to encourage investors to attach a high value to the business and invest their capital. With employees, the stories that businesses tell will be designed to get them excited about working for a company. With customers, business narratives are aimed at getting them to buy products and services, perhaps at premium prices. The stories told to each group may be different, and in some cases even inconsistent, a potentially troubling issue we will return to later in this book.

The most obvious use of storytelling in business is in selling and advertising. Not only are the very best salespeople effective storytellers but advertising is built on telling stories that not only prompt customers to buy your products and services but to remember (and value) brand names.

In business education, storytelling is a key part of all teaching and it has been formalized in the case study approach. Every good business case is a narrative or story that is meant to not only illustrate a key concept but also to do it in a way that students will remember that concept for long periods. As with any good story, the cases are written in ways that nudge students toward what the instructor believes is the right answer, and as with any good story, that nudging can turn to manipulation if misused.

In investing, storytelling is an integral part of both investment philosophies and recommendations. There are many investors who steer away from numbers and data and instead invest in story stocks, that is, businesses with compelling narratives. Even those analysts and investors who do look at the numbers often try to provide a structure for those numbers with stories. In sell-side equity research, for instance, it is the analysts who tell the most compelling stories about the sectors that they follow and the companies that inhabit that space who are most valued. With investment legends, it is striking that we remember famous investment feats as stories, rather than numbers. For instance, one of the most frequently repeated stories about Warren Buffett is that of his investment in 1964 in American Express. The company had been tarred by a scandal when it lent money to a commodity trader, Tino DeAngelis, who used contaminated salad oil as collateral; when the fraud was unearthed, American Express stock collapsed in value. Buffett made the assessment that the company's credit card business was not only unaffected by the scandal but worth many times more than what the company was trading for, and invested 40 percent of his investment partnership's money in the stock, which paid off as the stock rebounded. While Buffett's collective profits from this investment amounted to only $33 million, a paltry sum relative to his other winnings, the American Express story gets told and retold in value investing circles as a testimonial to how doing your research can pay off big time.

CASE STUDY 2.1: STEVE JOBS, MASTER STORYTELLER

As someone who has been a longtime Apple user, I watched Steve Jobs rise to mythical status, primarily because of his success at transforming not just Apple as a company but also the landscape of the music and entertainment businesses. While there are many aspects of the Jobs legend that you can point to, some good and some bad, one quality for which he stood out was storytelling. That quality came through in his famed annual presentations, when, clad in his signature black mock turtleneck, he used the latest Apple products to lay out his narrative for the company. In particular, his 1984 keynote (during which he introduced the Macintosh) and his 1997 presentation (during which he unveiled the iMac) stand not only as bookends to the process but showcase his ability to tell a story.

In 1984 computers were the domain of tech geeks, with the infamous Microsoft command lines separating the handful who were technologically savvy from those who were not. Steve Jobs saw a future in which the rest of the world would have to use computers and would have neither the willingness nor the inclination to learn these commands. Using the traditional desktop and file folders as his devices, his narrative was one that saw the computer as a tool that anyone would be able to use just as easily as they moved papers on their desks. In 1997 the world had bought into the idea of computers as essential business tools, useful for churning out documents and spreadsheets much more efficiently than typewriters. Again, Steve Jobs used the iMac, with its quirky shape and coloring, to tell the story of computers as vehicles for delivering music and entertainment into homes, laying the foundations for Apple's rise in the following decade.

Note that these two instances also illustrate another important truth about business storytelling. The stories that Steve Jobs told on both occasions were compelling and forward looking, but he (and Apple) did not benefit from the 1984 story reset. In fact, the Macintosh floundered under the weight of design choices and software limits, some of which arose from Jobs's own weaknesses, and it was Microsoft that learned the lesson, redesigned Windows, and almost drove Apple into oblivion. The 1997 launch of the iMac took a while to bear fruit and it was only five or six years after that Apple was able to reap any benefits. The lesson to be learned is that good storytelling is an integral part of building a business, but even the most compelling stories do not guarantee riches and rewards.

Storytelling in a Technology/Data Age

This should be the golden age for numbers, with increased access to immense amounts of data (big data) and improved data-analytic tools and machine power, and as we will see in the next chapter, there are signs that it is. Ironically, though, it is exactly this surge in number-crunching and computing powers that has created a greater demand for good storytelling, often as a counterpoint to masses of numbers. As we have access to more information, there is evidence that it is having the adverse effect of making it harder to retain that information. Assaulted by data overload, our brains stop processing the data and, as a *Scientific American* article points out, we are increasingly using the Internet as an external hard drive for our memories.[6] In an article in the *New York Times*, John Huth argues that our reliance on technology has made us break knowledge into pieces and lose sight of the big picture, perhaps creating a space for storytelling to fill.[7] I don't know whether these or other explanations hold water, but in financial markets, increased access to information has made investors feel less comfortable, not more so, when they make judgments. There is evidence that it has exacerbated many of the behavioral problems that have always afflicted investment decision making. As a consequence, investors seem to be more drawn to good storytelling now than in generations past.

We are also subject to more distractions in our lives, some digital but some not, and those are having an effect on how much attention we pay to what is happening around us. In fact there is evidence that as we increasingly multitask our way through the day, not only are we missing much of what is happening around us but the memories we form tend to be less robust and thus more difficult to retrieve. Again, storytelling may be what gets us to pay attention and remember.

Finally, the growth of social media has expanded the scope for storytelling. Not only do we have much larger audiences for our stories (all those Facebook friends), but there is always a chance that one or more of these stories can go viral, spreading across the globe at breathtaking speed. Businesses are quickly tapping into this trend as they try to get their stories on social media and spread virally. My colleague, Scott Galloway, has a Digital IQ Index that he uses to measure how companies are faring in digital space, and it is clear that those that lag are redoubling their efforts (and spending more money) to catch up.

The Dangers of Storytelling

As we noted in an earlier section, stories are powerful because they connect with people's emotions, get remembered, and elicit action from listeners. It is for each of these reasons that stories can be extremely dangerous, not just for listeners but also for storytellers. If the last section made a case for telling and listening to stories, you should consider this section a cautionary one about the dangers of letting stories alone drive decisions.

The Emotional Hangover

When master storytellers create fictional lands and take us to them, the perils of setting aside skepticism and following them into these lands are small. Thus, I can spend a weekend in J. R. R. Tolkien's Middle-earth or J. K. Rowling's Hogwarts and emerge none the worse for the immersion, and perhaps inspired by their creativity. In business, we face a different test for storytelling, since we are investing, accepting employment offers, or buying products, and if we make these decisions based just on stories, we are risking a great deal more.

The field of behavioral economics is of recent origin and represents the intersection of psychology and economics. Put succinctly, behavioral economics lays bare all of the quirks in human nature that lead people to make bad decisions, especially if they base these decisions on emotion, instinct, and gut feeling. Daniel Kahnemann, a father of this field, takes us on a romp through the fields of human irrationality in his book *Thinking, Fast and Slow* and notes some of the biases we bring to decision-making processes that stories can easily exploit.[8]

It is not just listeners, though, who are in danger of letting emotions run away from the facts. Storytellers face the same problem, as they start to believe their own stories and perhaps act on them. In effect, stories feed into the biases we already have, reinforce them, and make them worse. As Tyler Cowen pointed out in a TED Talk critiquing the wave of popular psychology books asking people to trust their instincts:

> The single, central, most important way we screw up [is that] we tell ourselves too many stories, or we are too easily seduced by stories. And why don't these books tell us that? It's because the books them-selves are all about stories. The more of these books you read, you're learning about some of your biases, but you're making some of your other biases essentially worse. So the books themselves are part of your cognitive bias.[9]

In an earlier section, I noted that one of the benefits of storytelling is that as listeners get more absorbed in stories, they tend to become much more willing to suspend disbelief and let questionable asser-tions and assumptions go unchallenged. Much as that may be a plus for storytellers, it is exactly what allows con men and fraudsters, usually master storytellers, to spin tales of big riches and separate listeners from their money. Quoting Jonathan Gotschall, "Master storytellers want us drunk on emotion so we will lose track of rational considerations and yield to their agenda," a benefit for a moviemaker but not a worthy testimonial for a business story.[10]

The Fickleness of Memory

It is true that many storytellers draw on personal memories in coming up with their stories, and if they tell their stories effectively, these stories will be remembered for far longer. As researchers are discovering, human memories are fragile and easily manipulated. In one study, researchers were able to convince 70 percent of their subjects that they had committed crimes as adolescents that resulted in police action, when in fact none of them had done so.[11] In another study, researchers were able to leave their subjects with the memory (false) of having been lost in a shopping mall as children, even though they had not.[12]

To the extent that business stories are often built around the experiences of the storytellers, it is easy to cross the line between real and imagined experiences. Founders who invent improbable rises from poverty, portfolio managers who claim to have had the foresight to get out just ahead of market collapses, and CEOs who invent struggles with nonexistent business challenges may, with repeated retelling of their stories, start believing them. This is not to suggest that stories are always made up or full of falsehoods but to show that even well-meaning storytellers can sometimes reinvent their memories and that those listening to those stories might not be remembering the stories the way they were actually told.

Numbers, the Antidote

A key difference between a story told purely to entertain and a business story is that the latter is (or should be) bounded by reality and the real world does not reward business storytellers for just being creative. In fact one of the perils of letting storytelling drive business decisions is that it is easy to cross the line and wander into fantasyland. In business storytelling, this can manifest itself in dysfunctional forms:

- The fairy tale: This is a business story that follows the standard script for the most part, but at some point in the story, the narrator lets his or her hopes replace expectations and the creative juices flow. Not surprisingly, these stories end well, with the narrator emerging the victor with a successful business as bounty.
- The runaway story: A close relative of the fairy tale, this story sounds so good and the protagonist is so likable that listeners overlook major gaps in the story or failures of logic because they want the story to be true.

The bottom line is that storytelling left unchecked can easily lose focus, and in the context of business stories, that can be dangerous for everyone involved.

If stories play to emotions and past experiences are skewed sometimes by false memories, you can see the advantages of introducing numbers into the conversation. When a storyteller has wandered into fantasyland, the easiest way to bring him or her back to Earth is with data that suggests the journey is either impossible or improbable. Similarly, when a story is so powerful that it overwhelms listeners, all it may take are a few pragmatic questions about what it will take to deliver the promised outcomes to bring listeners back to their senses.

CASE STUDY 2.2: THE CON GAME—STORYTELLING WITH A SUBVERSIVE END

Con games are as old as human existence, but what is it that allows them to survive? And what makes some con games so much better than others? While there are many answers, the one common element that all con artists seem to share is that they are master storytellers, capable of sensing the weakest spots in their listeners' emotional armor and exploiting the power of storytelling to get their victims to buy into the stories.

In his classic on market bubbles, Charles Mackay describes how salespeople through the ages have used stories to promote and push up prices on everything from tulip bulbs to shares in obscure companies, and why investors continue to fall for these stories.[13] The rise of financial markets and the growth of media have allowed storytellers to expand their audience and, with it, the potential for damage that they can create.

In more recent times, Bernie Madoff pitched an investment scheme in which he claimed he would buy about fifty of the hundred largest market cap stocks, timing his buys "opportunistically" (leaving investors with the impression that he had found a way to time markets well) and then using put options to limit potential losses. The key selling ingredients were threefold. The first was that the strategy was "too complicated for outsiders to understand" and too proprietary to be described in detail. The second was that it was supposedly so well designed that it would never lose money, even in bad months for the market. The third, and perhaps cleverest component, was that the strategy would make moderate rather than exceptionally high returns. Madoff's targeted risk-averse individuals and foundations, many of them Jewish, like he was, and by keeping his promised returns low enough to sound "reasonable" and his clientele "exclusive," he was able to get by for almost two decades without key questions being asked.

CASE STUDY 2.3: THERANOS—A STORY THAT SOUNDS SO GOOD THAT YOU WANT IT TO BE TRUE

The Theranos story has its beginnings in March 2004, when Elizabeth Holmes, a nineteen-year-old sophomore at Stanford, dropped out of college and started the company. The company was a Silicon Valley start-up with a non–Silicon Valley focus on an integral but staid part of the health-care experience, the blood test. Based on work she had been doing in a Stanford lab on testing blood for the SARS virus, Holmes concluded that she could adapt technology to allow for multiple tests to be run on much smaller quantities of blood than needed for conventional tests with a quicker and more efficient turnaround of results (to doctors and patients). In conjunction with her own stated distaste for the needles required for conventional blood tests, this became the basis for the Theranos Nanotainer, a half-inch tube containing a few drops of blood that would replace the multiple blood containers used by the conventional labs.

The story proved irresistible to just about everyone who heard it—her professor at Stanford who encouraged her to start the business, the venture capitalists who lined up to provide her hundreds of millions of dollars in capital, and health-care providers who felt this would change a key ingredient of the health-care experience, making it less painful and cheaper. The Cleveland Clinic and Walgreens, two entities at different ends of the health-care spectrum, both seemed to find the technology appealing enough to adopt it. The story was irresistible to journalists, and Holmes quickly became an iconic figure; *Forbes* named her the "the youngest, self-made, female billionaire in the world" and she was the youngest winner of the Horatio Alger Award in 2015.

From the outside, the Theranos path to disrupting the blood-testing business seemed smooth. The company continued to trumpet its claim that the drop of blood in the Nanotainer could run thirty lab tests and deliver them efficiently to doctors, going so far as to list prices on its website for each test, with costs dramatically lower (by as much as 90 percent) than the status quo. In venture capital rankings, Theranos consistently ranked among the most valuable private businesses with an estimated value in excess of $9 billion, making Holmes one of the richest women in the world. The world seemed truly at her feet, and to anyone reading the news stories, disruption seemed imminent.

The Theranos story started to come apart on October 16, 2015, when a *Wall Street Journal* article reported that the company was exaggerating the potential of the Nanotainer and that it was not using the Nanotainer for the bulk of the blood tests it was running in-house.[14] More troubling was the article's contention that senior lab employees at the company found that the Nanotainer's blood test results were not reliable, casting doubt on the science behind the product. In the following days, things got worse for Theranos. It was reported that the Food and Drug Administration, after an inspection at Theranos, had asked the company to stop using the Nanotainer on all but one blood test (for herpes) because the FDA had concerns about the data the company had supplied and the product's reliability. GlaxoSmithKline, which Holmes claimed had used the product, asserted that it had not done business with the start-up for the previous two years, and the Cleveland Clinic also backed away from its adoption. Theranos initially went into bunker mode, trying to rebut the thrust of the critical articles rather than dealing with the substantial questions. It was not until October 27, 2015 that Holmes finally agreed that presenting the data that the Nanotainer worked as a reliable blood-testing device would be the most "powerful thing" that the company could do. In the months following, the setbacks continued, as more evidence emerged of problems in the company's labs and with the blood testing technology. By July 2016, the company's future looked bleak as the FDA proposed a ban on Ms. Holmes from operating labs, and business partners (like Walgreens) abandoned the company.

If a Hollywood screenwriter were writing a movie about a young start-up, it would be almost impossible to come up with one as gripping as the Theranos story: a nineteen-year-old woman (that already makes it different from the typical start-up founder) drops out of Stanford (the new Harvard) and disrupts a business that makes us go through a health ritual we all dislike. Who among us has not sat for hours at a lab for a blood test, subjected to multiple needle pricks as a technician drew large vials of blood, waited for days to get the test back, and then blanched at the bill for $1,500 for the tests? To add to its allure, the story had a missionary component to it of a product that would change health care around the world by bringing cheap and speedy blood testing to the vast multitudes who cannot afford the status quo. The mix of exuberance, passion, and missionary zeal that animated the company came through both in speeches by and interviews with Holmes.[15] With a story this good and a heroine this likable, would you want to be the Grinch raising mundane questions about whether the product actually works?

Conclusion

Stories are critical in business. They allow businesses to connect to investors, customers, and employees at a level that pure facts or numbers cannot, and they induce action. They do come with negatives, especially when they are unchecked with facts. Storytellers tend to forget reality and make up imaginary worlds where success is guaranteed. Listeners who buy into the stories let them proceed without skeptical questioning, often setting aside doubts or inhibitions, because they want happy endings. If this book has a mission, it is to provide you with a template that will allow you to continue to be creative in your storytelling, while also introducing enough discipline into the process to warn you when you are crossing the line into wishful thinking. If you are someone listening to a business story, this book can act as a checklist to ensure that you don't let hope become expectations.

3

The Elements of Storytelling

There is a long-standing debate in creative writing circles about whether storytelling is an art or a craft. I think it is both. While there are some aspects of storytelling that cannot be taught, there are many components that are not only teachable but that can be improved with practice. In this chapter I look at the ingredients that go into a good story and examine how these ingredients need to be modified for a business story. I follow through by looking at types of stories, laying the foundation for the connection between narrative and numbers in later chapters, and at how narrators can use language and structure to evoke stronger reactions from listeners.

Story Structure

Most well-crafted stories follow a structure. In this section, I first look at the structuring of stories in general and then look at the same issue from the perspective of *business* storytelling. As you read this section, I should be honest and tell you that I was oblivious about much of the history of story structuring, which goes back millennia, until I started reviewing the literature. Recognizing that most of this story structure setup is constructed to help dramatists, novelists, and writers tell more gripping stories, my intent was simpler: to see whether I could extract lessons from the past that I could use in business storytelling.

It was Aristotle, in *Poetics*, who provided the first formal description of what a story requires.[1] In his telling, which he based on his observations of Greek theater, every story needs a beginning, a middle, and an end, and what keeps a story going is that the incidents within the story are linked together by cause and effect. For the story to have an effect, the protagonist should see a change in fortune over the course of the story. It is amazing how well that structure has held up through time.

In the nineteenth century, Gustav Freytag, a German novelist and playwright, fleshed out this story structure more and came up with his version, with five key ingredients:[2]

1. Exposition or the inciting moment: This is an event that gets the story started and introduces the main problem it will be addressing.
2. Complication or rising action: This is the phase in which the tension builds up in the story through additional events. In a tragedy, this is often the phase in which things are going well for the protagonist(s), and in a story with a happy ending, it is the interval of trying events.
3. Climax or turning point: This is the event that turns the tide, from good to bad in a tragedy and from bad to good in a happy ending story.
4. Reversal or falling action: In this phase, events occur that bring out the effects of the change initiated in the previous step.
5. Denouement: The story ends in catastrophe, if it is a tragedy, or in a resolution of some sort that shows the protagonist either winning or losing.

Freytag's structure is often depicted as a triangle, as shown in figure 3.1.

The Freytag storytelling structure is one in which the narrator controls the environment, acting as stage master who determines when surprises happen, to whom, and with what consequences. Thus, its direct use in business storytelling is limited, since so much of what happens is out of your control, your best-planned story can be rendered to waste by a real-world surprise, and the ending is not yours to script.

In the middle of the last century, Joseph Campbell, the famed researcher on mythology, looked at myths through the ages and concluded that they all shared a common structure: a journey a hero makes from humble

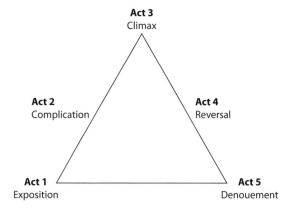

Figure 3.1
Freytag's pyramid of storytelling structure.

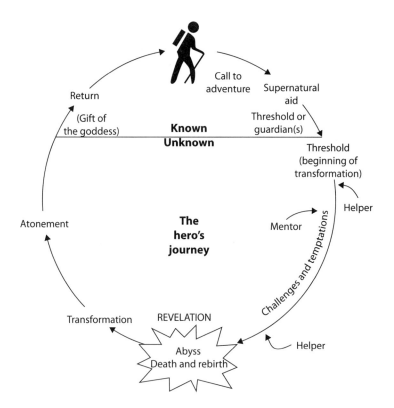

Figure 3.2
The hero's journey simplified.

beginnings to a triumphant ending.[3] In figure 3.2, you can see a simplified version of the hero's story.[4]

If you are a *Star Wars* fan, you will probably find this picture familiar, partly because George Lucas was influenced by it when writing the script for the movie. As with the Freytag structure, this one is clearly far too controlled for a business enviroment, but I think that it does provide an explanation for why some business stories get remembered far more than others. Again, think of Steve Jobs and his passage to mythic stature in business. Like the hero in Campbell's structure, Steve's call to adventure was in a garage in Silicon Valley where he and Steve Wosniak built the first Apple computer, and his challenges and temptations as he went on to make Apple a succesful company are well chronicled. It was, however, his ouster from Apple and his subsequent return (his death and rebirth) that set the stage for one of the greatest second acts in corporate history.

I am sure there are other structures that can be used for storytelling, but looking across time, the path from Aristotle's three-step structure to Joseph Campbell's hero's journey seems to be a short one. In effect, stories share more in common than we think and often just require updating to reflect modern sensibilities.

I would be lying if I said that I was thinking of the lessons of Aristotle, Freytag, and Campbell when I constructed the stories that animinate my valuations of Uber, Ferrari, and Amazon. In fact, I was not aware of much of their thinking until recently, but I have learned something from each of these structures that I can use in business storytelling. From Aristotle I learned the importance of keeping the story simple, with a beginning, middle, and end, and not getting distracted. Freytag made me understand the need to bring in both successes and reversals in a business story, since narratives without these are flat and boring. Campbell's structure highlighted the importance of characters in the story and how audiences relate to the key narrator's troubles and triumphs, a lesson that, in young companies at least, the story is as much about the founder or the person running the business as it is about the business. Finally, this version of the story brought home the realization that stories connect with audiences because they feed into all-too-human impulses.

The big difference between a fictional story, told primarily for entertainment, and a business story is that there are few limits on creativity in the former but far more in the latter. If you are writing a movie script or a story, you can create your own worlds, bizarre and unreal though they might be, and if you are skilled enough, you can take readers into those worlds. If you are telling a business story, you have to be more grounded in reality, since you will be measured not just on creativity but also on credibility and being able to deliver what you promise in the story. That said, there is no reason why you cannot adapt general storytelling structure to business storytelling.

Story Types

As with story structure, almost all stories we read or hear are recreations of old story lines. Much of the work on identifying types of stories has been with general storytelling, but there are parallels to the business world here as well.

General Types

In his book on storytelling, Christopher Booker contends that there are only seven basic plots for stories that have been mined for hundreds of years, and he lists them as follows:[5] In the first one, *overcoming the monster*, you have the underdog, usually smaller and perceived to be weaker, beating out an evil adversary. A *rebirth* is a story of renewal, in which a person is reborn to live a better life. In a *quest*, the protagonist goes on a mission to find an item or thing that will save him or her and perhaps the world. It is what makes myths like *Lord of the Rings* and *Star Wars* so appealing to audiences. A *rags-to-riches* story is about transformation, with someone or something who is poor and weak rising to become wealthy and powerful. In a *voyage and return*, the characters embark either intentionally or accidentally on a journey of discovery that ends with them returning, usually wiser, happier, or richer, to their point of origin. In *comedy* the intent is to make you laugh with the players or at them as they stumble through life's challenges, and in a *tragedy* you get the flip side: the objective here is to make you cry. Booker makes the compelling case that everything from high literature to pulp novels, opera to soap opera, and Shakespearean drama to James Bond movies draw from these seven themes.

Product Stories

Advertisers have drawn on general story types for decades in creating advertising narratives for products. Apple's 1984 advertisement for the Macintosh, with the personal computer business (IBM and Microsoft, in particular) playing the role of the heavy, can be viewed as a simple extension of the overcoming the monster story type. The Apple 1984 advertisement premiered on Super Bowl Sunday, and there is no better forum to observe this reliance on stories than on that day each year, when advertisers pay fortunes to get their chance to appeal to immense television audiences for very short time periods. In what has become a ritual for television watchers, both experts and audiences are polled to see which advertisements leave the biggest imprint on audience memories. While there is no one company or advertising agency that consistently comes out ahead, the one consistent finding is that ads that tell compelling stories, quite a feat to pull off within 30 or 60 seconds, are the ones most likely to be remembered.

Founder Stories

With young start-ups in particular, and even with some established businesses, the story of the business can be tightly tied to the story of the founder, and it is the founder's story that draws investors to the business. In particular, founder-based stories can be one of five types:

1. The Horatio Alger story: This is a classic, especially in the United States, and it is a variant of the rags-to-riches story. Investors are attracted to this story by the tenacity of the founder in making something of himself or herself in the face of immense odds.
2. The charisma story: In this narrative the founder's story is built around an epiphany, a moment when he or she gets a vision of business opportunity and then proceeds to fulfill that vision. Elon Musk has founded or cofounded many businesses, including SpaceX, Tesla, and SolarCity, but with each of these businesses, investors are as much drawn to him, as a charismatic founder, as they are to the companies themselves.
3. The connections story: In some businesses, it is who you know that gives you the advantage, and founders who have the right connections, either because of family background or due to their past roles as politicians or regulators, are given special deference.
4. The celebrity story: Investors are sometimes drawn to the celebrity status of a founder, in the belief this status will allow them to attract business and generate value. Jack Nicklaus, Magic Johnson, and Oprah Winfrey have all used their celebrity status to build successful businesses, with many investors being drawn to the celebrities' names as much as to the businesses themselves.

5. The experience story: It is the track record of some founders that draws investors to their businesses. The assumption, when investing in these businesses, is that if they have been successful in the past in building businesses, they will be successful in their new ventures.

There are two dangers of crossing the line and making a business story all about the founder or founders. First, a business that is too closely tied to its founder may not be able to survive personal failures on his or her part. When Martha Stewart was convicted of insider trading in 2003, the publicly traded company that shared her name suffered mightily in the aftermath, dropping almost 15 percent on her indictment. Second, while listeners are always attracted by the personal aspect of founder stories, these personal elements still have to be connected to business success. That perhaps explains why so many celebrities start off on the road to entrepreneurship and so few make it through successfully.

CASE STUDY 3.1: NARRATOR-BASED STORIES—UNDER ARMOUR AND KEVIN PLANK

Under Armour has been a success story in the apparel business, coming from small beginnings to mount a challenge to giants like Nike with its clothing and footwear offerings. The story of Under Armour is as much a story about the business as it is the story of its founder, Kevin Plank. Kevin, the youngest of five children, grew up in Maryland and walked on to the University of Maryland football team as a special teams player. He became captain of the team but noticed that he and his teammates were wearing heavy, sweat-soaked shirts after practice and came up with the idea of lightweight, sweat-wicking shirts using fabrics from women's undergarments.

After graduating in 1996, Plank started his business from the basement of his grandmother's house and built it up over the next decade into a worthy competitor to Nike, with revenues of $4 billion in 2015. He has been a very visible part of Under Armour's story, going so far as to put some of his teammates from the University of Maryland football team in early commercials for the company. He has also preserved his voting control of the company by issuing shares with different voting rights.

Business Stories

Business stories can range across the spectrum, and the one you use will depend on where the business is in the corporate life cycle and what the competition it is facing looks like. Again, at the risk of both overgeneralizing

Table 3.1
Types of Business Stories

Business story	Type of business	Investment pitch
The bully	Company with a large market share, a superior brand name, access to lots of capital, and a reputation for ruthlessness	They will steamroll competition to deliver ever-increasing revenues and profits.
The underdog	Company that is a distant second (or lower) in market share in a business, with claims to a better or cheaper product than the dominant company	They will work harder than the dominant player at pleasing customers, perhaps with a kinder, gentler corporate image.
The eureka moment	Company that claims to have found an unmet need in the market, usually in a serendipitous way, and then has come up with a way of meeting that need	They will succeed as a business by filling the unmet need.
The better mousetrap	Company that contends it has a better way of delivering an existing product or service that will be more desirable and better suited to the need	They will eat into the market share of the existing players in the market.
The disruptor	Company that changes the way a business is run, altering fundamental ways in which the product or service is delivered	The status quo is ineffective and inefficient, and disruption will change the business (while making money).
The low-cost player	Company that has found a way to reduce the cost of doing business and is willing to cut prices on the expectation that it can sell a lot more	Increased sales will more than make up for lower margins.
The missionary	Company that presents itself as having a larger, more noble mission than just making money	They will make money while doing good (for society).

and not spanning the spectrum of possible stories, a few classic business stories are presented in table 3.1.

This list is not a comprehensive one, but it does cover a large proportion of the businesses both in public and private capital markets, and there are two additional points worth making. The first is that it is possible for a company to have dual narratives, as is the case with Uber in September 2015, a company that is telling both a disruption story (it is changing the car service business) and a dominance story (it is presenting itself as unstoppable in the ride-sharing market). The second is that as a company moves through the life cycle, its narrative will change. Thus, when Google entered the search engine market in 1998, it was the scrappy underdog to the established players, but by 2015 it had made the transition to being the dominant player in the market, perhaps even a bully, with a reputation to match.

Steps for Storytellers

Through much of this chapter, I have looked at storytelling primarily from the perspective of listeners, investors gauging sales pitches by founders or using them to classify companies as investments, but what if you were starting a business and were the storyteller? Using the lessons from story structure and story types, here are the steps you can adopt to tell a better story.

1. Understand your business and know yourself: As a storyteller, it is difficult to tell a story about a business if you don't understand the business yourself. If your vision for the business in terms of what it does and where you see it going in the future is fuzzy or unformed, your story about it will reflect that confusion. This is true whether you are the CEO of a well-established business with a long history talking to equity research analysts or the founder of a start-up seeking venture capital money. In fact, as the founder of a start-up is so integral to the business, you are as much a part of the story as the business you have founded, and some introspection (on the role you hope to play in this venture) may be needed.

2. Understand your audience: Your business story may not be the same when you are talking to different stakeholders (employees, customers, or potential investors), because each has a different interest in the story. While employees may share your enthusiasm for the success of the business, they are just as interested or perhaps more so in how you plan to share that success with them and the personal risks they face from failure. Customers are more interested in your products than in your profits and want to hear the part of your story in which you explain how your product or service will meet their needs and what they will have to pay in return. Investors want to know about these same products and services,

but generally from the perspective of how you plan to convert potential into revenues and value. Even among investors there can be big differences in time horizon (short term versus long term) and how they expect to generate their returns (cash return versus growth in value), and your story may succeed with one while failing with the other.

3. Marshal the facts: Nothing will undercut your story more than mangling the facts. Thus, it will behoove you to do your homework on your company, its competitions, and the market you are trying to capture. To check your story before delivering it, you should consider adapting the five *W*s of journalism to business:

   - *Who* are your customers, your competitors, your employees?
   - *What* does your business look like now and what is your vision for what it will look like in the future?
   - *When* or over what time period do you see your business evolving to match your vision?
   - *Where* (in terms of markets and geographies) do you see yourself operating?
   - *Why* do you see yourself as the winner in this market?

   In a later chapter we will return to these questions and see how working with numbers can help you on each of these questions.

4. Talk in specifics: While your business story may be built around market opportunities or macroeconomic trends, you will need to be specific about how you plan to take advantage of these trends. Assume, for instance, that you are building a social media company. It is not enough, for instance, to argue that people are increasingly turning to social media to interact, to get their news, and even for entertainment. You need to specify what you are offering as a company that will draw these people to your products or services.

5. Show, don't tell: Steve Jobs's keynote speeches for Apple resonated because he was willing and eager to share Apple's new products on the stage, even at the risk of having some of them malfunction. In the same vein, being able to show how your products and services work can make your business story not only more memorable but also more effective.

6. Have a good ending: Taking Aristotle's advice to heart, you should craft an ending for your story that not only leaves your audience excited and eager to act but also encapsulates the message you were trying to deliver.

I have never pitched a business venture to investors, employees, or customers, and you should be skeptical about any advice I dish out on this question. I do teach, however, and I have always believed that good teaching requires every one of these six steps.

The Ingredients in a Good Story

So what is it that makes some stories more gripping than others? After all, stories come in many forms, are told by different characters, and have different twists, but good stories do share some commonalities. At the risk of missing some characteristics that you think belong on the list and adding some that you do not, my list of what makes for a good business story are the following:

1. The story is simple. Good business stories have a core message they deliver without distractions and eliminate complexities and complications that get in the way of that message.
2. The story is credible. A good story, in business, has to be actionable and deliverable, and consequently needs to meet the reality test. That may mean being open about your limitations as a business, while presenting the strengths that you bring to the game.
3. The story is authentic. Authentic is a much used word, with nebulous meaning, but it is undeniable that your stories resonate more when they reflect who you are as a person and what your business is truly about.
4. The story is emotional. I don't mean emotional in the sense that the storyteller cries on the stage, but emotional in the sense that it comes from the heart. If you are not passionate about your story, why would you expect anyone else to be?

Rather than go through the usual litany of business dos and don'ts, I decided to turn to Pixar, one of my favorite storytellers, for lessons. I remember watching *Toy Story* with my children and marveling at how well the storytelling kept both adults and children engrossed, and my admiration for the studio's storytelling capabilities have only increased over time. I was happy to discover that Emma Coats, who used to work at the studio, had put together a simple manual for storytelling based upon her experiences, titled the *22 Rules to Phenomenal Storytelling*. While not all of the rules she lists carry over directly into business stories, many can be adapted to the business setting. Bringing the Pixar rules to business storytelling, you would be well served to tailor your story to the interests of your audience, to simplify and focus that story, to find the most economical way to tell that story, and to keep working and reworking the story, rather than go for perfection. I found the last piece of advice the most important, because there is no better way to learn what works in your story and what does not than to tell it to different audiences. Practice does make for a better story.

On a personal note, I am a fan of *Shark Tank*, the television show featuring entrepreneurs who present their business ideas to and seek funding from successful venture capitalists and businesspeople (the sharks). One of my favorite activities when watching the show is to listen to the business stories told during the course of the show and think about why some stories connect and others do not and how that connection sometimes, but not always, translates into a willingness to invest.

Conclusion

A good story is magical in its capacity to create connections and evoke action. In this chapter I tried to look at the craft behind the magic. The way you structure stories has changed surprisingly little in the last two millennia and stories have been built around the same structures for centuries, whether it be Aristotle's theater-based structure or Joseph Campbell's discovery that a hero's quest lies at the heart of every enduring myth. In the same vein, there are only a handful of base story types that you return to over and over again, whether it be in fiction or in business.

Toward the end of the chapter, I probed the steps involved in constructing and telling good business stories. Good business storytellers, while learning from story structure and types, have to understand their businesses, their audiences, and themselves, and must craft simple stories that reflect reality, not fantasy. Those who listen to these stories should do so with open minds, always checking them against the facts and being willing to accept that, unlike fictional stories, business stories don't always have the desired endings.

4

The Power of Numbers

Stories create connections and get remembered, but numbers convince people. They give a sense of precision to even the most imprecise stories, and putting a number on a judgment call makes you feel more comfortable when dealing with uncertainty. In this chapter, I begin by looking at the history of numbers, tracing their origins from ancient civilizations to the quantitative models of today. I then look at the power that numbers have over us, why we use them, and how developments in the last three decades have made data easier to collect, analyze, and disseminate. I close the chapter by examining the dangers of trusting numbers too much and how they can lead you into mistakenly thinking that you are being objective and in control when in fact you are neither.

A History of Numbers

The very first number systems go back to prehistoric times and were tallying systems that you can see depicted in cave paintings. The ancient civilizations all had their own version of number systems, with the Mayan system built around a base of 60. The Egyptians are believed to have invented the base 10 system that underlies mathematics today, and the numbers we use today, while called *arabic* numerals, were first used by Indians. Along the way, the Arabs discovered the magical properties of zero, and the Chinese explored the possibility of negative numbers.

In spite of these advances, for much of human existence, the use of numbers was restricted to a few, because data was difficult to get and save, computation was time intensive, and analytical tools were limited. In the Middle Ages, the birth of the insurance business and the strides made in statistical theory expanded the use of numbers in business. It was the development of financial markets in the nineteenth century that supercharged the use of numbers and saw the growth of number crunching as a profession, with actuaries, accountants, and stockbrokers joining in.

The invention of the computer in the middle of the last century changed the game again; the scale of number crunching expanded as machines replaced human labor. Until the personal computer was invented in the 1970s, though, those with access to large, expensive computer systems (generally large corporations, universities, and research units) had a decided advantage over the rest of us. The personal computer has democratized not only access to data but also to the tools needed to analyze the data by allowing much greater numbers of businesspeople, investors, and journalists to do what only a select few could have done in a prior generation.

The Power of Numbers

As machine power continues to expand at an exponential pace, there are clear trends toward using numbers more in decision making. Businesses talk about using *big data* to guide what products they should produce, who they should sell them to, and at what price. Investors have also become more number oriented, with a subset of investors (the quants) putting their trust entirely in data and sophisticated tools for analyzing the data. In this section, I would like to focus on what it is about numbers that draws people to them.

Numbers Are Precise

Early in this book, I referenced *Moneyball*, the book about Billy Beane, manager of the Oakland As, a professional baseball team.[1] Baseball is a sport with a long history in the United States, and ironically for a sport that generates mounds of statistics about players, it has largely been run based on storytelling by scouts about young prospects, by managers about the right situational moves to make during a game, and by players on how to hit or pitch. Billy Beane revolutionized the sport by putting his faith in numbers, using the voluminous statistics that came out of games to determine who he would play on his teams and how the game would be played on the field. His success in creating a world-class team on a bare-bones budget not only made him a managerial star but led to others in baseball imitating him. In many ways, Michael Lewis encapsulates the tension between storytelling and numbers and makes the argument for numbers when he describes traditional baseball's reaction to Beane's efforts as "an example of how an unscientific culture responds, or fails to respond, to the scientific method."[2]

The notion that numbers are scientific and more precise than stories is deeply held, and as a result of this belief, the revolution that Billy Beane brought to baseball has spread far and wide. The field of sabermetrics, named by Bill James, the baseball statistician and Beane's intellectual mentor, has now found a place in other sports, with managers and players drawing from it. Nate Silver, a statistician by training, has upended the political punditry business, using numbers to challenge what he considers the fluffy stories told by conventional political experts. Not surprisingly, the field that has been upended the most by the data revolution has been business, partly because there is so much data available to analyze and partly because the payoff to using those data well can be immense.

In chapter 2 I pointed out how social media has created a platform for storytelling, but it is interesting that social media has also shown us how much we all care about numbers. You measure the content of Facebook posts by the number of likes and the reach of a Twitter tweet by its retweets, and there is evidence that you sometimes change what you write and say on social media to attract greater numbers of people.

Numbers Are Objective

At some point in time during our educational lives, we were taught (and often forgot) the scientific method. At least as described in a high school classroom, the essence of the scientific method is that you start with a hypothesis, conduct experiments or collect data, and then accept or reject the hypothesis based on the data. Implicit in this description is the message that a true scientist is unbiased and that it is the data that provides the answer to a question.

In chapter 2, when I looked at the dangers of storytelling, I noted how biases creep into stories and how difficult it is for listeners to push back in a storytelling world. One reason that people are so attracted to numbers is the perception, fair or unfair, that numbers are unbiased and thus agenda-free. While this presumption is not true, as you will see in the next section, it remains undeniable that while listeners may feel less connected with a person who presents a case primarily with numbers than with stories, they are also more likely to view the person as more objective.

Numbers Indicate Control

In *The Little Prince*, a children's book, the Prince visits an asteroid and meets a man who counts the stars, insisting that if he were able to count them all, he would own them. That children's tale has resonance, since many people seem to feel that measuring something or putting a number on it will allow them to control it better. Thus, even though a thermometer can only tell you that you have a fever and a blood pressure monitor provides a reading of your blood pressure at the time you take it, both seem to give you a sense of control over your health.

In business, the mantra has become: *if you cannot measure it, you cannot manage it*. That slogan is music to the ears of the firms that build, supply, and support measurement tools. There are areas of business in which being able to measure output and progress more accurately has led to significant progress. In inventory control, being able to track how much you have of each item in inventory in real time has allowed companies to simultaneously reduce their inventory and meet customer needs more promptly. In many segments of business, though, the reality is that the mantra has been modified to: *if you measure it, you have already managed it*. In other words, many businesses seem to have replaced serious analysis with more numbers.

CASE STUDY 4.1: THE POWER OF QUANT INVESTING

The power of numbers in investing is best seen in the growth of quant investing, whose promoters are open about the fact that their investing is based only on the numbers. In fact they compete with one another in explaining how much they have turned their investment processes over to the data and the power of their data-analytic tools. The roots of quant investing go back in time to a surprising source, Benjamin Graham, considered by many to be the father of modern value investing. Graham defined multiple screens for finding undervalued companies, and while applying these screens was difficult to do in his time, when data was often collected by hand and the screening was manual, screening for stocks today is easy and almost costless.

The Markowitz revolution that gave birth to modern portfolio theory also was a contributor to quant investing. The approach to finding efficient portfolios, that is, portfolios that delivered the highest returns for a given level of risk, that Harry Markowitz developed in the 1950s, was a computational nightmare at that time, given the limitations of both data access and analysis. Today it is possible for an individual investor, armed with a personal computer and online data, to generate efficient portfolios on stock samples that would have taken weeks to create a few decades ago.

In the late 1970s as historical returns data and accounting data became more accessible, a new strand of academic research emerged, in which researchers pored over past data, looking for systematic patterns. The initial findings from these studies, that small market capitalization stocks earned higher returns than larger market capitalization companies and that low price earnings (PE) stocks outperformed the market, were labeled anomalies by academics, because they did not fit the classical risk and return model predictions. For investors and port-folio managers, they became opportunities, market inefficiencies to exploit to generate higher returns.

In the last decade, as more data became available, some of it in real time, and computational power exploded, quant investing morphed into new and potentially troublesome forms. In his latest book, *Flash Boys*, Michael Lewis looks at a subset of investors called high-frequency traders who use high-powered computers to scan real-time price data for mispricing and trade on that mispricing. These dark pools are thus almost entirely number driven and are the logical end product of a purely number-driven invest-ment process.

The Dangers of Numbers

Just as the strengths of storytelling become its weaknesses, the strengths of numbers can very quickly become weaknesses that can be exploited by number crunchers to push their agendas.

The Illusion of Precision

I used to use the words "precise" and "accurate" interchangeably, until a mathematician pointed out to me that the two words measured different things. He used a dartboard to illustrate the difference, noting that the precision of a model is captured by how close results from the model are to each other, given the same inputs, whereas the accuracy of a model is best measured by looking at how the results of the model compare with the actual numbers (figure 4.1).

Put differently, you can create precise models that are inaccurate and accurate models that are imprecise. That contrast is worth noting, since the number-crunching disciplines often wrongly value precision over accuracy.

The more you work with numbers, the sooner you come to the realization that while numbers look or can be made to look precise, they are anything but precise, especially in the context of forecasting the future. In fact, statistics tries to make this imprecision explicit through its estimation process, wherein you are taught that when you make an estimate, you should also reveal the potential error in that estimate in the form of a *standard error*. In practice, and especially so in business and investing, that advice is ignored, and estimates are treated as facts, often leading to disastrous consequences.

There is a final aspect of numbers that adds to the imprecision. One of the key findings in behavioral economics is that our response to numbers depends not only on their magnitude but also on how they are *framed*. That is the weakness that retailers exploit when they mark up the price on an item to $2.50 and take 20 percent off, since shoppers seem more inclined to buy that item than a similar one priced at $2.00. In one of the more famous

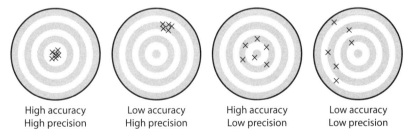

High accuracy	Low accuracy	High accuracy	Low accuracy
High precision	High precision	Low precision	Low precision

Figure 4.1
Accuracy versus precision.

Table 4.1
The Effect of Framing

Framing	Treatment A	Treatment B
Positive	Saves 200 people	33.33% chance of saving all 600 people, 66.67% chance of saving no one.
Negative	Kills 400 people	33.33% chance that no one will die, 66.67% chance that everyone will die.

examples of this framing bias, subjects in an experiment were asked to choose between two treatments for 600 people affected by a deadly disease with the results for each of the treatments as shown in table 4.1. With positive framing, treatment A was chosen by 72 percent of the subjects over treatment B, though they had exactly the same numerical end results. With negative framing, treatment A was chosen by only 22 percent of the subjects over treatment B, again with the same end results. In the context of business, the analogies would be making money (positive) and losing money (negative) and businesses surviving (positive) and businesses failing (negative), with the implication that framing the same numbers differently can lead to different responses.

CASE STUDY 4.2: THE "NOISY" HISTORICAL
EQUITY RISK PREMIUM

The equity risk premium, simply put, is the price investors charge for investing in equities (which are a risky investment class) as opposed to keeping their money in a riskless investment. Thus, if investors can earn an annual, guaranteed (making it riskless) return of 3 percent, the equity risk premium is what they will demand over and above that number for investing in stocks. Intuitively, you would expect the equity risk premium to be a function of how risk-averse investors are, with more risk aversion translating into a higher premium, and how risky they perceive equities to be as an investment class, with the perception that there is more risk leading to a rise in the equity risk premium.

Given that the equity risk premium is a key input for both corporate finance and valuation, how can you estimate this number? Most practitioners turn to history, looking at what investors have earned in the past on stocks relative to a riskless investment. In the United States, that database goes back a century or longer, though the stock market has expanded and matured over that period. If you assume that the U.S. Treasury cannot default and that the securities that it issues (Treasury bills and Treasury bonds) are thus guaranteed, risk-free investments, you can estimate historical equity risk premiums from past data. For instance, in the 1928–2015 time period, U.S. equities earned 11.41 percent on average each year, and the annual return on Treasury bonds was 5.23 percent over the same period. The difference of 6.18 percent is labeled a historical equity risk premium and used by practitioners as the estimate for the future.

Probing that number a little more, it should be noted that this average comes from stock returns that are volatile, with returns ranging from a high of almost 50 percent in 1933 to a low of close to −44 percent in 1931. Figure 4.2 captures this volatility in stock returns.

The equity risk premium estimate of 6.18 percent now comes with a warning label in the form of a standard error of 2.30 percent. What does that mean? Loosely speaking, it suggests that your estimate could be wrong by as much as 4.60 percent in either direction, meaning that your true equity risk premium could be as low as 1.58 percent or as high as 10.78 percent.[3]

The numbers get even shakier if you bring in the fact that your estimation choices affected your estimate. Rather than use the 1928–2015 time period, you could have used a shorter period (say the last ten or fifty years) or a longer one

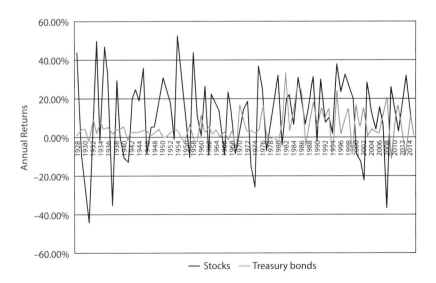

Figure 4.2
Annual returns on U.S. stocks and Treasury bonds from 1928 to 2015.
Source: Damodaran Online (http://pages.stern.nyu.edu/~adamodar).

Table 4.2
Estimates of Annual Equity Risk Premium for the U.S. Estimation Choices

	Arithmetic average		Geometric average	
	Stocks—Treasury bills	Stocks—Treasury bonds	Stocks—Treasury bills	Stocks—Treasury bonds
1928–2015	7.92%	6.18%	6.05%	4.54%
1966–2015	6.05%	3.89%	4.69%	2.90%
2006–2015	7.87%	3.88%	6.11%	2.53%

(since you have some databases that go back to 1871). Instead of using the ten-year Treasury bond, you could have used a three-month Treasury bill or a thirty-year bond. Finally, you could have replaced the arithmetic average with a compounded or geometric average. Each of these choices would have yielded different estimates of the equity risk premium, as evidenced in table 4.2.

Thus, using a different time period, a different measure for a riskless investment, and even a different manner of averaging returns can yield very different estimates of the equity risk premium for the United States. The equity risk premium is definitely an estimate, not a fact.

The Illusion of Objectivity

The fact that the way you frame numbers can change the way people respond to them provides a segue into the second delusion about numbers—numbers are objective and number crunchers have no agendas. Really? As you will see in detail in the next chapter, the process of collecting, analyzing, and presenting data provides multiple opportunities for bias to enter the process. To make things worse, in the hands of a skilled number cruncher, this bias can be hidden far better with numbers than with stories.

From the listeners' perspective, there are different biases that come into play, in which the way you look at the numbers and the ones you choose to focus on will depend on your prior beliefs. To provide an example, I estimate the effective tax rates paid by publicly traded companies in the United States at the start of every year on my website. In the interests of providing comprehensive statistics, I report the average tax rates for each sector using three different approaches for averaging: a simple average of the tax rates across companies in the sector, a weighted average of the tax rates across companies in the sector, and a weighted average of the tax rates across only money-making companies in the sector. Each year there are journalists, politicians, and business trade groups that use my tax rate data, often to support very different agendas. The business trade groups, intent on showing that they pay their fair share of taxes, pick the tax rate measure that yields the highest value to make their case. Advocacy groups that believe U.S. corporations don't pay their fair share in taxes look at the same table and find the tax rate measure that yields the lowest value to bolster their arguments. Both sides argue that the facts (and numbers) are on their side and neither will admit to the existence of bias.

CASE STUDY 4.3: NUMBERS AND BIAS WITH THE EQUITY RISK PREMIUM

In case study 4.2, I explained how making different estimation choices can yield very different estimates of the equity risk premium, with estimates ranging from 2.53 percent (a ten-year geometric average premium for stock over Treasury bonds) as a low number to 7.92 percent (the arithmetic average premium for stocks over Treasury bills from 1928 to 2015) as the high number. That should not surprise you, given the standard error of 2.30 percent that I estimated for the risk premium from 1928 to 2015.

The equity risk premium that you choose to use has consequences, and one venue where the effects can be large is in the regulation of utilities (power, water) in the United States. For decades, the companies in these businesses have been allowed to operate as monopolies in their regional domains, but in return, regulatory commissions determine how much utilities can increase the prices of their products. In making this judgment, these commissions look at what a fair rate of return should be for investors in these companies and then allow the product price to rise to deliver this return. That fair rate of return for much of the last few decades has been computed with the equity risk premium as a key ingredient, with the rate of return increasing as the equity risk premium goes up.

Not surprisingly, the regulated companies and the regulatory authorities have very different perspectives on which number they should be using from table 4.2. The companies push for the highest premium they can get away with, perhaps even the 7.92 percent, because the higher premium translates into a higher rate of return and more substantial price increases. The regulatory commission, on the other hand, would prefer the use of a lower premium, since that will then keep a lid on product price increases and make consumers happier. Each side claims that its estimate of the premium is a fact and it is often left to legal forums or arbitration panels to split the difference.

The Illusion of Control

Measuring something does not mean that you are controlling it. Just as a thermometer can tell you that you have a fever but cannot treat it, measuring the standard deviation of a portfolio only tells you that it is risky but does not protect you from that risk. That said, it is true that you may feel more in control when you are able to measure something and that the more time you spend with numbers, the more you may use measurement tools as a crutch.

In corporate finance and valuation, areas in which I spend most of my time, I notice this phenomenon play out in many places. The first is in the use of *what if* or *sensitivity analysis*, often as an addendum to a valuation or a project analysis. In most cases, these analyses happen after the decision has already been made, and the only explanation I can provide for why analysts spend so much time on them is that it makes them feel more in control. The second is in the attention that analysts give to small and often irrelevant details. I say, only half jokingly, that when in doubt, I add decimals to my final numbers, whether they be valuations of companies or rates of return for projects.

The danger with deluding yourself that you are in control, just because you have a sophisticated measurement tool, is that you may not only let the numbers overwhelm your common sense but that you will not prepare yourself properly for the dangers ahead. That, unfortunately, was what happened at banks around the world during the banking crisis in 2008. In the two decades prior to the crisis, these banks had developed a risk measure called "value at risk" (VAR), which allowed them to see in numerical terms their worst-case scenarios in terms of losses from their businesses. In the intervening period, risk-management experts and academics refined VAR to make it more powerful and more complex, with the stated intent of making it more effective. As bank managers became increasingly reliant on VAR, they also let down their guards and concluded that if the computed VAR was within their defined safe limits, their risk taking was also under control. In 2008 that delusion fell apart, as the weaknesses in VAR's core assumptions were exposed and banks that thought they were protected from catastrophic risk found that they were not.

CASE STUDY 4.4: THE SAD (BUT TRUE) STORY
OF LONG-TERM CAPITAL MANAGEMENT

If you trust numbers too much, you should pay heed to the experiences of Long-Term Capital Management (LTCM). The firm, which was founded in the early 1990s by ex–Salomon Brothers trader John Meriwether, promised to bring together the best minds in finance to find and take advantage of mispricing opportunities in the bond market. Delivering on the first part of the promise, Meriwether lured the best bond traders from Salomon and brought on board two Nobel Prize winners, Myron Scholes and Bob Merton. In the first few years of its existence, the firm also lived up to the second part of the promise, earning extraordinary returns for the elite of Wall Street. In those years, LTCM was the envy of the rest of the Street as it used low-cost debt to augment its capital and earn substantial returns on mostly safe investment opportunities.

As the funds at their disposal got larger, the firm had to widen its search to include riskier investments, though it did find those investments by analyzing the data. By itself, this would not have been fatal, but the firm continued to use the same leverage on these riskier investments as it did on its safe investments. It did so because the complex models it had built told it that while the individual investments were risky, based on their history, they would not move together and that the portfolio was therefore a safe one.

In 1997, the strategy unraveled as collapses in one market (Russia) spread into other markets as well. As the portfolio dropped in value, LTCM found itself facing the downside of its size and high leverage. Unable to unwind its large positions without affecting market prices and facing the pressures of lenders, LTCM faced certain bankruptcy. Fearing that it would bring down other investors in the market, the Federal Reserve engineered a bank-led bailout of the firm.

What are the lessons we can learn from the fiasco? Besides the cynical one that it is good to have friends in high places, you could argue that the fall of LTCM teaches you that having access to the most brilliant minds, the most up-to-date data, and the best models in investing or business does not equate to success.

The Intimidation Factor

If you are a corporate financial analyst, a consultant, or a banker facing a skeptical audience, one simple technique to silence the room is to open up a complex spreadsheet filled with numbers. This works particularly well if your audience is not comfortable with numbers, but even if you have a numerically literate audience, the human mind is generally incapable of looking at a hundred numbers on a page and making sense of them.

The fact that numbers can be intimidating is not a secret to either number crunchers or to their audiences. For number crunchers, that intimidation works at cutting off debate and preventing probing questions that may uncover large and potentially fatal weaknesses embedded in the numbers. For those in the audience, the numbers offer an excuse for not doing their homework. When things fall apart, as they did with VAR in 2008, both the number crunchers and the number users blame the model for their failures.

I know that I am capable of using numbers to bludgeon those who disagree with me on my valuations or investment judgments. When asked a question that cuts to the heart of my investment thesis, perhaps exposing its weakness, I feel the urge to pull up an equation that will either deflect the question or leave the questioner uncertain about the basis for his or her question, but I also know that doing so will only make my judgments less sound.

The Imitation Problem

If the numbers are all that drive your decisions, as some purist number crunchers claim, you are in big trouble as the decision maker, for two reasons. The first is that you have positioned yourself perfectly for being outsourced, replaced not just by a cheaper number cruncher in a different location but by a machine. After all, if your strong point is that you can be machine-like in your decision making, objective and driven just by the numbers, a machine would be better at that task than you will ever be. That, of course, is the promise of young financial technology firms that offer robo-investing advice: they ask investors for numbers (age, income, financial savings, and retirement plans) just as a financial advisor would, and the computer then generates an investment portfolio based upon the numbers.

If your defense against the outsourcing is that you have better data and more powerful computers than most other people, you open yourself up to a second problem, which is that a purely number-driven decision process is easy to imitate. Thus, if you are a "quant hedge fund" and build an elaborate quantitative model to find the best stocks to buy and sell, all I would need to do is be able to see the stocks you buy and sell, and with a powerful enough computer of my own, I should be able to replicate your strategy.

The Lemming Problem

Let's assume that you live in big data heaven, where you and everyone else has huge databases and powerful computers to analyze and make sense of the data. Since you all share the same data, and perhaps even use the same tools, you are going to highlight the same opportunities, generally at about the same time, and seek them out for profit. That process is going to create "herding," when you buy and sell the same stocks at the same time. So what? That herding will create momentum, which will reinforce your decisions at least in the short term but will also cause you to be collectively wrong if there is a structural shift in the underlying process (business, market, or economy). The data, after all, comes from the past, and if the future is going to be different from the past, the consequence of the structural shift, the predictions based upon the data will come apart.

The implications are sobering. As we move increasingly to a data-driven world, and more and more people have access to that data, it stands to reason that we will see more booms and busts than we have historically. Bubbles in markets will be bigger than they used to be and when these bubbles burst, as they inevitably will, the carnage is going to be greater as well.

Storytelling as Antidote

If numbers are dangerous because they come with the illusions of control, precision, and objectivity and can be easily imitated, how will adding stories to numbers reduce those problems? First, the nature of stories is that they are fuzzy and remind us that precise as the numbers look, changing your story will change the numbers. Second, that recognition also will dispel the notion that you somehow can deliver the numbers you have forecast, since stories can be changed by forces out of your control. Third, when you are forced to unveil the story that backs your numbers, your biases are visible not just to the rest of the world but to yourself. I also believe that the capacity to combine stories with numbers makes it more difficult for others to imitate you, if you are successful. Unlike models that can be easily copied, storytelling is more nuanced, personal, and difficult to replicate.

The one problem that adding stories to numbers will not solve, at least in the near term, is herding. The groupthink that leads people to pile into the same stocks and investments because the numbers lead them there will also lead to them to reinforce one another's stories. There is an argument to be made, though, that the best way to break the madness of crowds is with a combination of an alternative (and more realistic) story, backed up by numbers to give it credibility.

CASE STUDY 4.5: THE FALL OF QUANT INVESTING

In case study 4.1, I presented quant investing as the positive culmination of the data revolution, a version of *Moneyball* for financial markets, in which number crunching replaced the hand waving and storytelling of an earlier age. In this follow-up, I want to look at how the dangers of numbers—they are imprecise, are vehicles for bias, and provide the illusion of control—have played out in the downfall of at least some aspects of quant investing.

Let's start with the imprecision of the numbers. The good news, if you are a money baller in financial markets, is that they create immense amounts of data, some from companies' financial filings but far more from the market itself (price changes, trading volume). The bad news is that the data is extraordinarily noisy, as you can see, even at the market level, in my computations of standard errors for the equity risk premium in case study 4.2. Almost every quant strategy is built on past data, and its promise (usually taking the form of an alpha or excess return) comes with the qualifier that the past is not a predictor of the future and that even if it is, there is a great deal of uncertainty about outcomes.

As for bias, much as we try not to, it is impossible not to let your biases creep into not only how you crunch the numbers but also in how you read the data entrails. Once you create a quant strategy, attach your name to it, and sell it to clients, you are irrevocably on a biased path, where you will find confirmation that your strategy works, even when it is on the verge of collapse.

Finally, it took the market crisis in 2008 to reveal to hedge funds how little control they had over investment outcomes. As developed markets went through contortions that had never been seen in recent history, models that had been built carefully on historical data not only gave false signals but did so for lots of investors at the same time.

I am not ready to bury quant investing yet, since the forces that brought it to the forefront are still around us, but I think that its successes and failures reveal both the promise and peril of numbers. Quant investing, to succeed and prosper, has to find a place for storytelling and narrative in conjunction with the numbers, and if it does, it will not only be more successful but it will also be more difficult to imitate and outsource.

Conclusion

I am naturally drawn to numbers but one of the ironies of working with numbers is that the more I work with them, the more skeptical I become about purely number-driven arguments. In my work with financial data, both accounting and market driven, I have learned about how much noise there is in that data and how difficult it is to make predictions based on that data. I believe in the scientific method, but I don't believe there are many pure scientists out there. All research is biased, with the only questions becoming about the direction and magnitude of the bias. Thus, it is my job when presented with a numbers-driven argument to probe for the biases of the person making the argument, and once I find them, to adjust the numbers to reflect that bias. Finally, I have learned that it takes hubris on my part to believe that just because I put a number on a process or variable, I control it or even understand it. Thus, I can offer you a dozen different numerical measures for risk, most with great academic pedigrees, but I struggle on a daily basis to understand what exactly risk is and how it affects us as investors.

5

Number-Crunching Tools

If you are a numbers person, this should be the golden age, as tasks that would have taken you months to complete a few decades ago can be done in a few seconds with the help of technology. The ease of access to numbers and tools has also made everyone a number cruncher, with mixed results; as we noted in the last chapter, numbers can be misused, manipulated, or just misread. In this chapter I break the number-crunching process into three parts, starting with the collection of data, moving on to the analysis of that data, and ending with presenting the data to others. At each stage, I look at practices that you can use to minimize bias and error when working with numbers or to detect bias and error when presented with numbers and models.

From Data to Information: The Sequence

Is this the data age or is it the information age? I am not sure, and the reason is that data and information are used as interchangeable words when they represent very different concepts. The data is what we start with, the raw numbers, and defined as such, we are in the data age, when it is possible to collect and store massive quantities of these numbers.

Data has to be processed and analyzed for it to become information, and it is here that we face a conundrum. The proliferation of data has also meant that not only do we have far more data to process but that data can offer contradictory signals, making it more difficult to convert it into information. Thus, it is data overload that we face, not information overload.

There are three steps in the data-to-information process, and this chapter will be built around these steps, since at each step there is both promise and peril.

1. Data collection: The first step is collecting the data. In some cases, this can be as simple as accessing a computerized database. In others, it will require running experiments or surveys.
2. Data analysis: Once the data has been collected, not only does it have to be summarized and described, but you have to look for relationships in the data that you can use in your decision making. It is at this stage that statistical analysis comes into play.
3. Presentation: Having analyzed the data, you have to present it, not only so others can see and use the information you have gleaned from the data, but so you yourself have a sense of what that information is.

At each stage in the process it is easy to get lost in the details as you get drawn into data-collection debates, statistical arguments, and discussions about whether you should use bar graphs or pie charts. You have to remember that your endgame is to use the information to make better decisions and that anything that helps you do that is good and anything that leads you away from it is a distraction.

Collecting Data

The first step in the process is collecting data, a time-consuming and manual process for much of mankind's history. Broadly speaking, that data can either come from records maintained by an organizing entity (government, security exchange, regulator, private business), from surveys, or from experiments. As more and more of our transactions are done on or with computers, the data is generally recorded online, making the job of creating and maintaining databases simpler.

The Choices in Data Collection

In using data, a fundamental question is how much data is enough. At the risk of oversimplifying this choice, you often will have to decide between a smaller sample of meticulously collected and curated data and a larger sample with noisy and potentially erroneous data. In making that decision, you should be guided by the *law of large numbers*, one of the building blocks of statistics. Put simply, the law of large numbers states that as sample sizes get larger, your computed statistics from that sample get more precise. If that sounds unreasonable, the intuition is that as sample sizes get larger, the mistakes you may have on individual data points get averaged out.

Assuming that you are getting a sampling of the process you want to understand, you then have to make decisions on what will constitute the sample. In the context of financial data, for instance, here are some choices you will face:

1. Public company versus private company data: Publicly traded companies in most of the world face information disclosure requirements; they have to make their financial statements available to the public. As a consequence, it is far easier to access data on public companies than their privately owned counterparts.

2. Accounting versus market data: With public companies, not only do you have access to financial statement data but you also can obtain data from financial markets on price movements and transactions data (bid-ask spread, trading volume).

3. Domestic versus global data: Many researchers, and especially those in the United States, tend to stay focused on U.S. data, partly because they trust and understand it more and partly because it is easier to access, for most of them. As both companies and investors globalize, that domestic focus may no longer be appropriate, especially if the decisions you are making have global consequences.

4. Quantitative versus qualitative data: Databases tend to be skewed heavily toward quantitative data, partly because that is the bulk of the data collected and partly because it is so much easier to store and retrieve than qualitative data. Consequently, it is easy to obtain data on the number of directors at each publicly traded company but much more difficult to get data on how much dissension there is at board meetings at companies. One of the outgrowths of the surge in social media sites is the development of more sophisticated techniques for reading, analyzing, and storing qualitative data.

Your choices in what types of data you collect can affect the results you obtain, because your choices can create bias in your samples, often implicitly.

Data-Collection Biases

For those who still hold onto the belief that data is objective, a closer look at the data-collection process is often all that is needed to dispel that belief. In particular, when sampling, there are at least two biases that represent clear and present danger if your objective is to be unbiased and great opportunity if you have an agenda that you want to advance.

SELECTION BIAS

As we are all taught in our introductory statistics classes, it is perfectly reasonable to sample from a larger population and draw conclusions about that population, but only if that sample is random. That may sound like a simple task, but it can be very difficult to accomplish in the context of business and investing.

- In some cases, the sampling bias you introduce can be explicit when you pick and choose the observations in your sample to deliver the result you want. Thus, a researcher who starts off with the objective of showing that companies generally take good investments may decide to use only companies in the S&P 500 in his sample. Since these are the largest market capitalization companies in the United States and they reached that status because of their success in the past, it should not be surprising that they have a history of taking good investments, but that result cannot be generalized to the rest of the market.
- In other cases, the bias can be implicit and embedded in what you may believe are innocuous choices that you had to make in what data you would collect. For instance, restricting your sample to just publicly traded companies may be a choice that is thrust upon you, because the databases you use contain only those companies. However, the results you get from this data may not be generalizable to all businesses, since privately owned businesses tend to be smaller and more localized than public companies.

As a general rule, I find it useful when I sample data to also take a look at the data I exclude from my sample, just to be aware of biases.

Survivor Bias

The other challenge in sampling is survivor bias, that is, the bias introduced by ignoring the portions of your universe that have been removed from your data for one reason or another. As a simple example of survivor bias, consider research done by Stephen Brown, my colleague at New York University, on hedge fund returns. While many studies looking at hedge fund returns over time had concluded that they earned "excess" returns (over and above expectations), Professor Brown argued that the mistake many analysts were making was that they were starting with the hedge funds in existence today and working backward to see what returns those funds earned over time. By doing so, the analysts were missing the harsh reality of the hedge fund business, which is that the worst-performing hedge funds go out of business and not counting the returns from those funds pushes up the computed return for the sample. His research concluded that survivor bias adds about 2–3 percent to the average hedge fund return. In general, survivor bias will be a bigger issue with groups that have high failure rates, thus posing a more significant problem for investors looking at tech start-ups than for those looking at established consumer product companies.

Noise and Error

In this age of computer data, when less of the data is entered by hand, we have learned to trust the data more, perhaps too much. Even in the most carefully maintained databases, there will be *data input errors*, some of which are large enough to alter the results of your study. Consequently, it behooves researchers to do at least a first pass at the data to catch the big errors.

The other problem is *missing data*, either because the data is not available or because it did not make it into the database. One solution is to eliminate observations with missing data, but not only will this reduce your sample size, it may introduce bias if missing data is more common in some subsets of the population than in others. It is a problem that I face increasingly, as I have chosen to move away from U.S.-centric to global data. To provide an example, I consider lease commitments to be debt and convert them when looking at how much a company owes; U.S. companies are required to reveal these commitments for disclosure purposes, but in many emerging markets, especially in Asia, there is no such disclosure requirement. I have two choices. One is to go back to a conventional debt definition, which does not include leases, but I will then be settling for a much poorer measure of financial leverage than I could be using for the half of my global sample that does report leases. The other is to eliminate all firms that don't reveal lease commitments from any sampling for financial leverage and not only lose half of my sample but create significant bias. I settle for an intermediate choice; I use lease commitments as debt for U.S. firms and I make an approximation of future commitments, based on the current year's lease expense, for non-U.S. firms.

Data Analysis

I enjoyed my statistics classes in college, but I did find them abstract, with few real-world examples that I could relate to. That is a pity, because if only I had known then how critical statistics is to making sense of data, I would have paid more attention.

Tools for Data Analysis

When faced with a large data set, you want to start by summarizing the data into summary statistics before you embark on more complex analysis. The first two statistics you start with are the *mean* and the *standard deviation*, with the mean representing the simple average of all of the data points and the standard deviation capturing how much variability there is around the average. If the numbers are not distributed evenly around the average, the mean may not be the most representative number for the sample, and thus you may estimate the *median* (the 50th percentile of the numbers in your sample) or the *mode* (the number that occurs most frequently in your sample). There are other summary statistics designed to capture the spread of numbers in your sample, with the *skewness* measuring the symmetry in your sample numbers and the *kurtosis* the frequency of numbers that are very different from your mean.

For those who prefer a more visual description of the data, you will often see the numbers graphed out in a distribution. If your data is discrete, that is, it can take only a finite number of values, you can count the number of times each value occurs and create a *frequency table*, which you can then graph as a *frequency distribution*. For example, in the frequency table and distribution in figure 5.1, I report on the bond ratings

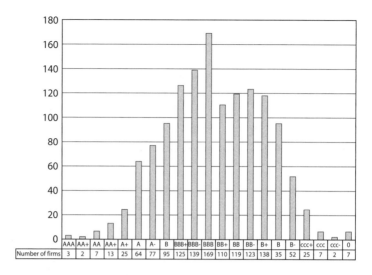

Number of firms	AAA	AA+	AA	AA+	A+	A	A-	B	BBB+	BBB-	BBB	BB+	BB	BB-	B+	B	B-	CCC+	CCC	CCC-	0
	3	2	7	13	25	64	77	95	125	139	169	110	119	123	138	35	52	25	7	2	7

Figure 5.1
S&P bond ratings for U.S. companies, January 2016. *Source*: S&P Capital IQ (for raw data).

(S&P rating, a discrete measure that takes on alphabetical values) for U.S. companies at the start of 2016.

If your data is continuous, that is, it can take any value between a minimum and maximum value, you can classify your numbers into smaller groupings, count the number in each group, and graph the results in a *histogram*. If the histogram that you have is close to a standardized probability distribution (normal, lognormal, exponential), you can then draw on the properties of these standardized distributions to make statistical judgments about your data. To illustrate, I have graphed out the distribution of price-earnings (PE) ratios for all companies in the United States for which a PE ratio could be computed at the end of 2015 (figure 5.2).

Finally, there are statistical measures and tools designed to measure how two or more variables move with each other. The simplest of these is the *correlation coefficient*, a number that is bounded between +1 (when two variables move in perfect harmony, in the same direction) and −1 (when two variables move in perfect harmony, in opposite directions). A close variant is the *covariance*, which also measures the comovement of two variables but is not bounded by −1 and +1. The easiest way to visualize the relationship between two variables is with a scatter plot, where the values of one variable are plotted against the other. In figure 5.3, for instance, I plot the PE ratios for U.S. companies against expected growth rates in earnings

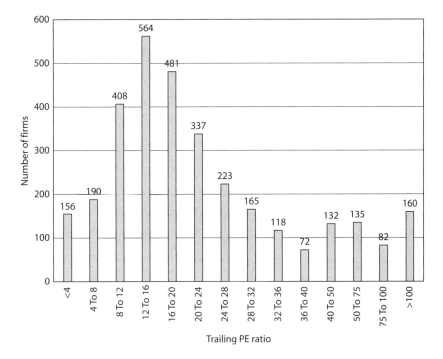

Figure 5.2
PE ratio for U.S. companies, January 2016. *Source*: Damodaran Online (http://www
.damodaran.com).

(as estimated by analysts) to see whether there is any truth to the conventional wisdom that higher-growth companies have higher PE ratios.

The good news for conventional wisdom is that it is true, in the aggregate, since the correlation between PE and growth is positive, but the bad news is that it is not that strong, since the correlation is only 20 percent. If the objective is to use one variable to predict another, the tool that fits well is a regression, with which you find a line that best fits the two variables. Graphically, a *simple regression* is most easily visualized in the scatter plot, and I report the results of a regression of PE against expected growth rates in (figure 5.3). The numbers in brackets in the regression are *t* statistics, with *t* statistics above 2 indicating statistical significance. Based on the regression, every 1 percent increase in expected growth translates into an increase of 0.441 in the PE ratio, and you can use the regression to predict the PE ratio for a firm with an expected growth rate of 10 percent:

$$\text{Predicted PE} = 19.86 + 44.10\ (0.10) = 23.27$$

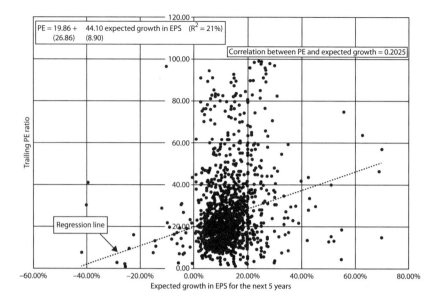

Figure 5.3
Trailing PE versus expected growth in earnings per share (EPS) for the next five years for U.S. companies, January 2016.

Note that this predicted PE comes with a wide range, reflecting the low predictive power of the regression (captured in the R-squared of 21%). The biggest advantage of a regression is that it can be extended to multiple variables, with a single dependent variable (the one you are trying to explain) linked to many independent variables. Thus, if you wanted to examine how the PE ratios of companies are related to the risk, growth, and profitability of those companies, you could run a multiple regression of PE (dependent variable) against proxies for growth, risk, and profitability (independent variables).

Biases in Analysis

The fact that we have statistical tools at our disposal that will do all of what we described in the last section and more is a mixed blessing, since it has opened the door to what can be best classified as "garbage in, garbage out" analysis. Looking at the state of data analysis in business and finance, here are a few of my observations:

1. We put too much trust in the average: With all of the data and analytical tools at our disposal, you would not expect this, but a

substantial proportion of business and investment decisions are still based on the average. I see investors and analysts contending that a stock is cheap because it trades at a PE that is lower than the sector average or that a company has too much debt because its debt ratio is higher than the average for the market. The average is not only a poor central measure on which to focus in distributions that are not symmetric, but it strikes me as a waste to not use the rest of the data. While an analyst in the 1960s could have countered with the argument that using all of the data was time-consuming and unwieldy, what conceivable excuse can be offered in today's data environment?

2. Normality is not the norm: One of the shameful legacies of statistics classes is that the only distribution most of us remember is the normal distribution. It is an extremely elegant and convenient distribution, since it can not only be fully characterized by just two summary statistics, the mean and the standard deviation, but it lends itself to probability statements such as "that has only a 1 percent chance of happening since it is 3 standard deviations away from the mean." Unfortunately, most real-world phenomena are not normally distributed, and that is especially true for data we look at in business and finance. In spite of that, analysts and researchers continue to use the normal distribution as their basis for making predictions and building models and are constantly surprised by outcomes that fall outside their ranges.[1]

3. The outlier problem: The problem with outliers is that they make your findings weaker. Not surprisingly, the way researchers respond to outliers is by ridding themselves of the source of the trouble. Removing outliers, though, is a dangerous game; it opens the door to bias, since outliers that don't fit your priors are quick to be removed, but outliers that do fit your priors are maintained. In fact, if you view your job in business and investing as dealing with crises, you can argue that it is the outliers you should be paying the most attention to, not the data that neatly fits your hypothesis.

Data Presentation

If you are collecting and analyzing data for your own decision making, you may be ready to make your best judgments after your data analysis. However, if you are crunching numbers for a decision maker or team or have to explain your decision to others, you will need to find ways to present the data to an audience that is neither as conversant with nor as interested in the data as you are.

Presentation Choices

The first way you can present the data is in tables, and there are two types of tables. The first is *reference tables*, which contain large amounts of data and allow people to look up specific data on individual segments. Thus, the tax rate data that I have, by sector, on my website is an example of a reference table. The second is *demonstration tables*, which are summary tables, whose objective is to show differences (or the lack thereof) between subgroups of the data.

The second way you can show data is in charts, and while there are a multitude of different charts, the three most commonly used are listed below:

1. Line charts: Line charts work best for showing trend lines in data across time and for comparing different series. In figure 5.4, I look at the equity risk premium for U.S. stocks and the U.S. Treasury bond rate for each year from 1960 to 2015. It allows me to not only describe how equity risk premiums have risen and fallen over different time periods but also how they have moved with risk-free rates.

2. Column and bar charts: Column and bar charts are most suited for comparing statistics across a few subgroups. For illustration, you can compare the PE ratios for companies in five different markets or five different sectors to see whether one or more of them is an outlier.

3. Pie charts: A pie chart is designed to illustrate the breakdown of a whole into component parts. Thus, I can use a pie chart to illustrate the parts of the world where a company gets its revenues or the businesses that a multibusiness company is in.

I am a fan of Edward Tufte, a visionary when it comes to presenting data, and I agree with him that we need to go beyond the restrictive and dull bounds of spreadsheet programs to create pictures that better convey the story in the data. In fact, presenting data more creatively is a discipline in itself and has spawned research, new visualization tools (infographics), and new businesses to further the use of these tools.

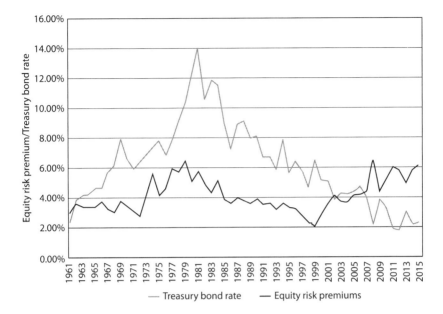

Figure 5.4
Equity risk premiums and Treasury bond rate, 1961–2015. *Source*: Damodaran Online (http://pages.stern.nyu.edu/~adamodar).

Presentation Biases and Sins

All through this chapter we have noted how bias creeps into the process, either implicitly or explicitly. At the data-collection stage, it shows up in biased samples designed to deliver the results you want, and in the data-analysis stage, in how you deal with outliers. Not surprisingly, it finds its way into the data-presentation stage as well, in small but still significant ways, ranging from changing the scaling of axes to making changes look bigger than they are to the use of infographics that are meant more to mislead than to inform.

If there is one message that you should heed at the data-presentation stage, it is that less is more and that your objective is to not drown decision makers in three-dimensional graphs with dubious content but to build up to better decisions. So do not use a table when mentioning two numbers in the text will do; do not insert a graph when a table will suffice; do not give a graph a third dimension when two dimensions are all you need.

I have been guilty of violating all of these rules at some time in my life and I perhaps will do so later in this book; if I do, I hope that you will call me out on my transgressions.

CASE STUDY 5.1: THE PHARMACEUTICAL BUSINESS—R&D
AND PROFITABILITY, NOVEMBER 2015

To understand the drug business, I started my analysis in 1991, toward the beginning of a surge in spending on health care in the United States. The pharmaceutical companies at the time were cash machines, built on a platform of substantial upfront investments in research and development (R&D). The drugs generated by R&D that made it through the Food and Drug Administration (FDA) approval process and into commercial production were used to cover the aggregated cost of R&D and to generate significant excess profits. The key to this process was the pricing power enjoyed by the drug companies, the result of a well-defended patent process, significant growth in health-care spending, splintered health insurance companies, and lack of accountability for costs at every level (from patients to hospitals to the government). In this model, not surprisingly, investors rewarded pharmaceutical companies based on the amounts they spent on R&D (secure in their belief that the costs could be passed on to customers) and the fullness and balance of their product pipelines.

So how has the story changed over the last decade? The growth rate in health-care costs seems to have slowed down and the pricing power of drug companies has waned for many reasons, with changes in health-care laws being only one of many drivers. First, we have seen more consolidation within the health insurance business, potentially increasing its bargaining power with the pharmaceutical companies on drug prices. Second, the government has used the buying clout of Medicaid to bargain for better prices on drugs, and while Medicare still works through insurance companies, it can put pressure on drug companies to negotiate lower costs. Third, the pharmacies that represent the distribution networks for many drugs have also been corporatized and consolidated and are gaining a voice in the pricing process. The net effect of all of these changes is that R&D has much more uncertain payoffs and has to be evaluated like any other large capital investment: it is good only when it creates value for a business.

To test the hypotheses that pharmaceutical companies have lost pricing power between 1991 and 2014 and that R&D no longer has the revenue punch it used to have, I started by looking at the average profit margins at pharmaceutical companies in figure 5.5, using different measures of profit (net income, operating income, earnings before interest, taxes, depreciation, and R&D) for each year:

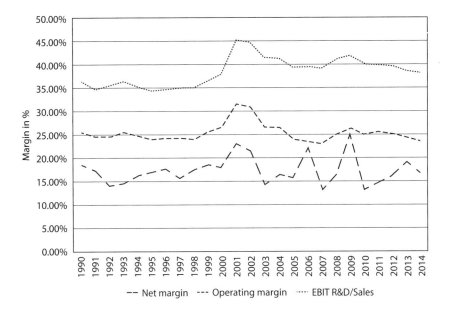

Figure 5.5
Pharmaceutical companies: profit margins.

The evidence is only weakly supportive of the hypothesis that pricing power has waned over the period, since margins, while down slightly, have not changed much over the time period.

I followed up by looking at whether the payoff to R&D in terms of revenue growth has slowed over time by looking at R&D spending as a percent of sales each year and revenue growth in the same year from 1991 to 2014 in table 5.1.

I know there is a substantial lag between R&D spending and revenue growth, but as a simplistic measure of the contemporaneous payoff to R&D, I computed a growth to R&D to sales growth:

$$\text{Growth to R\&D ratio} = \text{revenue growth rate/R\&D spending as percent of sales}$$

Notwithstanding its limitations, this ratio illustrates the declining payoff to R&D spending at pharmaceutical firms, dropping close to zero in the 2011–2014 period.

What can we learn from this analysis? First, pharmaceutical companies remain profitable, notwithstanding the significant changes in the health-care

Table 5.1
Payoff to R&D in Revenue Growth

Year	R&D/sales	Revenue growth rate	Growth to R&D ratio
1991	10.17%	49.30%	4.85
1992	10.64%	6.40%	0.60
1993	10.97%	3.58%	0.33
1994	10.30%	15.85%	1.54
1995	10.37%	17.32%	1.67
1996	10.44%	11.38%	1.09
1997	10.61%	13.20%	1.24
1998	11.15%	19.92%	1.79
1999	11.08%	15.66%	1.41
2000	11.41%	8.15%	0.71
2001	13.74%	−8.17%	−0.59
2002	13.95%	4.80%	0.34
2003	14.72%	16.26%	1.10
2004	14.79%	8.17%	0.55
2005	15.40%	1.49%	0.10
2006	16.08%	2.86%	0.18
2007	16.21%	8.57%	0.53
2008	15.94%	6.21%	0.39
2009	15.58%	−4.87%	−0.31
2010	15.17%	19.82%	1.31
2011	14.30%	3.77%	0.26
2012	14.48%	−2.99%	−0.21
2013	14.28%	2.34%	0.16
2014	14.36%	1.67%	0.12
1991–1995	10.49%	18.49%	1.80
1996–2000	10.94%	13.66%	1.25
2001–2005	14.52%	4.51%	0.30
2006–2010	15.80%	6.52%	0.42
2011–2014	14.36%	1.20%	0.08

business in the United States. Second, pharmaceutical companies have not cut back on internal R&D spending as much as some stories suggest they have. Third, the R&D table suggests that pharmaceutical companies should be spending less money on R&D, not more, as the growth payoff to R&D becomes lower and lower. Finally, it provides at least a partial explanation for why some pharmaceutical companies have embarked on the acquisition path, focusing on buying younger, smaller companies for the products in their research pipelines.

CASE STUDY 5.2: EXXONMOBIL'S OIL PRICE EXPOSURE, MARCH 2009

In chapter 13, I will describe a valuation of ExxonMobil in March 2009, in which the primary problem I faced was that oil prices had dropped significantly (to $45 a barrel) in the six months leading up to the valuation, but much of the financial data (including revenue and earnings) that ExxonMobil was reporting reflected a prior year, when oil prices had averaged almost $80 a barrel. While the obvious insight is that the trailing twelve-month earnings are too high, given the drop in oil prices, I still faced the challenge of trying to adjust the company's earnings to the lower oil price.

To see how sensitive ExxonMobil's earnings were to oil prices, I collected historical data on its operating income and the average oil price each year from 1985 to 2008. The numbers are in figure 5.6.

I also ran a regression of ExxonMobil's operating income on the average oil price each year. Not only is the company's operating income determined almost entirely by oil price levels (with an R-squared exceeding 90%), but you can use the regression to get an adjusted operating income for it at the prevailing oil price of $45 a barrel.

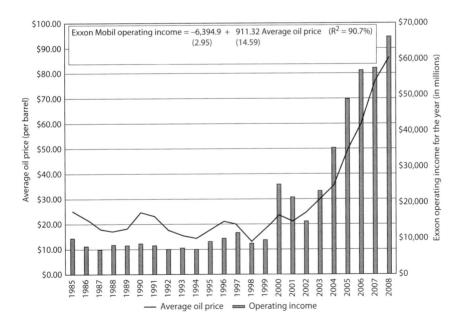

Figure 5.6
ExxonMobil operating income versus average oil price.

ExxonMobil oil-price-adjusted operating income = −$6,394.9 million
+ $911.32 million (45) = $34,615 million

While this operating income of $34.5 billion was substantially lower than the reported income over the prior twelve months, this is the operating income that you will see me use in my Exxon valuation.

CASE STUDY 5.3: A PICTURE OF VALUE DESTRUCTION—PETROBRAS

I am not particularly creative when it comes to converting data analyses into presentations that tell a story. I do remain proud of an analysis I did in May 2015 of how Petrobras, the Brazilian oil company, put itself in a cycle of value destruction that reduced its market capitalization by close to $100 billion (see figure 5.7).

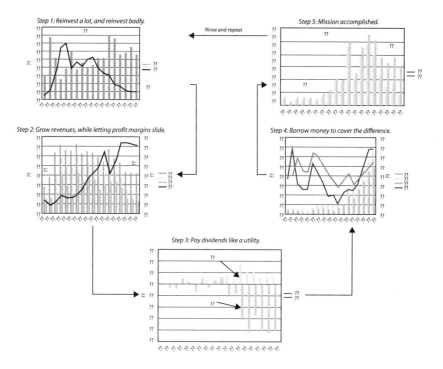

Figure 5.7
A roadmap to destroying value: Petrobras, 2015.

I undoubtedly violated many data-visualization rules and tried to pack too much into one picture, but I was trying to convey not only the collection of actions that Petrobras took that led to the value destruction but how these actions logically led one to the other. Thus, the massive investments in new reserves without regard to profits had to be financed with new debt issues because the company wanted to continue paying high dividends. The net effect was a value-destruction cycle that occurred over and over and destroyed value at an exponential pace.

Conclusion

In this chapter I looked at the three steps in using data, starting with data collection, moving on to analysis of that data, and finishing with how best to present that data. At each step you have to fight the urge to mold the data to fit your preconceptions. If you are willing to keep an open mind and learn from the data, it will augment your storytelling skills and lead to better investment and business decisions.

6

Building a Narrative

Now that I have laid out the broad processes for storytelling and number crunching, it is time to get specific. In this chapter I begin by looking at business narratives, that is, the stories that are told about businesses and the process of building these stories. As you read this chapter, you will notice that much of it is focused on the storyteller, and if you are a listener, you may wonder whether these same lessons apply to you. After all, the interests of the storyteller and the investor can sometimes diverge. Thus, if you are a founder or a manager, you often want to push soaring narratives about your venture, since it may result in a higher value being attached to it. As the investors to whom the pitch is made, you not only have to examine the same narrative for credibility, since it is your money at risk, but you have to develop your own narrative for the company, which may diverge from the founder's story. In my view, a good business story, that is, one that has staying power and backs up a successful business, is one in which listener and storyteller interests converge. If you are a potential investor in a publicly traded company, you often have to be both a storyteller, developing a narrative that underpins value, and a listener, probing your own story for its weakest links. The bottom line is that there is no room in investing for passive listeners and whether you are a founder, a manager, or an investor, you ultimately have to play the storyteller role.

The Essence of a Good Narrative

In chapter 4 I looked at the ingredients of a good story, and I can draw on some of those lessons when constructing narratives to back a business or an investment. In particular, a business narrative needs the following ingredients to work:

1. It has to be simple: A simple story that makes sense will leave a more lasting impression than a complex story in which it is tough to make connections.
2. It has to be credible: Business stories need to be credible for investors to act on them. If you are a skillful enough storyteller you may be able to get away with leaving unexplained loose ends, but those loose ends will eventually imperil your story and perhaps your business.
3. It has to inspire: Ultimately, you don't tell a business story to win creativity awards but to inspire your audience (employees, customers, and potential investors) to buy into the story.
4. It should lead to action: Once your audience buys into your story, you want them to act, employees by choosing to come to work for your company, customers by buying your products and services, and investors by putting their money in your business.

The bottom line for a business narrative is that it is less about specifics and details and more about big picture and vision.

The Pre-work

Before a story is constructed for a business, there is homework to be done by both storytellers and listeners. You have to review the history of the business for which you are telling the story, understand the market in which the company operates, and have a measure of what the competition looks like.

The Company

The logical place to start building the narrative is with the company you are trying to tell the story about. If the company has been in operation for a while, you can start with its history, trying to get measures of past growth, profitability, and business direction. While you may not be bound by that history in constructing your narrative for the company's future, you still have to be aware of the past.

With young companies, there will be less to learn from examining the past. Poring over the financial statements for a young start-up will usually yield the unsurprising conclusion that it did not generate much (if any) in revenue in the most recent periods and it reported losses while doing so. With these companies, you may learn more as an investor by looking at the founders/owners running the businesses and their histories and other more established companies in the same business.

The Market

The second step is looking at the larger market in which the company is operating or plans to operate. Table 6.1 contains a checklist of some of the questions for which you are trying to find answers.

With established companies in mature businesses, this analysis is relatively simple, since the market characteristics are observable (market growth, profitability, trend lines) and often forecastable. Your job gets more difficult if you have companies in evolving or changing businesses, with that change coming from a maturing of the business, a shift in consumer behavior (as is the case with the entertainment content business as consumers shift to streaming), changes in regulatory rules/restrictions (for example, the telecommunication business after deregulation), or geographic shifts. In these cases, you will not only have to make a judgment about the current state of the business but also how you see it evolving over time.

Perhaps the most challenging scenario is when you are trying to build a narrative for a young company in an evolving and shifting business. Thus, in valuing Twitter in 2013, I had to make a judgment about whether Twitter's business would remain online advertising (its primary source of revenues in 2013) or whether it could leverage its user base to expand into retail or even convert to a subscription-driven model. As an investor looking at Twitter, you may be tempted to ask Twitter's owners and managers for the answers, but recognize that they are as uncertain as you are and often more biased.

Some businesses are easier to assess and understand than others. In general, you will have an easier time assessing and understanding settled

Table 6.1
Market Analysis

Category	Questions	Comments
Growth	How quickly is the overall market growing? Are some parts of the market growing faster than others?	In addition to looking at the average growth rate over time, you also want to detect shifts in the market across product lines and geographies.
Profitability	How profitable is this business, in the aggregate? Are there any trends over time in the profitability?	Look at profit margins (gross, operating, and net) and accounting return trends over time.
Investing for growth	What assets do companies in this business have to invest in, to grow? How much investment are companies making collectively in this business to generate their growth? How easy is it to scale up?	With manufacturing companies, investment is generally in plant, equipment, and assembly lines, but with technology and pharmaceutical companies, the investment may take the form of R&D.
Risk	How much do revenues and earnings vary across time? What are the forces that cause these operating numbers to change? How much debt (or fixed commitments) do companies in this business tend to carry? What are the risks that companies in this business may fail? What is the trigger (debt payments due or running out of cash) that cause failure?	Volatility in your revenues/earnings can be caused by macroeconomic variables, which can include interest rate, inflation, commodity price, and political risk, or from company-specific variables.

businesses than transitional ones and businesses represented by mostly publicly traded firms than businesses dominated by small, private companies. That said, the payoff to assessing and understanding businesses is greater when they are more difficult to assess than when they are simple to analyze.

The Competition

The final piece of this pre-work is to assess your competition, current and potential. Building on the dimensions of growth, profitability, investment, and risk that you estimated for the entire sector or business, you now look at variations on those dimensions across companies within the market.

Table 6.2 contains questions that may better help you understand this process.

After you have assessed the companies in the businesses, you will have to examine how your company fits into the competitive landscape and what you see as your pathway to profits. In making these judgments, it is easy to assume that while the rest of the world stays still, your company will move quickly from opportunity to opportunity, blazing new trails and generating profits, but that assumption is usually unrealistic. When you see large market opportunities, rest assured that much of the rest of the world does as well, and when you move decisively to take advantage of them, be ready for others to be making the same moves. You can learn from game theory, the branch of economics that looks at multiplayer games and tries to forecast how these games will play out, as a function of not just your moves but also those of the other players. You may not always be the best capitalized, cleverest, or quickest player in the game, and if you are not, it is good (though hard) to be honest in your assessment.

Table 6.2
Competitive Analysis

Category	Questions	Comments
Growth	Are there big differences in growth across companies within the business? If there are big differences, what are the determinants of these differences?	If companies in the business are growing at different rates, you are trying to assess whether it is related to size, geography, or market segment.
Profitability	Are there big differences in profitability across companies within the business? If there are big differences, what are the determinants of these differences?	If there are big differences in profit margins across companies, you are looking to see what types of companies earn the most and which ones the least.
Investing for growth	Is there a standardized investment model that is used by all companies in the market? If not, are there differences in profitability and growth across companies with different models?	As companies grow in this business, you are checking to see whether their investing needs decrease (economies of scale and networking benefits) or increase (with more competition).
Risk	Are there big differences in risk (earnings variability and survival) across companies within the business? If there are big differences, what are the determinants of these differences?	You are interested in whether there are variations in risk (operating and survival) across companies, and if so, what causes those variations.

CASE STUDY 6.1: THE AUTO BUSINESS, OCTOBER 2015

In the chapters to come, I will value two automobile companies: Ferrari, in the next four chapters, to illustrate the sequence from narrative to value; and mention Volkswagen, in passing, to examine how a scandal may (or may not) upend a narrative. For both companies, I will be drawing on the auto business as it exists today and make assumptions about changes that are coming.

The auto business has a long history, tracing back to the early part of the twentieth century. Its growth provided the base for the building of industrial economies, and there was a time when as auto companies performed, so did the nation's economy. Those glory days are now in the past, and the auto business today bears the characteristics of a bad business in which companies collectively earn less than their cost of capital and most companies destroy value. If that sounds like a brash overgeneralization, it is a view shared by Sergio Marchionne, CEO of Fiat Chrysler, one of the largest auto companies. Marchionne is not afraid to talk the language of investors and is open about the problems confronting not only his company but also the entire automobile business. While he has been arguing that case for a while, sometimes in public and sometimes with other auto company executives, he crystallized his arguments in a presentation titled "Confessions of a Capital Junkie" that he made in an analyst conference call.[1] In this presentation he argues that the auto business has earned less than its cost of capital for much of the last decade and that without significant structural changes, it will continue to underperform.

So, what is it that makes the auto business so bad, at least collectively? Looking at the business broadly, here are three characteristics that underpin the business:

1. It is a low-growth business: The auto business is a cyclical one, with ups and downs that reflect economic cycles, but even allowing for its cyclic nature, the business is a mature one. That is reflected in the growth rate in revenues at auto companies in table 6.3.

    During this period, the emerging market economies in Asia and Latin America provided a significant boost to sales, but even with that boost, the compounded annual growth rate in aggregate revenues at auto companies between 2005 and 2014 was only 5.63 percent.

2. It has poor profit margins: A key point that Marchionne made about the auto business is that operating margins of companies in this business were much too slim, given their cost structures. To illustrate this point, and to set up my valuation of Ferrari, I computed the pretax operating margins of all auto companies listed globally with market capitalizations exceeding $1 billion (see figure 6.1).

Table 6.3

Revenues and Growth at Auto Companies, 2005–2014

Year	Total revenues	Percent growth rate (%)
2005	$1,274,716.60	11.54
2006	$1,421,804.20	30.44
2007	$1,854,576.40	−1.94
2008	$1,818,533.00	−13.51
2009	$1,572,890.10	15.47
2010	$1,816,269.40	8.06
2011	$1,962,630.40	7.54
2012	$2,110,572.20	2.28
2013	$2,158,603.00	−3.36
2014	$2,086,124.80	5.63
Compounded growth: 2005–2014		

Source: S&P Capital IQ.

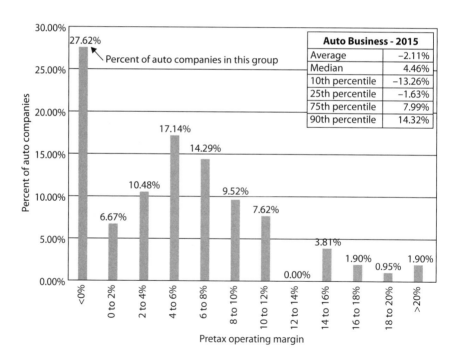

Figure 6.1

Operating margin for auto companies, October 2015. *Source*: S&P Capital IQ.

Not only do more than a quarter of all automobile firms lose money, the median pretax operating margin is 4.46 percent.

3. It has high reinvestment needs: The auto business has always required significant plant and equipment investments, but in recent years the growth of auto-related technology has also pushed up R&D spending at auto companies. One measure of the drag this puts on cash flows is to look at net capital expenditures (capital expenditures in excess of depreciation) and R&D as a percent of sales for the entire sector (see figure 6.2).

In 2014, auto companies collectively reinvested almost 5 percent of their revenues back into their businesses, with R&D comprising the bulk of that reinvestment.

It is this combination of anemic revenue growth, slim margins, and increasing reinvestment that causes this business to deliver returns that are lower than its cost of capital, as is evidenced in table 6.4.

In nine of the ten years between 2004 and 2014, auto companies have collectively earned returns on their invested capital that are less than their costs of capital.

Defenders of the status quo will undoubtedly argue that this poor performance is in the overall sample and that subsets of companies are performing better.

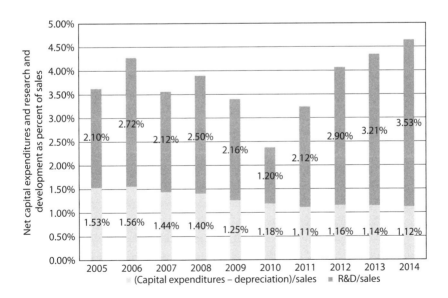

Figure 6.2

Reinvestment as percent of sales for auto companies, 2005–2014. *Source*: S&P Capital IQ.

Table 6.4

Return on Invested Capital (ROIC) and Cost of Capital: Auto Companies

	ROIC	Cost of capital	ROIC – cost of capital
2004	6.82%	7.93%	−1.11%
2005	10.47%	7.02%	3.45%
2006	4.60%	7.97%	−3.37%
2007	7.62%	8.50%	−0.88%
2008	3.48%	8.03%	−4.55%
2009	−4.97%	8.58%	−13.55%
2010	5.16%	8.03%	−2.87%
2011	7.55%	8.15%	−0.60%
2012	7.80%	8.55%	−0.75%
2013	7.83%	8.47%	−0.64%
2014	6.47%	7.53%	−1.06%

Table 6.5

Auto Company Profitability by Market Capitalization, October 2015

Size class	Number of firms	Operating margin	Net margin	Pretax ROIC
Largest (>$10 billion)	31	6.31%	5.23%	6.63%
2	16	5.24%	5.57%	10.72%
3	14	2.43%	3.19%	3.40%
4	20	1.51%	−0.40%	2.02%
Smallest (<$1 billion)	26	2.46%	2.56	2.74%

To address this argument, I looked across auto companies in terms of market capitalization, geography, and market focus (luxury versus mass market); here is what I found:

1. Small versus large: When the auto companies are classified by market capitalization into five classes (see table 6.5), the largest auto companies have, on average, delivered higher margins than smaller companies, but the returns on capital are underwhelming across the board.
2. Developed versus emerging: Since much of the growth in auto sales has come from emerging markets in the last decade, there is the possibility that emerging market auto companies perform better than developed market auto companies. In table 6.6 I compare the two groups on profitability.

Again, the results are underwhelming. Emerging market auto companies are less profitable than developed market auto companies on an operating

Table 6.6
Developed Versus Emerging Market Auto Companies, October 2015

Classification	Number of firms	Operating margin	Net margin	Pretax ROIC
Emerging auto	73	5.01%	6.13%	7.54%
Developed auto	34	6.45%	4.91%	6.52%

margin basis and score only a little better than developed market companies on net margin and return on invested capital.

3. Mass market versus luxury: The super–luxury car manufacturers (Ferrari, Aston Martin, Lamborghini, Bugatti, etc.), with huge price tags on their offerings, cater to the superrich and have seen sales grow faster than the rest of the auto industry and have been much more profitable. Much of the additional growth is coming from the newly minted rich in emerging markets in general and in China in particular.

In my valuation of Ferrari, I will draw on these general findings about the auto business in crafting a narrative for the company.

CASE STUDY 6.2: THE RIDE-SHARING LANDSCAPE, JUNE 2014

I became interested in Uber after reading a news story in June 2014 that indicated that Uber had been valued at $17 billion in a venture capital round. I posted my first valuation of Uber in June 2014, viewing it as an urban car service company with local (but not global) networking benefits. At the time my initial task was to assess the size and makeup of that market. One significant problem I ran into is that, at least in mid-2014, the car service market was localized, with different rules and structures in different cities and little in terms of organized information, making it a much more difficult business to assess than the auto business.

1. Market size: I started with an attempt at estimating the size of the total market by looking at the largest taxi market cities in the world (Tokyo, London, New York, and a few other large cities) and checking out both trade group sites and regulatory estimates of market sizes. Thus, for New York, I was able to get a measure of the total revenues in 2013 from yellow cabs and licensed car service companies from the New York City Taxi & Limousine Commission. Unfortunately, that information was not available for many emerging market cities, and my initial estimate of the urban car service market of $100 billion is partially based on guesstimates.

2. Market growth: The records also indicate that the growth in the market is low, about 2 percent in developed markets and perhaps 4–5 percent in emerging markets. That information again comes from markets where regulatory authorities keep tabs on and report cab revenues.

3. Profitability: The private cab companies that make up this market are generally reluctant to open up their books, but I used two numbers to back into the conclusion that this was a relatively profitable market, at least prior to the arrival of the ride-sharing businesses. The first comes from looking at the handful of publicly traded cab companies across the world and the pretax operating profit margins they report, generally 15–20 percent. The second is a judgment based on looking at the market prices of the rights to operate a cab, which is public information in some cities. In New York, for instance, a yellow cab medallion in December 2013 was trading at about \$1.2 million, yielding an imputed profit of about \$100,000–\$120,000 per year.

4. Investment: The conventional way in which this business has been run is for an investor to pay for and win the rights to operate a medallion (an upfront investment), which is followed by buying a cab and, if the investor does not plan to drive the cab, hiring a driver (paying either a fixed salary or sharing a portion of the cab receipts). The investments are therefore in the cab medallion primarily, and in the automobile secondarily, and to grow, you have to invest in both.

5. Risk: The regulatory constraints on entry into the car service business had resulted in generally stable earnings and cash flows, though the state of the local economy can still exercise its effects on cab revenues. In 2002, when the New York city economy was in the doldrums, taxi receipts also dropped off, and more generally, the cab service business in the city has reflected the health of the financial service business over this period. The only reason that some cab companies were more exposed to this risk than others was because they had borrowed more money or leased their cars, and these fixed payments had to be made out of reduced revenues.

The car service business in June 2014, with its regulation and splintered competition, also meant that the big differences across competitors were created by regulatory restrictions rather than company characteristics.

The Story

Once you understand the structure of the market in which your business operates, you are ready to take the first step in valuation and construct a narrative about your company. Since it is an iterative process, my advice, if you are uncertain, is to start with a story and then revisit it as you run into roadblocks or contradictory data. Along the way, you will have to make choices, since your story can be big and soaring or narrow and focused, it can stay with the status quo or be built on challenging the established ways of doing business (disruption), it can be about a business that you expect to continue in the long term (going concern) or it can be for a finite period, and it can cover the spectrum of growth (from high growth to decline). Obviously the story you tell has to match the company, and I will look at ways to test for mismatches in the next chapter.

Big Versus Small

In a big story, you describe a business with an expansive vision that plans to be in many businesses and/or many geographic regions, whereas in a small one, your vision of the company is restricted to a specific business and/or a specific geographic area. No contest, you say? It is true that big stories create more excitement among employees and investors and may allow you to get a higher price attached to your business, especially early in the process. But big stories also create two costs. The first is that you will be drawn to be in many businesses at a time when you cannot afford to lose your focus, and that can have devastating effects on your company. The second is that you push expectations up, and if you fail to meet them, you will be punished.

I am jumping the gun here, but this contrast is one that I saw playing out in September 2015, with Uber and Lyft, two ride-sharing companies. While my initial valuation of Uber in June 2014 valued it as an urban car service company, its words and actions in the year following led me to rethink my narrative and treat it as a global, logistics company instead, thus expanding its potential market. In the same periods, Lyft narrowed its focus, first in its business (by asserting that it would limit itself to ride sharing) and then in its geographic focus (by deciding to grow just in the United States). I will revisit these companies in chapter 14 to see the effect these contrasting narratives have on their valuations.

Establishment Versus Disruption

If you are describing a company that follows established business models, that is, the status quo, in how it operates, your story is a simple one.

You will still have to find a business dimension, such as having a lower cost structure or being able to charge a price premium, where you can differentiate yourself from the competition. In contrast, a company that plans to challenge established business practices is following a disruption model. Again, which one you pick will depend on the company you are valuing and the business you are targeting.

If a company already makes up a significant part of the status quo, it is very difficult to credibly make a disruption story about the company. This, for instance, would be why a story of Tesla as a disruptive company is easier to make than one about Volkswagen upending the status quo. In fact, if you follow Clayton Christensen's adage that disruption generally comes from companies that have little to lose, you can more easily tell disruptive stories about companies early in the life cycle.

There is another part of the argument that also needs to stand up to scrutiny. It is very difficult to disrupt businesses that are being run efficiently. Not only will these established companies be better positioned to push back against disruption, but customers will be less likely to shift. If a business is badly run, insofar as the players in the business make little or no money while delivering products and services that leave their customers dissatisfied, you have the perfect storm for disruption. Thus, your case for disruption becomes much stronger with Uber, where the traditional cab business is an overregulated, underperforming mess and no one (cabdrivers, customers, regulators) is happy.

Going Concern Versus Finite Life

One of the advantages of telling stories about publicly traded companies is that you can keep them going in perpetuity, legal entities with infinite lives. While that is often the path you will choose when valuing publicly traded companies, there are times when an alternate vision may work better. If you are valuing a privately owned legal or a medical practice or a publicly traded royalty trust (where you get a share of a natural resource reserve until it is exhausted), your story should have a finite life span, and when that span is over you tie up loose ends (liquidate your assets) and end the story.

There are some who would argue that all stories about natural resource companies (oil, mining) should always be finite life stories, since these natural resource reserves will be exhausted at some point in time. Thus, if the story that you are telling about ExxonMobil is that it is an oil company, you may decide that a finite life span better fits the story. In contrast, if your story about ExxonMobil describes it as an energy company, where once the oil gets exhausted ExxonMobil will move into whatever the next energy source may be, the constraint may be lifted and you can treat it as a going concern.

The Growth Spectrum

The final choice you will face is where to put your company on the growth spectrum. With a start-up in a big market, the sky can be the limit in terms of growth, but with a declining company in a shrinking business, your narrative may very well require you to make the company smaller over time. Using just some of the companies that I will be analyzing in the next few chapters, a high-growth story clearly works for Uber or Tesla but not for Volkswagen. For companies like Amazon, this may be the most debated component of the narrative, with those who feel Amazon's already large size will make high growth elusive attaching a lower value to the company, and those who believe Amazon will find new markets and businesses convinced it will be able to maintain its double-digit revenue growth. With JCPenney, a company that I will value in chapter 14, the question is not how high the growth will be but how much shrinkage the company will see as its base business continues to deteriorate.

CASE STUDY 6.3: THE UBER NARRATIVE, JUNE 2014

In June 2014, when I first tried to value Uber, I did not have much experience with the company's products and its practices. In my research on how the company operates, I quickly came to the conclusion that Uber was not in the taxi business, at least in the conventional sense, since it owned no cabs and had no cabdrivers as employees. Instead, it played the role of matchmaker, matching a driver/car with a customer looking for a ride and taking a slice of the fare for providing the service. Its value, to its riders, comes from its screening of the drivers/cars (to ensure both safety and comfort), its pricing/payment system (customers choose the level of service and are quoted a fare), and its convenience (you can track the car that is coming to pick you up on your phone screen).

Figure 6.3 captures the steps in the Uber business model as I saw it in mid-2014, with comments on what it is that Uber offers at each stage and whether that offering is unique.

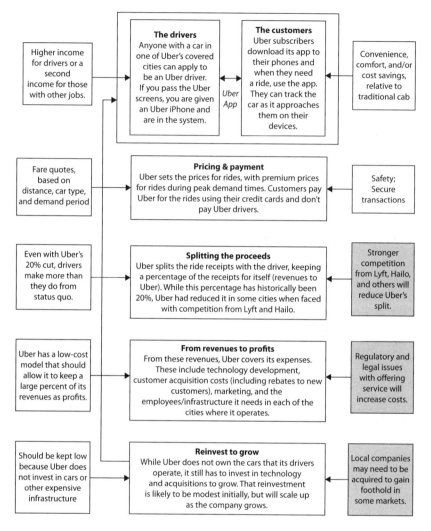

Figure 6.3
The Uber business model, June 2014.

Uber had been able to grow at exponential rates since its founding in 2009, with its CEO, Travis Kalanick, claiming that it was doubling its size every six months.

To get to a story for Uber, I went through a sequence of key parts of the narrative, and here were the judgments that I made on each one, at least in June 2014:

1. The business: Uber is and will remain an urban car service company. While it can expand into suburbia and into other businesses, the demand will be muted and it will not be cost-efficient for Uber to expand.

2. Market growth: Uber (and other ride-sharing services) will draw new customers into the urban car service markets, some from mass transit and some from private cars. That will push up growth in the urban car service market.

3. Networking benefits: Uber's networking benefits will be local, that is, if Uber becomes the largest player in a particular city, it will find it easier to get even bigger in that city. However, that success will not benefit it in a different city, where a competing ride-sharing company may be the biggest player and enjoy local networking benefits of its own.

4. Competitive advantages: The decision to split the taxi receipts, 80 percent for the driver and 20 percent for the ride-sharing company, is arbitrary, but it is accepted as the standard, at least in the United States. Uber's competitive position is strong enough that it will be able to maintain this sharing agreement and hence its pricing power.

5. Business model: Uber has a low–capital intensity model in which it does not own the cars that its service uses and has minimal infrastructure investment in the cities into which it expands. That model is assumed to be sustainable and Uber will continue with it.

6. Risk: Uber is a young company, losing money and in constant need of new capital. Its success in delivering growth and access to a healthy private capital market will keep the probability that the company will run out of money low, but it is still a business with substantial operating risk.

Could this story be wrong? Of course, but that is the nature of investing and business. In the next chapter I will start building the numbers that are consistent with the story.

CASE STUDY 6.4: THE FERRARI NARRATIVE, OCTOBER 2015 (AHEAD OF ITS INITIAL PUBLIC OFFERING)

The Ferrari story started with Enzo Ferrari, a racing car enthusiast who established a business in 1929 to assist and sponsor race car drivers driving Alfa Romeos. While Enzo manufactured his first racing car (the Tipo 815) in 1940, Ferrari as a car-making company was founded in 1947, with its manufacturing facilities in Maranello in Italy. For much of its early existence, it was privately owned by the Ferrari family, though it is said that Enzo viewed it primarily as a racing car company that happened to sell cars to the public. In the mid-1960s, in financial trouble, Enzo Ferrari sold a 50 percent stake in the company to Fiat. That holding was subsequently increased to 90 percent in 1988 (with the Ferrari family retaining the remaining 10 percent). Since then, the company has been a small, albeit very profitable, piece of Fiat (and Fiat Chrysler).

To illustrate how exclusive the Ferrari club is, in all of 2014, the company sold *only 7,255 cars*, a number that had barely budged over the previous five years. The company has its roots in Italy but is dependent on a superrich clientele globally for its sales, as evidenced in figure 6.4, where I graph out Ferrari's sales by region in 2014.

Note that a significant slice of the revenue pie came from the Middle East, and that Ferrari, like many other global companies, became increasingly dependent on China for growth. As a by-product of this exclusivity and the pricing power bestowed by it, Ferrari also reported an operating margin of 18.20 percent in the twelve months leading into the IPO, more than triple the global auto industry average. Finally, the company had weathered the market crises of the prior decade remarkably well, with little damage to its sales, pricing power, and profit margins.

Building on this data, my story for Ferrari at the time of its IPO in 2015 was that it would remain an extra-exclusive automobile company, keeping production low and prices high. The benefits of this strategy are high operating margins, partly because of the high prices and partly because the company did not have to spend much on expensive ad campaigns or selling. It also will keep reinvestment needs to a minimum, since capacity expansion will not be necessary, though the company will continue spending on R&D to preserve its edge (on speed and styling).

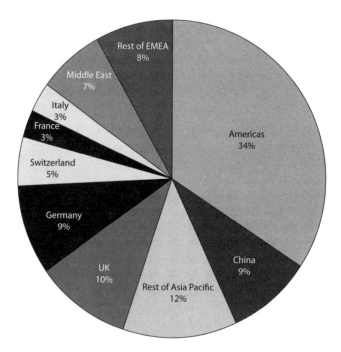

Figure 6.4
Ferrari revenue breakdown.

In addition, by focusing on a very small group of superrich people around the world, Ferrari may be less affected by macroeconomic forces than other luxury auto companies. In the next two chapters, I will convert this story into valuation inputs and value for the company.

CASE STUDY 6.5: AMAZON, THE *FIELD OF DREAMS* MODEL, OCTOBER 2014

Amazon is a truly extraordinary success story. Starting as an online bookstore in the 1990s, the company became the poster child for the dot-com boom in the last part of that decade and then, more impressively, survived the dot-com bust. In January 2000, close to the peak of the boom, I valued Amazon, on the assumption that it would grow its revenues fortyfold over the following decade and convert its operating losses to profits.[2] In the years thereafter, the company more than delivered on the revenue growth but fell well short of my profit targets (set in 2000), as evidenced in table 6.7.

Table 6.7

Amazon Revenues and Profits: Forecasts Versus Actuals

Year	Revenues ($ millions) My forecast, 2000	Actual	Operating income ($ millions) My forecast, 2000	Actual	Operating margin My forecast, 2000	Actual
2000	$2,793	$2,762	−$373	−$664	−13.35%	−24.04%
2001	$5,585	$3,122	−$94	−$231	−1.68%	−7.40%
2002	$9,774	$3,392	+$407	−$106	4.16%	2.70%
2003	$14,661	$5,264	+$1,038	−$271	7.08%	5.15%
2004	$19,059	$6,921	+$1,628	−$440	8.54%	6.36%
2005	$23,862	$8,490	+$2,212	−$432	9.27%	5.09%
2006	$28,729	$10,711	+$2,768	−$389	9.63%	3.63%
2007	$33,211	$14,835	+$3,261	−$655	9.82%	4.42%
2008	$36,798	$19,166	+$3,646	−$842	9.91%	4.39%
2009	$39,006	$24,509	+$3,883	−$1,129	9.95%	4.61%
2010	$41,346	$34,204	+$4,135	−$1,406	10.00%	4.11%
2011	$43,827	$48,077	+$4,383	−$862	10.00%	1.79%
2012	$46,457	$61,093	+$4,646	−$676	10.00%	1.11%
2013	$49,244	$74,452	+$4,925	−$745	10.00%	1.00%
2014 (last 12 months)	$51,460	$85,247	+$5,146	−$97	10.00%	0.11%

Note, though, that the absence of profits was not the result of miscalculation or bad circumstances but the consequence of a strategy Amazon had followed of going for higher revenues at the expense of profits. To accomplish this, Amazon had consistently offered new products and services (Amazon Prime, Kindle, Fire) at below cost to attract and keep customers.

In October 2014 my story for Amazon is that it is pursuing a *Field of Dreams* story line, promising investors that if the company builds it (revenues), they (profits) will come. In my narrative, I argue that Amazon will continue on its path of delivering high revenue growth by continuing to sell products or offer services at or below cost for the near future and will eventually start to use its market power to deliver profits, but its market power will be checked by the entry of new players into the retail business.

CASE STUDY 6.6: ALIBABA, THE CHINA STORY, SEPTEMBER 2014

To understand Alibaba, you should visit their flagship site, Taobao, a chaotic and colorful hub where both individuals and businesses can offer their goods, used or new, for sale, at fixed or negotiable prices. Though modeled on eBay, Taobao is different on two counts. The first is that it is far more tilted toward small and midsized retailers offering new products for sale than to individuals selling used items. The second is that Alibaba, unlike eBay, does not charge a transaction fee but instead makes its revenues primarily from advertising.

In 2010 Alibaba opened a new front in its business with Tmall, a site for a selective list of larger retailers, playing an expanded role in the process for a larger slice of the transaction pie. On this site, retailers pay a deposit to Alibaba to reimburse buyers who receive counterfeit goods, a technical service fee to cover the fixed costs of maintaining the store, and a sales commission determined by transactions value. Alibaba also developed Alipay, a third-party online payment platform akin to PayPal that has grown in the last few years to dominate the Chinese online payment market. As we value Alibaba for its IPO, though, it should be noted that investors will not be getting a share of Alipay, because it has been separated from the company and will be operated as an independent entity.

Alibaba has been phenomenally successful both in terms of helping online retailing find its legs in China and becoming extremely profitable while doing so. In 2013 the company generated almost $4 billion in operating profit on revenues of approximately $8 billion and its rapid evolution from small start-up to profitable behemoth are traced in figure 6.5.

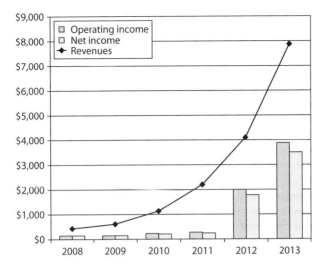

Figure 6.5
Alibaba—the rocket takes off!

There are four ingredients that I see as key to Alibaba's successful climb to the top of the Chinese online retail business.

1. Enter a growth market early and mold it to your strengths: In 1999, when Alibaba was founded, online retailing in China was in its infancy. While the largest U.S. online players (Amazon, eBay, etc.) either ignored or mishandled the market, Alibaba not only adapted to Chinese conditions but played a key role in the evolution and growth of the Chinese e-commerce market, as China has become the second-largest online market in the world. One key difference between the Chinese e-tailing market and U.S. online retail is that the former has historically been much more dependent on online marketplaces (as opposed to retailer-based online sites), largely because of Alibaba's influence.

2. Differentiate and dominate: The story of how Alibaba beat eBay and Amazon is grist for strategic storytellers, but at its core, there are three reasons why Alibaba won (and eBay lost). The first is economic. By charging no transactions fees initially and depending entirely on modest advertising charges, Alibaba made itself a bargain to retailers, relative to competitors. The second is that Alibaba molded its offerings to Chinese culture and consumer behavior. The *Economist*'s characterization of Taobao as an online bazaar is apt, since the site is set up for online haggling between buyers and sellers. Third, the site is also attuned to the fact that the Chinese retail market is splintered,

with thousands of small and midsized retailers who lack visibility, credibility, and payment-processing skills online, and Taobao offers all of those. The visibility comes from the traffic on the site; the credibility from Alibaba's system of independent verification, paid for by sellers; and payment processing from Alipay. In 2013 about 75 percent of all online retail business in China was routed through one of Alibaba's sites.

3. Don't be greedy: While most online retail transactions in China go through Alibaba sites, the slice that Alibaba keeps for itself is very small. For Taobao in particular, revenues are just advertising charges paid by retailers to list on the site, a very small portion of the total transaction value. In Tmall, Alibaba does get a larger slice of the transaction revenues, because it charges a transaction fee, but it is still only 0.5 percent to 1.5 percent of revenues. While this small share may seem like a negative, it has proved to be one of Alibaba's competitive advantages, since it has made it difficult for competitors to undercut Alibaba and offer better deals to customers and retailers.

4. Avoid pretense: Alibaba seems to generate these revenues with little effort (and marketing costs), and since the company does not aspire to be a technological innovator, its R&D and development costs are negligible. These factors result in the company's most impressive statistic: in 2013 it had a pretax operating margin of almost 50 percent and a net profit margin of close to 40 percent, high by any standards.

In my story line for Alibaba at the time of their IPO in 2014, I see them continuing on the same path, with a dominant market share of the Chinese market and high profit margins. At the same time, I see their strengths in the Chinese market as potential weaknesses if they try to move into other markets, and consequently will value them as a Chinese online retail giant rather than as a global player. In chapter 7 I will consider Alibaba as a global player in an alternative narrative.

Conclusion

A good business story is simple, credible, and persuasive. Telling one, though, requires that you understand both the business and the market in which it operates. That requires not only collecting data about both but using the tools developed in chapter 5 to convert that data into information. The key to this process, though, is realizing that the data will not tell the story. You are the storyteller, and that means you have to be willing to make judgments, which though based on data and information, are still judgments. You can and will be wrong, but that is not a reflection of your weaknesses but a consequence of uncertainty.

If you are listening to stories told by those who seek your approval or your money, you have to replicate what storytellers do in terms of home-work (understanding the business, market, and competition) and use that knowledge to find the weakest links. Ultimately, if you decide to invest in a business based upon a story, you have to make it your story, thus erasing the line between storytellers and listeners.

7

Test-Driving a Narrative

Unlike fictional storytelling, where you are bounded only by your own imagination in how far you can roam, a business story must be grounded in reality. In this chapter I will start the process of reality—checking by testing stories for possibility, plausibility, and probability, in that order. Along the way, I will look at how stories can get off track, starting with impossible stories (fairy tales), and how and why both founders and investors sometimes go along; moving on to implausible stories and the reasons why they sometimes gain traction; and ending with improbable stories and how some of them can come true.

The Three Ps: Possible, Plausible, and Probable

Once you have a story to tell about a company, the first test is to make sure your story is *possible*. As you will see later in this chapter, there are narratives that fail this very weak test, and these stories of course are destined for the business fairy-tale book. How, you might ask, would anyone be delusional enough to tell an impossible story? Caught in the heat of storytelling and surrounded by people who think like you, it can happen.

The second test is determining whether the story you are telling is plausible, a stronger test. For a story to be plausible, you have to provide some evidence that it can happen, by pointing first to other companies that have pulled it off and then to your own history to make a case that you are similar to these successful companies.

The third and toughest test is determining whether the story you are telling is probable, and that requires that you be willing to quantify your story and make your best estimates of how your story will play out in numbers. Not everything that is possible is plausible and many stories that pass the plausibility test flounder when put to the probability test.

Why should you care? Much of conventional valuation is built around the probable, wherein you formulate expected values in the form of revenues, earnings, and cash flows based upon probabilities. There is an opening for the plausible, primarily in your expected future growth rates. As for the possible, that is, things that may happen but you are so unsure that you don't even know what those things might be, conventional valuation tends to break down and you have to draw on what are called real options models. I capture these differences in figure 7.1.

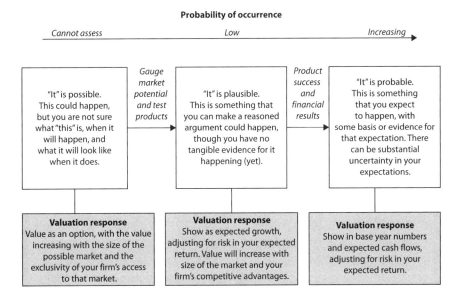

Figure 7.1
Valuing the possible, plausible, and probable.

To provide an example, consider the story I told about Uber in June 2014, in which I described it as an urban car service company. That characterization clearly met the possibility and the plausibility tests, since Uber was already operating in dozens of cities at the time. In my forecasts of revenues and cash flows for the future, I was drawing on probabilities and making my best estimates of the probable outcomes. However, at the time of the valuation, there was talk of Uber entering suburban markets and competing with rental car companies, plausible extensions of its existing business model, and I allowed for an expansion of the total market and higher growth in that market. Finally, there were a few who were arguing that Uber would encroach on the automobile markets, perhaps causing urban buyers to not buy automobiles and suburban families to skip acquiring second vehicles. That sounds like a possibility, but in June 2014 I saw no evidence of that happening and did not incorporate it into my initial estimate of value, although I would consider adding an option value. Figure 7.2 summarizes the three categories for Uber.

The lines between the possible, plausible, and probable are not always easy to draw, but one simple technique I have found useful is to think about the distinction between *im*possible, *im*plausible, and *im*probable. Impossible and improbable are quantifiable, the first because you are assigning

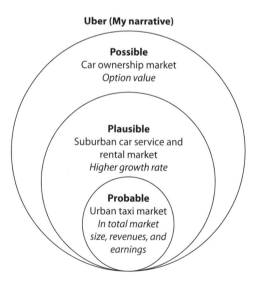

Figure 7.2
Possible, plausible, and probable for Uber, June 2014.

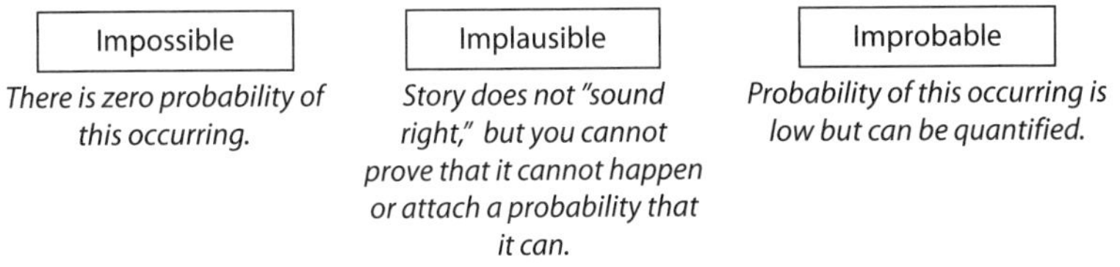

Impossible	Implausible	Improbable
There is zero probability of this occurring.	Story does not "sound right," but you cannot prove that it cannot happen or attach a probability that it can.	Probability of this occurring is low but can be quantified.

Figure 7.3
The continuum of skepticism.

a zero probability to an event happening and the latter because you are attaching a probability (albeit a low one) that an event will happen. Implausible lies in the muddled middle, since proving that it cannot happen is not feasible and attaching a probability judgment to it is just as difficult. At the risk of sounding fuzzy, these are the parts of stories that just don't sound right, and figure 7.3 shows where I would put it in what I call the "continuum of skepticism."

Breaking down stories by using this spectrum also allows us to get perspective on how different investment philosophies think about investing stories and, by extension, investment value. Old-time value investors, weaned on the dividend-based valuation models in Ben Graham's book on security analysis[1] and brought up on the adage that you only invest in the known and predictable, will invest in "highly probable" narrative companies, complaining even then that they would prefer total certainty for those companies. More aggressive value investors may venture a little further down the probability path and invest in companies with lower probability outcomes at the right price. Growth investors have to be more willing to bet on plausible story lines and build them into growth projections, accepting the fact that these projections come with more risk. Later-stage venture capitalists tend to be bunched up toward the lower end of the plausibility spectrum, investing in companies that have promise and potential (another way to think of low-plausibility narratives). Early-stage venture capitalists are taking their chances on possibilities, knowing full well that only some of these possibilities will become plausible and fewer still will make it all the way to the probability end of the spectrum. Figure 7.4 captures the range of investment philosophies and where they fall in the possible to probable spectrum.

Why should you care? For a narrative to work, you have to find the right audience. A great pitch for a young, tech start-up with an unformed business model will fall flat, if made to a group of value investors at Omaha for the Berkshire Hathaway annual meeting, and an equally good pitch for

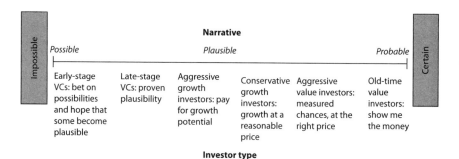

Figure 7.4
Narrative and investor type.

a cash-generating, low-growth business will not be well received by venture capitalists in Silicon Valley.

The Impossible Stories

What makes a story impossible? The company described in the story, at some point in time, breaks a mathematical, market, or accounting constraint that cannot be violated. In many cases, the storyteller does not even realize that a line has been crossed, because the assumption causing the violation is made implicitly or on autopilot. I will list a few of these impossible stories in this section.

Bigger than the Economy

It is perfectly reasonable to tell growth stories in which you argue that your company will get bigger over time, but I think that we can all agree that *no company can grow so much that it becomes larger than the economy in which it operates.* That may be stating the obvious, but I am surprised at how often I see this simple mathematical constraint violated in valuation.

When you look at a company's intrinsic value, or its most common form, a discounted cash flow valuation (DCF), the biggest cash flow in almost any business valuation is the terminal value. That number, usually estimated five or ten years down the road, is supposed to capture the intrinsic value of the company at a future point in time. In a true intrinsic valuation, that terminal value can be estimated in one of only two ways. It can be a *liquidation value*, if you have a business with a finite life and plan to liquidate all your assets at the end of the company's life. More frequently, at least with going concerns, the terminal value is estimated by assuming that cash flows grow at a constant rate forever, yielding an infinite series in mathematics and a perpetual growth equation for the present value of all cash flows beyond that point:

Terminal value in year n = Expected cash flow in year $n + 1$/
(Discount rate – Expected growth rate)

This equation, taught in finance classes around the world and often reproduced with little thought by analysts, is the source of valuation angst for all the wrong reasons.

It is not uncommon to see analysts become unglued when they use this equation to value a business with an 8 percent cost of capital and a 9 percent expected growth rate and arrive at a negative terminal value. Before they unleash their fury on the model, they should realize that the expected growth rate in this model is a growth rate forever, and assuming a growth rate of 9 percent (in U.S. dollars) in perpetuity is pushing an impossible narrative. If a company grows at a 9 percent rate for a long enough period, it will become the economy, and even with the benefits of globalization, it will reach a point where it cannot grow any more. Put simply, any perpetual growth rate that exceeds the nominal growth rate of the economy is impossible.

Bigger than the Market

The estimation of earnings and cash flows usually starts with estimates of revenues in future years. When companies have high growth potential, it should not be surprising to see revenues grow exponentially over time. But there is one caveat: *No matter how successful you think a company will be in capturing market share, its eventual market share cannot exceed 100 percent.*

That obvious constraint is also violated in many valuations, and one reason for it is our trust in past growth. When building a narrative for a company, it is natural (and good sense) to check out how quickly it has grown in the past, and these past growth rates can be astronomical for companies early in the life cycle, partly because these firms grow from a small base. Thus, a company that sees its revenues increase from $1 million to $5 million reports a 400 percent growth rate. If your story is built on the assumption that this company can maintain this growth rate over long periods, your revenues will very quickly start approaching that of the total market and then move beyond.

To keep a check on this, you should build in the assumptions that scaling up will get more difficult as a company gets bigger and that the growth rates you use in future years will have to be lower than past growth rates. Just as a sanity check, it is also good to get a measure of the total market you are going after and the market share you are attributing to your company in future years.

More than 100 Percent Profit Margins

The profit margin is estimated by dividing a company's generated earnings by its revenues. If you are valuing a company with strong pricing power, it is reasonable to build a narrative of high profit margins driving value. That said, those profit margins cannot exceed 100 percent, no matter how much pricing power a company has.

The narratives that are most likely to violate this impossibility rule are efficiency stories, in which you argue that improving efficiency at a company (either from new processes or new management) will allow that company to deliver high growth in earnings over time, even with flat or slow-growing revenues. While that story is a reasonable justification for a short period of growth, it can pass into fantasy when that growth is projected out for very long periods. Remember that as you cut costs (by becoming more efficient), your profit margins improve, and if you assume that they keep improving for very long periods, you should not be surprised to see your profit margins break through 100 percent.

Costless Capital

Businesses need capital to grow, and those who supply capital invest to earn a return. With debt, that required return is explicit and takes the form of an interest rate, but with equity, there is scope for wishful thinking, since the bulk of the cost is implicit. In other words, when investors buy your equity, they hope to get their returns in one of two ways: as dividends while they hold the stock and in price appreciation when they sell the stock. The dividends represent an explicit cash flow for the company but the price appreciation portion is implicit.

It is the implicit portion of equity returns that allows some companies to view their equity as costless or close to costless. I have heard some CFOs argue that the dividend yield (the dividend as a percent of the price) is the true cost of their equity, thus making costs of equity not only very low numbers but zero for the 60 percent of U.S. companies that do not pay dividends. It is an argument that does not hold up to scrutiny, because it does not factor in the expected price appreciation that is part of the required return on equity.

The Implausible

It is on the plausibility question that many stories get entangled, especially when they make assumptions about market dynamics, particularly assumptions about how competitors, customers, employees, and regulators will behave in response to the actions of a company.

Market Dynamics

Assume you are telling your story about a company that operates in a very competitive sector, and in your story, you see the company capturing a higher market share of this market. That is a plausible story, but not if you also claim that the company will be able to simultaneously raise prices on its products and have higher profit margins. After all, in a competitive product market, if you raise prices, you will lose market share, not gain it. With almost every part of your narrative, you have to think through how others will react and whether your results will continue to hold, given their reactions. If your narrative is built around cutting employee wages and benefits, and thus increasing profits, it will work only if employees will continue to work for you at the reduced compensation.

The Big Market Delusion

In some cases, stories that are plausible at the individual-company level can become implausible in the aggregate. One classic example is what I term the *big market delusion*, in which companies notice a big market (China, the Cloud, ride sharing, online advertising) and are drawn to it by the opportunities they see. To see how (almost) rational and (mostly)

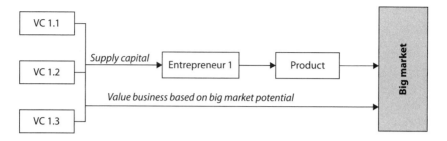

Figure 7.5
Entrepreneur sees big market.

smart individuals can be fooled by big market potential into being collectively irrational, assume you are an entrepreneur who has come up with a product you see as having a large potential market and, based on that assessment, you are able to convince venture capitalists (VCs) to fund your business (as shown in figure 7.5).

Note that everyone in this picture is behaving sensibly. The entrepreneur has created a product that he or she sees as fulfilling a large market need and the VCs backing the entrepreneur see the potential for profit from the product.

Now assume that six other entrepreneurs see the same big market potential at about the same time you do and create their own products to fulfill that market need and that each finds VCs to back his or her product and vision. Figure 7.6 illustrates this world.

To make the game interesting, let's make these entrepreneurs bright and knowledgeable about their products and let's also make the VCs smart and business savvy. If this were a rational marketplace, each entrepreneur and his/her VC backers should be valuing his/her business based on assessments of market potential and success and the existence of current and future competitors.

Let's now add the twist that causes the deviation from rationality and makes both the entrepreneurs and VCs overconfident, the former in the superiority of their products over the competition and the latter in their capacity to pick winners. This is neither an original assumption nor a particularly radical one, since there is substantial evidence already that both groups (entrepreneurs and VCs) attract overconfident individuals. The game now changes, since each business cluster (the entrepreneur and the VCs that back his or her business) will now overestimate its capacity

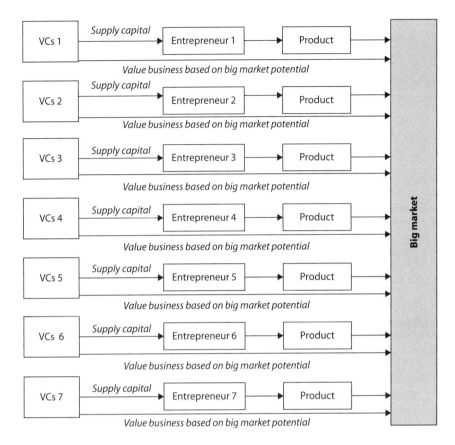

Figure 7.6
Many entrepreneurs see big market.

to succeed and its probability of success, resulting in the following. First, the businesses targeting the big market will be collectively overvalued. Second, the marketplace will become more crowded and competitive over time, especially with new entrants being drawn in because of the overvaluations. Thus, while revenue growth in the aggregate may very well match expectations of the market being big, the revenue growth at individual firms will fall below expectations and operating margins will be lower than expected. Third, the aggregate valuation of the sector will eventually decline and some of the entrants will fold, but there will be a few winners, and those entrepreneurs and VCs will be well rewarded for their investments.

The collective overvaluation of the companies in the big market will look like a bubble, and the correction will lead to the usual hand-wringing about bubbles and market excesses, but the culprit is overconfidence, a characteristic that is almost a prerequisite for successful entrepreneurship and venture capital investing. That said, the extent of the overpricing will vary, depending on the following factors:

1. The degree of overconfidence: The greater the overconfidence exhibited by entrepreneurs and investors in their own products and investment abilities, the greater the overpricing. While both groups are predisposed to overconfidence, that overconfidence tends to increase with success in the market. Not surprisingly, therefore, the longer a market boom lasts in a business space, the larger the overpricing will tend to get in that space. In fact, you can make a reasonable argument that overpricing will increase in markets where you have more experienced VCs and serial entrepreneurs, since experience often adds to overconfidence.

2. The size of the market: As the target market gets bigger, it is far more likely that it will attract more entrants, and if you add in the overconfidence they bring to the game, the collective overpricing will increase.

3. Uncertainty: The more uncertainty there is about business models and the capacity to convert them into end revenues, the more overconfidence will skew the numbers, leading to greater overpricing in the market.

4. Winner-take-all markets: The overpricing will be much greater in markets in which there are global networking benefits (i.e., growth feeds on itself) and winners can walk away with dominant market shares. Since the payoff to success is greater in these markets, misestimating the probability of success will have a much bigger effect on value.

Every decade or so, this phenomenon of collective overpricing plays out in a young market—PC companies in the 1980s, dot-com companies in the 1990s, and social media companies in the last few years. Each time that overpricing is corrected, often characterized as the bubble bursting, the words "never again" are used by investors, regulators, and onlookers, suggesting that lessons have been learned that will prevent a reoccurrence of the cycle. I believe that as long as you have markets, this collective overpricing is a feature of markets—and not always an undesirable one.

CASE STUDY 7.1: THE ONLINE ADVERTISING BUSINESS IN NOVEMBER 2015—A BIG MARKET DELUSION?

The market that best lends itself to run this experiment in 2015 is the online advertising market, with the influx of social media companies into the market-place in the preceding few years. To run my experiment, I took the market capi-talization of each company in the online advertising space and backed out of the expected revenues ten years from now. To do this, I had to make assumptions about the rest of the variables in my valuation (the cost of capital, target operat-ing margin, and sales-to-capital ratio) and hold them fixed, while I varied my revenue growth rate until I arrived at the current market capitalization.

Figure 7.7 illustrates this process using Facebook with the enterprise value of $245,662 million from August 25, 2015, base revenues of $14,640 million (trailing twelve months), and a cost of capital of 9 percent. Leaving the existing margins un-changed at 32.42 percent, I can solve for the imputed revenue in year 10 in figure 7.7.

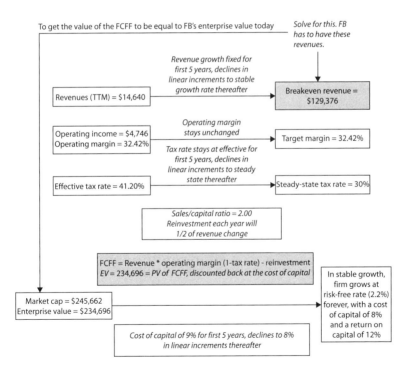

Figure 7.7
Facebook breakeven revenues.

I assume that Facebook's current proportion of revenues from advertising (91 percent) will remain unchanged over the next decade, yielding imputed revenues from advertising for Facebook of $117,731 million in 2025. The assumption that the advertising proportion will remain unchanged may be questionable, at least with some of the other companies on the list, for which investors may be pricing growth in new markets into the value.

I repeat this process with other publicly traded companies with significant online advertising revenues, using a fixed cost of capital and a target pretax operating margin of either the current margin or 20 percent, whichever is higher, for every firm. Note that both assumptions are aggressive (the cost of capital may have been set too low and the operating margin is probably too high, given competition) and both will push imputed revenues in year 10 down (see table 7.1).

The collective online advertising revenues imputed into the market prices of the publicly traded companies on this list in August 2015 was $523 billion. Note that this list is not comprehensive, since it excludes some smaller companies that also generate revenues from online advertising and the not-inconsiderable secondary revenues from online advertising generated by firms in other businesses, such as Apple. It also does not include the online advertising revenues being imputed into the valuations of private businesses like Snapchat, that were waiting in the wings in November 2015. Consequently, I am understating the imputed online advertising revenue being priced into the market right now.

To gauge whether these imputed revenues were viable, I looked at both the total advertising market globally and the online advertising portion of it. In 2014, the total advertising market globally was about $545 billion, with $138 billion from digital (online) advertising. The growth rate in overall advertising is likely to reflect the growth in revenues at corporations, but online advertising as a proportion of total advertising will continue to increase. In table 7.2 I allow for different growth rates in the overall advertising market over the 2015–2025 time period and varying proportions moving to digital advertising to arrive at the estimates of the global digital/online advertising market in 2025.

Even with optimistic assumptions about the growth in total advertising and the online advertising portion of it climbing to 50 percent of total advertising, I estimate the total online advertising market in 2025 to be $466 billion. The imputed revenues from the publicly traded companies on my list is already in excess of that number, and it seems reasonable to conclude that these companies are being overpriced relative to the market (online advertising).

Table 7.1

Breakeven Revenues for Online Advertising Companies

Company	Market cap	Enterprise value	Current revenues	Breakeven revenues (2025)	Percent from online advertising	Imputed online ad revenue (2025)
Google	$441,572.00	$386,954.00	$69,611.00	$224,923.20	89.50%	$201,306.26
Facebook	$245,662.00	$234,696.00	$14,640.00	$129,375.54	92.20%	$119,284.25
Yahoo!	$30,614.0	$23,836.10	$4,871.00	$25,413.13	100.00%	$25,413.13
LinkedIn	$23,265.000	$20,904.00	$2,561.00	$22,371.44	80.30%	$17,964.26
Twitter	$16,927.90	$14,912.90	$1,779.00	$23,128.68	89.50%	$20,700.17
Pandora	$3,643.00	$3,271.00	$1,024.00	$2,915.67	79.50%	$2,317.96
Yelp	$1,765.00	$0.00	$465.00	$1,144.26	93.60%	$1,071.02
Zillow	$4,496.00	$4,101.00	$480.00	$4,156.21	18.00%	$748.12
Zynga	$2,241.00	$1,142.00	$752.00	$757.86	22.10%	$167.49
United States	**$770,185.90**	**$689,817.00**	**$96,183.00**	**$434,185.98**		**$388,972.66**
Alibaba	$184,362.00	$173,871.00	$12,598.00	$111,414.06	60.00%	$66,848.43
Tencent	$154,366.00	$151,554.00	$13,969.00	$63,730.36	10.50%	$6,691.69
Baidu	$49,991.00	$44,864.00	$9,172.00	$30,999.49	98.90%	$30,658.50
Sohu.com	$18,240.00	$17,411.00	$1,857.00	$16,973.01	53.70%	$9,114.51
Naver	$13,699.00	$12,686.00	$2,755.00	$12,139.34	76.60%	$9,298.74
Yandex	$3,454.00	$3,449.00	$972.00	$2,082.52	98.80%	$2,057.52
Yahoo Japan	$23,188.00	$18,988.00	$3,591.00	$5,707.61	69.40%	$3,961.08
Sina	$2,113.00	$746.00	$808.00	$505.09	48.90%	$246.99
Netease	$14,566.00	$11,257.00	$2,388.00	$840.00	11.90%	$3,013.71
Mail.ru	$3,492.00	$3,768.00	$636.00	$1,676.47	35.00%	$586.76
Mixi	$3,095.00	$2,661.00	$1,229.00	$777.02	96.00%	$745.76
Kakaku	$3,565.00	$3,358.00	$404.00	$1,650.49	11.60%	$191.46
Total non–United States	**$474,131.00**	**$444,613.00**	**$50,379.00**	**$248,495.46**		**$133,415.32**
Global total	**$1,244,316.90**	**$1,134,430.00**	**$146,562.00**	**$682,681.44**		**$522,387.98**

As more companies line up to enter this space, this gap between the size of the market that is priced in and the actual market will continue to grow, but investors will continue to fund these companies, even if they are aware of the gap. After all, the nature of overconfidence is that founders and investors are convinced that the overpricing is not occurring in their firms but in the rest of the market. There will be a day of reckoning, when markets will realize the gap and stock prices will correct, but there will still be winners within this group.

Table 7.2
Online Advertising Revenues in 2025

Online as percent of total market	Compounded annual growth rate (CAGR) in total ad spending				
	1.00%	2.00%	3.00%	4.00%	5.00%
30%	$182.49	$203.38	$226.42	$251.81	$279.76
35%	$212.90	$237.27	$264.15	$293.77	$326.38
40%	$243.32	$271.17	$301.89	$335.74	$373.01
45%	$273.73	$305.07	$339.63	$377.71	$419.64
50%	$304.15	$338.96	$377.36	$419.68	$466.26

The Improbable

I believe that no one, no matter how well informed, has a monopoly on narratives and that it is reasonable for sensible, well-informed people to disagree about the value of a company. As you will see in the case studies that follow, while I have my narratives for Uber, Ferrari, Amazon, and Alibaba, there are acceptable and plausible counternarratives for each company. That said, there are some narratives for these and any other companies that cross the line into being improbable.

So what is it that makes a story improbable? It is not that you disagree with the storyteller's views on revenue growth, profit margins, reinvestment, or risk, but that the storyteller's views on these are internally inconsistent, that is, they are at war with one another. The simplest device that I have for finding these inconsistencies is what I call the iron triangle of value (shown in figure 7.8).

The three corners of the triangle—growth, risk, and reinvestment—are the drivers of the value of a business, as you will see in the next chapter. For each variable, the effects on value are predictable. As growth increases, value will go up, but as risk or reinvestment increases, value will go down. Not surprisingly, a storyteller with an agenda of making a company more valuable will tell a story that combines high growth with low risk and low reinvestment, but that story is usually implausible because it is inconsistent. A company with high growth will generally need to have high reinvestment to deliver that growth, and it will be riskier than average much of the time.

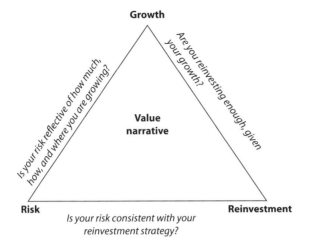

Figure 7.8
The iron triangle of value.

CASE STUDY 7.2: FERRARI, THE EXCLUSIVE AUTO CLUB

In my narrative for Ferrari, I assumed that it would strive to stay an exclusive club, not trying to increase production and units sold but preserving its limited reach and aiming for ultrarich clientele. The upside in the narrative is that Ferrari will be able to preserve its high profit margins and reduce its exposure to macroeconomic risk, but the downside is that there will be low revenue growth.

Consider an alternative strategy that I will title the "rev it up" strategy. In this one, Ferrari expands its customer base, perhaps by introducing a lower-priced version; this would mirror what Maserati did with its Ghibli model. That will allow for higher revenue growth, but like Maserati, Ferrari will have to yield some of its operating margin, since this strategy will require lower prices and higher selling costs. Seeking a larger market will also expose it to more market risk, since some of its customers now will just be rich (not superrich) and thus more exposed to economic downturns. This is clearly a viable alternative strategy that passes the plausibility test.

For an example of an implausible narrative, you could argue that Ferrari will increase sales by introducing a new model, like Maserati has, but be able to maintain the margins it has had historically and not affect risk. That strategy yields a value-increasing combination of numbers (high revenue growth + high operating margin + low risk), but it is an implausible combination. Finally, for an improbable narrative, you could spin the tale of Ferrari generating billions of dollars in revenues and profits from selling merchandise, including clothes, watches, and toys. While that narrative could happen, the probability of it unfolding seemed low, at least from my perspective in late 2015.

CASE STUDY 7.3: AMAZON—ALTERNATIVE NARRATIVES, OCTOBER 2014

In case study 6.5, I described my base narrative for Amazon as a *Field of Dreams* story, in which the company would continue to pursue high revenue growth with no or low profits before eventually turning its attention to improving profitability. Since this company evokes strong responses, pro and con, it should not be a surprise that there are many who disagreed with me, some arguing that my narrative was too optimistic and some that it was too pessimistic.

One more optimistic and plausible counternarrative was that Amazon was not a retail company and that its push into cloud computing and entertainment would allow it to have the best of both worlds, experiencing high revenue growth from penetrating and gaining market share in these markets, while earning the higher margins that companies in these markets enjoyed.

A more pessimistic story was that Amazon would continue to pursue revenue growth, managing to drive existing competition from brick-and-mortar retail firms out of business, but would then find itself facing a new wave of online competitors who would keep it in price-cutting mode. In this narrative, Amazon would end up with high revenues but continue to generate pencil-thin margins in the long term.

There is also an almost paranoid tale that some wove of Amazon as the ultimate competition buster, using its access to capital and patient investor base to bludgeon existing competition. In this story, Amazon becomes so powerful that it can charge whatever it wants, because customers have nowhere else to go. At the end of this story, Amazon would end up with high revenues and much higher margins than the companies in the businesses today.

CASE STUDY 7.4: ALIBABA, THE GLOBAL PLAYER

In case study 6.6 I described Alibaba as the China story, a company through which 75 percent of all online retail traffic in China flowed in 2014, and one that I saw as continuing to dominate Chinese online commerce for the future, while being unable to extend its reach into other markets geographically. There were many who took issue with this narrative, arguing that Alibaba's strengths, which include a charismatic CEO, Jack Ma, and access to capital, would allow it to grow in other markets, starting with Southeast Asia but expanding into developed markets. That story, to be plausible, has to incorporate the consequences of this more ambitious growth agenda and these include:

1. Lower profit margins: Alibaba's margins in China reflect its dominance of the market and the strong networking benefits that it controls. Its margins will be much slimmer in other markets, where it will be competing against more established players.

2. More reinvestment: To enter these new markets, Alibaba will have to either invest capital in entering these markets on its own or, more likely, acquire existing players in the market. These reinvestments will have a lower payoff than the investments Alibaba makes in China.

The net effects of this global story for Alibaba will be a higher total market (and revenues) for the company coupled with lower profitability and higher reinvestment, setting up a trade-off that may or may not push Alibaba's value upward.

To provide a measure of what an implausible story would look like, it would be one in which Alibaba is assumed to be able to become a global player while maintaining the sky-high operating margins that it commands in its Chinese operations and without having to invest significant amounts to get a global footprint.

Conclusion

A business story has to be credible to convince investors. In this chapter I proposed a three-level test for a story, starting with whether the story is possible, followed by an assessment of whether it is plausible, and finishing with an analysis of probabilities. I looked at impossible stories, ones in which companies are projected to become larger than the market they operate in (more than 100 percent market share) or earn margins that exceed 100 percent. I followed up with implausible stories, in which you have stories that may happen but have only a slim chance of occurring. I end with improbable stories, in which each piece of the story makes sense but the overall story does not, because the parts are at war with one another.

8

From Narratives to Numbers

Let's say you have a business story, grounded in reality and tested for plausibility. In this chapter, I look at connecting the story to numbers that determine the value of a business. I begin this chapter with a very quick introduction to valuation, not so much to delve into the theory, but to link value to key drivers that cut across businesses in different industries and different stages in the corporate life cycle. I then describe the value drivers for different narratives, ranging from big-market stories to low-risk stories. In the last part of the chapter, I take my chosen companies (Uber, Ferrari, Alibaba, and Amazon), which range the spectrum on life cycle, growth and sector, to illustrate the use of the process.

Breaking Down Value

To make the link between stories and value, you have to start with the basics of intrinsic valuation. While there are far more in-depth reviews of the topic that you can find elsewhere, the fundamentals of intrinsic value are not difficult to summarize. The intrinsic value is the value you would attach to an asset based upon its fundamentals: cash flows, expected growth, and risk. The essence of intrinsic value is that you can estimate it for a specific asset, without any information on how the market is pricing other assets (though it does certainly help to have that information). At its core, if you stay true to its principles, a DCF model is an intrinsic valuation model, because you are valuing an asset based upon its expected cash flows, adjusted for risk. Even a book value approach can be an intrinsic valuation approach in which you are assuming that the accountant's estimate of what fixed and current assets are worth is the true value of a business.

In a DCF valuation, the intrinsic value is estimated in an equation that ties value to expected cash flows, and these expected cash flows incorporate your estimates of growth and a discount rate that carries the weight of reflecting risk (see figure 8.1).

This picture also keys in on the drivers of value for any business. The first is the capacity of existing assets to generate cash flows, with assets with stronger earning power creating more value than assets with weaker earnings power. The second is the value of growth, the net effect of the trade-off

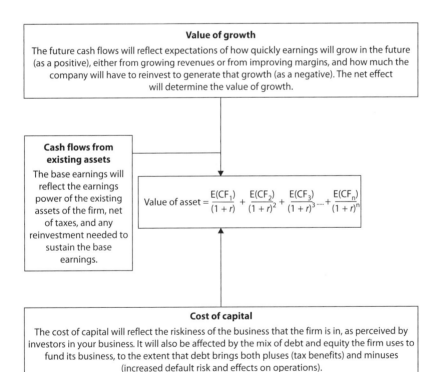

Value of growth
The future cash flows will reflect expectations of how quickly earnings will grow in the future (as a positive), either from growing revenues or from improving margins, and how much the company will have to reinvest to generate that growth (as a negative). The net effect will determine the value of growth.

Cash flows from existing assets
The base earnings will reflect the earnings power of the existing assets of the firm, net of taxes, and any reinvestment needed to sustain the base earnings.

$$\text{Value of asset} = \frac{E(CF_1)}{(1+r)} + \frac{E(CF_2)}{(1+r)^2} + \frac{E(CF_3)}{(1+r)^3} \cdots + \frac{E(CF_n)}{(1+r)^n}$$

Cost of capital
The cost of capital will reflect the riskiness of the business that the firm is in, as perceived by investors in your business. It will also be affected by the mix of debt and equity the firm uses to fund its business, to the extent that debt brings both pluses (tax benefits) and minuses (increased default risk and effects on operations).

Figure 8.1
The "theory" of intrinsic value.

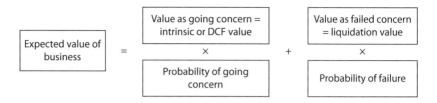

Figure 8.2
Value and truncation risk.

of its benefits, which include rising revenues and earnings, against what it costs the firm in reinvestment to generate this growth. The third is risk, with higher risk translating into a higher discount rate and lower value.

One of the limitations of DCF valuation is that it is designed to value *going concerns*, that is, businesses you expect to stay operating for long periods, and that the value that you get will be too high if there is a significant chance the company will not make it. This failure risk is high for young companies that have to make it through a gauntlet of tests to become operating businesses and for older, declining businesses that are overburdened with debt. In these cases, to estimate an expected value, you should consider the probability and consequences of failure for investors in the company explicitly, which leads to an adjusted value shown in figure 8.2.

This may seem like a cursory explanation of intrinsic value, but it does provide the big-picture perspective that I will return to as I value individual companies.

Connecting Stories to Inputs

The chapters leading into this one have been focused on telling a story about a company, one that fits the company's circumstances and the business arena in which it operates, and the challenge you face is in how to reflect that story in value. While there are many ways you can do this, the most versatile framework, in terms of being capable of incorporating almost any story, is one that uses the structure of a valuation model. Thus, if you think of cash flows as your endgame, you can start by first estimating revenues as the product of the *total market* that you see the company aiming at and the *market share* that you estimate it will be able to command within this market. Multiplying these revenues by the *pretax operating margin* yields the operating income of the company, and netting out *taxes* generates the after-tax operating income. Netting out what the company has to *reinvest to*

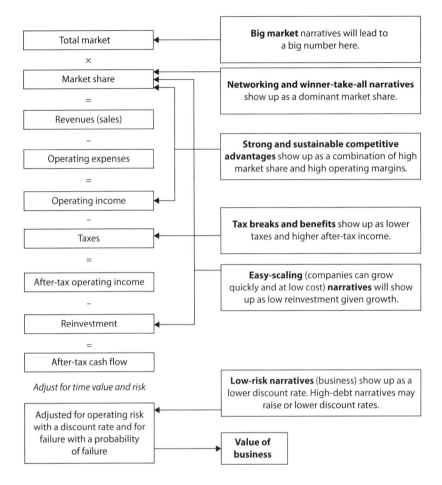

Figure 8.3
Connecting stories to valuation inputs.

generate growth will result in the free cash flow. Finally, discounting these cash flows back to today at a *risk-adjusted discount rate* gives you value.

Every story has an input that is best suited to reflect its impact on value. If you have a *big market* story, it is the total market that will reflect it; even a small share of this market will generate big revenues. If you are pushing a *strong networking benefit story*, one that promises that your company will find it easier to grow as it gets larger, or a *market dominance story*, in which your company will overpower its competitors, the market share is the input that will allow you to incorporate this effect in value. If the business you are valuing has *strong and sustainable competitive advantages*, you will see the payoff in high operating margins and income. If a business will *benefit from tax breaks*, the tax rate will be lower, pushing up after-tax income and cash flows. If your business is built on low capital intensity, that is, it can *scale up easily*, it is the reinvestment that will show that advantage, remaining low for big increases in revenues. If a business is *low risk*, the discount rate that you use to bring the cash flows back to today will be lower (and the value higher). Figure 8.3 summarizes the effects.

Simplistic though this framework may be, it is remarkably flexible in terms of being able to factor in story lines for companies across the life cycle and in different businesses.

CASE STUDY 8.1: UBER—FROM STORY TO NUMBERS

Lead-in case studies:

Case Study 6.2: The Ride Sharing Landscape
Case Study 6.3: The Uber Narrative

In case studies 6.2 and 6.3, I told my story for Uber in June 2014, describing it as an urban car service company that would draw new users into the car service business, while using its competitive advantages (access to capital, first mover) to maintain local networking benefits and its revenue-sharing model, doing all this with its existing low-capital business model. Converting this story into valuation inputs:

1. As an urban car service company, the market that it is pursuing is the taxi-cab and car service market in cities. Aggregating the taxicab and car service revenues of cities, I obtain a value of *$100 billion* for the urban car service market.

2. The local networking benefits will allow Uber to emerge as the dominant player in a subset of cities, while facing competitors (both domestic and foreign) in others. The market share that I assign in steady state for the company is 10 percent. While this is far higher than the highest market share of any of the existing players in this splintered business, it is capped at 10 percent rather than 30 or 40 percent because my story does not presume global networking benefits.

3. Uber's first-mover status, its strong capital position, and its technological edge will allow the company to maintain the revenue-sharing agreement that it has with drivers (80 percent to the driver, 20 percent to Uber) and sustain strong operating margins (40 percent in steady state).

4. Continuing on its prevailing path of not owning cars or investing in infra-structure, the company will be able to generate $5 in revenues for every dollar in capital invested. To provide some perspective, the median value for this statistic across all U.S. companies is about 1.5 ($1.50 in sales for every dollar

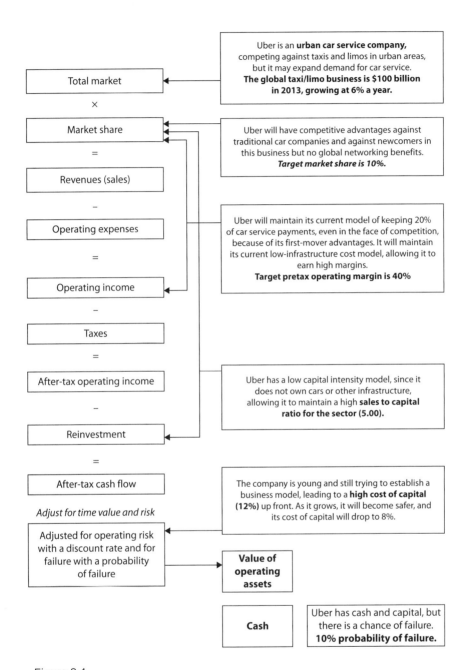

Total market

×

Market share

=

Revenues (sales)

−

Operating expenses

=

Operating income

−

Taxes

=

After-tax operating income

−

Reinvestment

=

After-tax cash flow

Adjust for time value and risk

Adjusted for operating risk with a discount rate and for failure with a probability of failure

Value of operating assets

Cash

Uber is an **urban car service company,** competing against taxis and limos in urban areas, but it may expand demand for car service. **The global taxi/limo business is $100 billion in 2013, growing at 6% a year.**

Uber will have competitive advantages against traditional car companies and against newcomers in this business but no global networking benefits. **Target market share is 10%.**

Uber will maintain its current model of keeping 20% of car service payments, even in the face of competition, because of its first-mover advantages. It will maintain its current low-infrastructure cost model, allowing it to earn high margins. **Target pretax operating margin is 40%**

Uber has a low capital intensity model, since it does not own cars or other infrastructure, allowing it to maintain a high **sales to capital ratio for the sector (5.00).**

The company is young and still trying to establish a business model, leading to a **high cost of capital (12%)** up front. As it grows, it will become safer, and its cost of capital will drop to 8%.

Uber has cash and capital, but there is a chance of failure. **10% probability of failure.**

Figure 8.4
Uber, 2014—valuation inputs.

invested in capital) and a sales-to-capital ratio of 5.0 would be around the 90th percentile of all companies. Figure 8.4 summarizes these inputs.

That story can of course be challenged at almost every turn, and in chapter 10 I will look at those challenges.

CASE STUDY 8.2: FERRARI—FROM STORY TO NUMBERS

Lead-in case studies:

Case Study 6.1: The Auto Business
Case Study 6.4: The Ferrari Narrative
Case Study 7.2: Ferrari, the Exclusive Auto Club

In chapter 6 I outlined my basic story for Ferrari and described it as a superexclusive automobile company, with that exclusivity restricting it on its revenue growth but helping it sustain its high profit margins and low risk profile. In figure 8.5, that story finds its connection to valuation inputs.

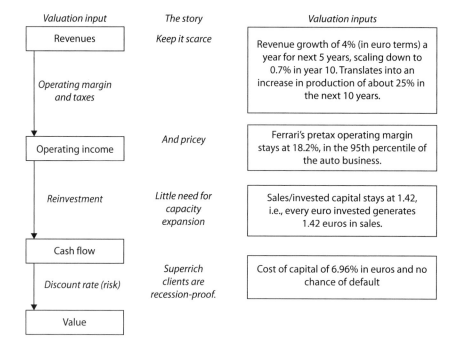

Figure 8.5
Ferrari: the exclusive club—valuation inputs.

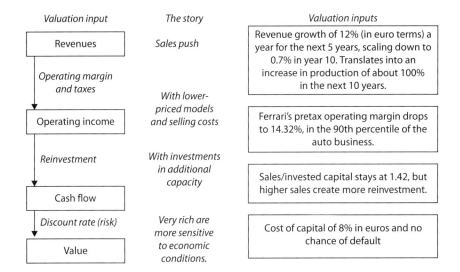

Valuation input	The story	Valuation inputs
Revenues	Sales push	Revenue growth of 12% (in euro terms) a year for the next 5 years, scaling down to 0.7% in year 10. Translates into an increase in production of about 100% in the next 10 years.
Operating margin and taxes	With lower-priced models and selling costs	
Operating income		Ferrari's pretax operating margin drops to 14.32%, in the 90th percentile of the auto business.
Reinvestment	With investments in additional capacity	
Cash flow		Sales/invested capital stays at 1.42, but higher sales create more reinvestment.
Discount rate (risk)	Very rich are more sensitive to economic conditions.	
Value		Cost of capital of 8% in euros and no chance of default

Figure 8.6
Ferrari: the rev it up narrative—value inputs.

In chapter 7 I outlined a plausible counternarrative, in which Ferrari aspires for higher growth and, to deliver that growth, introduces a lower-cost model and increases advertising spending. Figure 8.6 shows the conversion of that narrative into valuation inputs.

While these narratives are both plausible, neither dominates in terms of value effects. The exclusive club scenario has lower sales, but it also has higher margins and lower risk. In chapter 9 we will look at the resulting valuations for both narratives.

CASE STUDY 8.3: AMAZON—FROM STORY TO NUMBERS

Lead-in case studies:

Case Study 6.5: Amazon, the *Field of Dreams* Model
Case Study 7.3: Amazon—Alternative Narratives

In my initial narrative for Amazon, I described it as a *Field of Dreams* company, one that would accept low or even no profits in return for high revenue growth in multiple businesses (retail, entertainment, cloud computing) on the expectation that it would be able to generate higher profit margins in the future. Figure 8.7 shows the conversion of that story into valuation inputs.

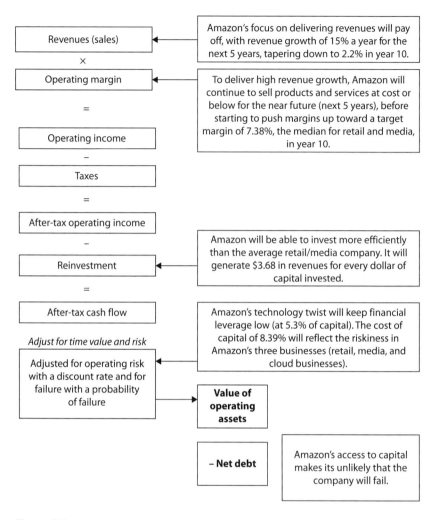

Figure 8.7
Amazon: the *Field of Dreams* narrative—valuation inputs.

As I noted in chapter 7, Amazon is a company for which there are many plausible counternarratives with widely divergent value consequences. I presented two extreme cases: one in which the revenue growth with no profits becomes the steady-state model and another in which Amazon's relentless expansion decimates the competition, allowing Amazon significant pricing power. In figure 8.8, I look at both stories.

While there are differences on the revenue growth rates across the narratives, the most significant divergence is in the target operating margins, with

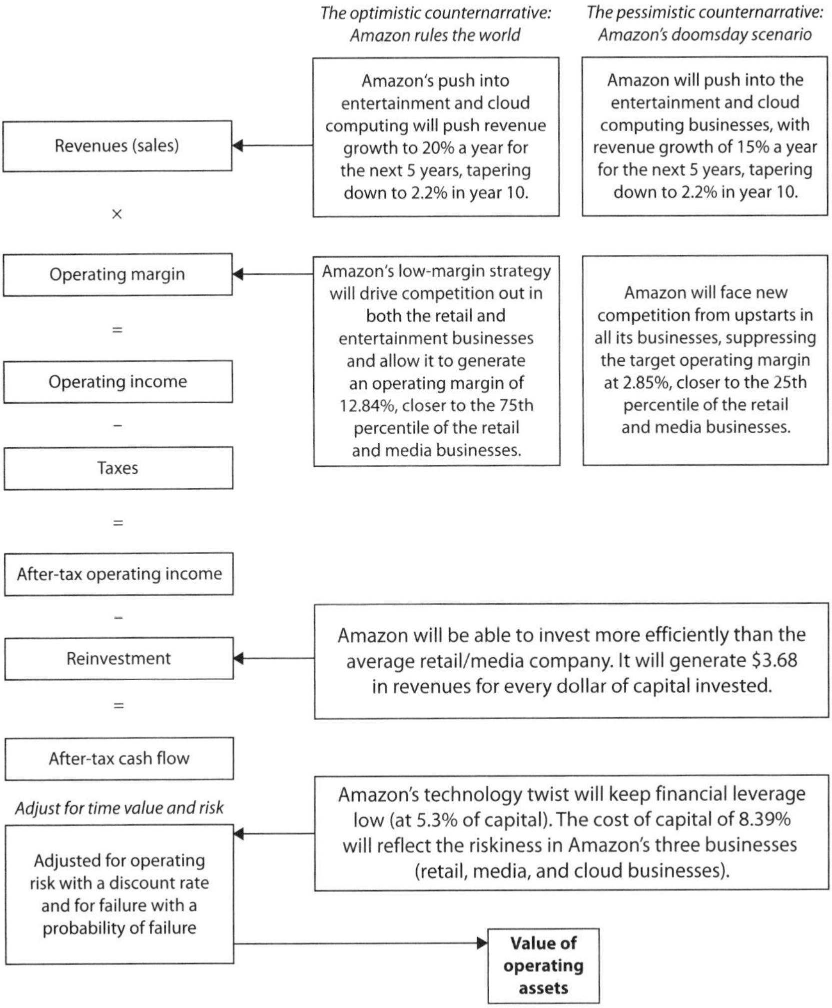

The optimistic counternarrative: Amazon rules the world	The pessimistic counternarrative: Amazon's doomsday scenario

Revenues (sales)

Amazon's push into entertainment and cloud computing will push revenue growth to 20% a year for the next 5 years, tapering down to 2.2% in year 10.

Amazon will push into the entertainment and cloud computing businesses, with revenue growth of 15% a year for the next 5 years, tapering down to 2.2% in year 10.

×

Operating margin

Amazon's low-margin strategy will drive competition out in both the retail and entertainment businesses and allow it to generate an operating margin of 12.84%, closer to the 75th percentile of the retail and media businesses.

Amazon will face new competition from upstarts in all its businesses, suppressing the target operating margin at 2.85%, closer to the 25th percentile of the retail and media businesses.

=

Operating income

−

Taxes

=

After-tax operating income

−

Reinvestment

Amazon will be able to invest more efficiently than the average retail/media company. It will generate $3.68 in revenues for every dollar of capital invested.

=

After-tax cash flow

Adjust for time value and risk

Adjusted for operating risk with a discount rate and for failure with a probability of failure

Amazon's technology twist will keep financial leverage low (at 5.3% of capital). The cost of capital of 8.39% will reflect the riskiness in Amazon's three businesses (retail, media, and cloud businesses).

Value of operating assets

Figure 8.8
Amazon: counternarratives.

my narrative built around the presumption that Amazon's margin will converge on 7.38 percent, the median of the retail and entertainment businesses, the optimistic counternarrative arguing for a 12.84 percent margin (the 75th percentile), and the pessimistic one settling for a 2.85 percent margin (the 25th percentile).

CASE STUDY 8.4: ALIBABA—FROM STORY TO NUMBERS

Lead-in case studies:

Case Study 6.6: Alibaba, the China Story
Case Study 7.4: Alibaba, the Global Player

In chapter 6, my story for Alibaba was a China story, with Alibaba continuing to dominate, grow, and profit from the Chinese online retail market for the long term. The size and growth in China's online retail business forms the basis for Alibaba's value proposition, augmented by Alibaba's dominant market share and low cost structure. Figure 8.9 shows how closely my Alibaba revenue growth story tracks the Chinese online retail market.

In figure 8.10 I summarize the links between this story and my valuation inputs (with all the estimates in U.S. dollar terms, partly to reflect the fact that Alibaba's IPO was planned for the United States and partly for convenience).

That story, though, may be missing Alibaba's global ambitions, and there is a plausible counterstory that I developed in chapter 7, in which Alibaba extends its success in China into other markets, including the United States, and perhaps even into other businesses. In this alternate story, Alibaba could generate

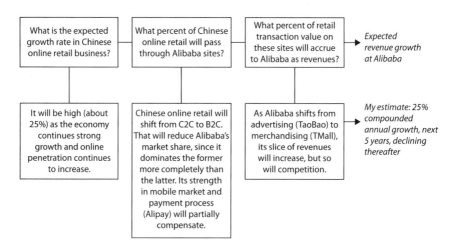

Figure 8.9
Alibaba revenue growth and Chinese online retail.

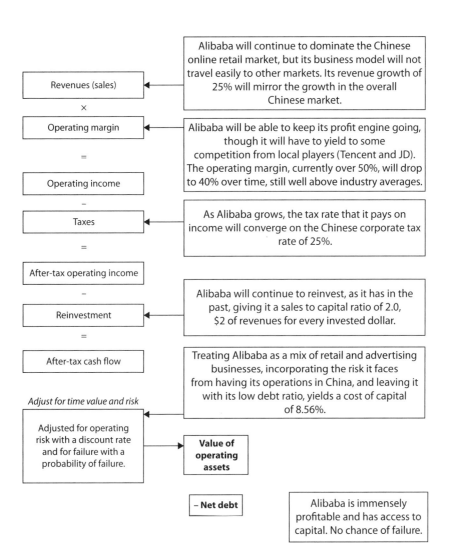

Figure 8.10
Alibaba, the China story.

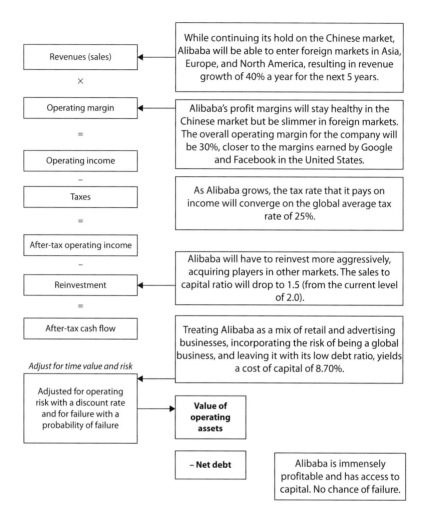

Figure 8.11
Alibaba, the global player.

higher revenue growth than in my narrative, albeit with lower operating margins and more reinvestment. Figure 8.11 summarizes the effects of this global player story.

As noted before, it remains to be seen whether the net effect of this global push adds or takes away value from Alibaba.

Qualitative Meets Quantitative

The chasm between story people and numbers crunchers is most visible when the discussion turns to qualitative factors. To the storytellers, the obvious weakness of valuation models seems to be their failure to consider corporate culture, the quality of management and employees, and a multitude of soft factors that affect the value of a business. To the number crunchers, the raising of qualitative factors is a red flag, an indication of shallow thinking and the use of buzzwords to justify premiums. I find myself in the middle on this one, since I believe that both sides have a point.

Do qualitative factors affect value? Of course! How could the value of a business not be determined by whether its management can think strategically, how loyal and well trained its work force is, and the brand name that it has built up over time? Before you put me in the storytellers' camp, let me hasten to add that as an investor, you cannot collect your dividends in corporate culture units, strategic considerations, or brand name bragging rights. The key, then, is to bridge the gap, and at the risk of inviting the scorn of both sides, I think that any qualitative factor, no matter how fuzzy, can be converted into numbers.

If you look back at the valuations I am setting up just in this chapter, each of the companies I have valued has qualitative strengths that are at the core of their success. Uber is managed by a risk-taking team that aggressively seeks out opportunities and is backed by skilled technology, but that is why I feel comfortable making the assumption that they will conquer the ride-sharing market over the next decade. Ferrari has one of the best-known brand names in the world, but it is that brand name that gives them the pricing power to charge more than a million dollars per car and earn a profit margin in the 95th percentile of the auto business. Amazon has Jeff Bezos as CEO, a visionary who is also pragmatic, and this may explain why investors have been willing to go along with the *Field of Dreams* model, in which revenues get delivered today but you have to wait for profits. Alibaba has the benefit of being the largest player in China, a market with immense potential, but that potential is what allows me to assume a revenue growth rate of 25 percent a year in conjunction with sky-high margins for the company for the next few years.

I think that both sides will benefit from this conversation. Storytellers, who naturally gravitate to qualitative factors, will be forced to be more specific in their stories and be able to check them for plausibility. Thus, arguing that a company has good management means little until you start to explain what it is that management does that makes them "good." For number crunchers, bringing in qualitative factors will bring depth to their numbers and perhaps even lead to a reassessment of whether those numbers will hold up.

Finally, connecting the qualitative to the quantitative can allow investors a way of scrutinizing claims made by founders and managers about a business. A brand name story for a company whose profit margins are below the median for a sector should be viewed with skepticism, as should a high-growth story for a company that has consistently reported single-digit revenue growth for the last decade.

Pricing a Story

In this chapter, I have focused on converting stories into numbers in an intrinsic valuation framework. However, there are many investors who feel that the intrinsic value process is too complex and that it is simpler and more effective to price companies, rather than value them. That pricing usually takes the form of computing a pricing multiple (of revenue drivers, revenues, earnings, or book value) and comparing this multiple across "comparable" firms. In this section, I will lay out the structure for connecting pricing to storytelling, a well-worn path followed by many equity research analysts, and explain potential dangers with the approach.

The Essence of Pricing

To set the table for the comparison, let me start with an assessment of the differences between the valuation and pricing processes. The value of a business is determined by the magnitude of its cash flows, the risk/uncertainty of these cash flows, and the expected level and efficiency of the growth that the business will deliver. The price of a traded asset (stock) is set by demand and supply, and while the value of the business may be one input into the process, it is one of many forces, and it may not even be the dominant force. The push and pull of the market (momentums, fads, and other pricing forces) and liquidity (or the lack thereof) can cause prices to have a dynamic entirely their own, which can lead to the market price being different from value.

The tools for estimating value and price reflect the differences in the processes. To estimate value, as we noted in the previous section of this chapter, we use DCF models, make assumptions about the fundamentals that drive value, and estimate a value. To figure out a price, we take a much simpler path. We look at how "similar" assets are being priced in the market today and try to estimate a price that the market would attach to the company in question, given its characteristics. There are three steps in pricing:

1. Find comparable or similar assets in the market: While the conventional practice for doing relative valuation, at least in the context of stocks, is to look at other companies in the same sector as the company you are pricing, it is ultimately a subjective judgment and will depend largely on how investors in the market classify a company. Thus, if Tesla is being treated by investors as a tech company and not an automobile company, the pricing may very well have to do the same.

2. Look for the pricing metric that investors use in pricing these companies: When pricing companies, it is not your place or mine to determine what investors *should be using* to price companies, but what they actually *are using*. Thus, if the metric investors focus on when pricing social media companies is the number of users these companies have, you should focus on that metric in pricing your company.

3. Price your company: Now that you have the metric or metrics that investors are using to price companies, you can price your company based on that metric and the pricing ratios across the comparable companies. Using the social media example again, if social media companies are being priced based on users, and the average price that the market was paying was $100/user in 2013, you would have priced Twitter, which had 240 million users in October 2013, at approximately $24 billion.

The pricing process can yield a very different number for your company than the valuation process. As to which number you would use, it depends on whether you are an investor or a trader, with no negative connotations on the latter intended. Investors focus on value and invest on the faith that

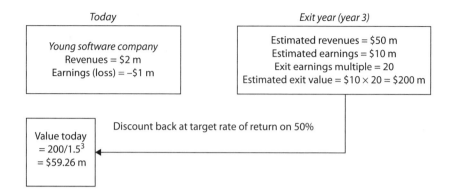

Figure 8.12
Venture capital valuation (pricing).

price will move toward value. Traders focus on price and are judged on whether they get the direction of price movements right.

Connecting Stories to Prices

It is my view that most individuals in public markets, including many who call themselves value investors, are really traders, afraid to accept that labeling because they view it as a reflection of shallow analysis and are afraid of being called speculators. In the private capital markets, the delusion is even deeper, as most venture capitalists have little interest in value and are relentlessly focused on pricing. In fact, the venture capital (VC) valuation model is a pricing tool in which the pricing is consigned to the exit multiple, as can be seen in figure 8.12.

Since the exit multiple is obtained from the pricing of comparable firms and the target rate of return is a made-up number (more a negotiating tool than a discount rate), there is very little pricing in this process.

If you are playing the pricing game, your challenge with stories is to bring them into the pricing game. To do so, you will have to mold the story around the pricing metric, whatever that might be, a simpler and more straightforward task than the full-fledged connections that were made in the intrinsic value process. Thus, if your start-up is a social media company and the market is indeed focused on users, your story should revolve around users. Alternatively, if the market's basis for pricing is earnings, you have to tie your story to future earnings.

Dangers of Pricing Stories

We are drawn to pricing stories for their simplicity and directness. They do come with their own set of weaknesses, perhaps as a consequence of the shortcuts taken along the way:

1. Intermediate variable: No matter what metric is used in the pricing, it is, at best, an intermediate step on the way to value or, at worst, a proxy for nothing substantial. Pricing a social media company on the basis of the number of users implicitly assumes that future revenues, earnings, and ultimately value are correlated with the number of users today. Even with more value-driven metrics like earnings, there is the assumption that earnings today are good indicators of future earnings, a dangerous leap of faith in unstable and volatile sectors.

2. Markets are fickle: If your defense is that it is your job to deliver what markets want (users, revenues, or earnings), it is worth remembering that markets are fickle. Young companies, particularly, will be faced with what I call "bar mitzvah" moments, where the market suddenly shifts its attention from one variable to an entirely different one. I will come back to this question in chapter 14, when I talk about corporate life cycles.

3. Game playing by companies: If investors do become focused on a metric, companies will start to not only mold their stories around the metric but may start changing their business models to focus on delivering on that metric. If you add in the possibility of gaming the numbers, where accounting and measurement tools are twisted to deliver higher numbers on the metric in question, you have the makings of a disaster.

Conclusion

If valuation is a bridge between stories and numbers, this chapter is the girder that brings them together. It converts the words in stories into inputs in valuation models and will allow you to make the final steps to get to value in the next chapter. The process is not always sequential, and it is entirely possible that as you attach valuation inputs to your story, you may feel the need to revisit earlier parts of the story and tweak or change them. I believe that the process will make your stories stronger and your valuations more credible.

9

Numbers to Value

I went from telling a story in chapter 6 to testing that story for plausibility in chapter 7 to connecting the story to value drivers in chapter 8. In this chapter I bring the process to fruition by using the value drivers to estimate value. I begin the chapter by returning to the valuation model introduced in chapter 8 and exploring the mechanics of valuing a company and presenting that valuation. Using the companies that I introduced in chapter 8 as illustrative examples, I arrive at estimates of value that are consistent with the stories that I told about each company. In the second part of the chapter, I reverse the process and look at how you can extract stories from existing valuations (often presented just as numbers) and use these stories to judge whether the valuations make sense.

From Inputs to Value

If you have converted your stories into valuation inputs, the bulk of the heavy lifting in valuation is already done, because making the connection between value inputs into value is mechanics, for the most part.

Valuation Basics

When valuing a business, you start by valuing its existing investments and then augment that value with the value created or destroyed by growth, before adjusting for risk in the cash flows. The steps involved are described in figure 9.1.

As you review the mechanics of this story, it is worth emphasizing that the inputs are interconnected, that is, changes in one almost always trigger changes in the others. Thus, if you decide to increase the growth rate in a valuation, you have to consider how much your reinvestment will need to change to deliver that growth and whether you will have to alter your business mix (and the risk of that mix) and financial leverage to deliver that growth.

One aspect of DCF valuation that both trips up and troubles those using it is the role of the terminal value. If you are valuing a business, it is almost inevitable that the terminal value will be a substantial contributor to

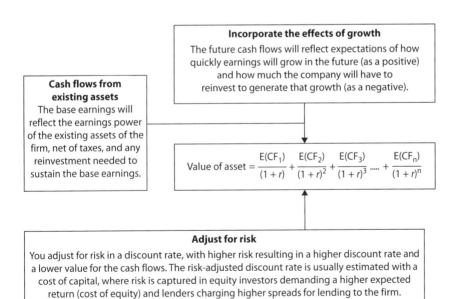

Figure 9.1

The steps in valuation.

the value that you estimate for the value today, accounting for 60 percent, 70 percent, or even more than 100 percent of the current value. Rather than view that as a weakness of the model, as some are apt to do, consider it a reflection of how you make money as an equity investor in a business. Equity investors generate cash flows while they hold onto their investments in the form of dividends or cash payouts, but the bulk of their returns comes from price appreciation. The terminal value stands in for this price appreciation, and not surprisingly, as the growth potential of a business increases, the terminal value's contribution to current value will also increase. If you accept that interpretation of terminal value, the second concern you might have is about how assumptions you make in your terminal value can hijack your entire valuation. Consider again the equation for estimating terminal value, estimated for a going concern:

$$\text{Going concern terminal value}_n = \text{E(Cash flow}_{n+1})/\text{Stable growth cost of capital} - \text{Growth rate)}$$

In chapter 7 we introduced the first constraint on this computation, arguing that the growth rate in the terminal value equation has to be less than or equal to the nominal growth rate in the economy (domestic or global) in which the company operates. I would tighten that constraint by suggesting that the risk-free rate be used as the proxy for nominal growth in the economy, thus bringing the currency choice into the growth estimate; if you are working with a higher-inflation currency, both your risk-free rate and expected growth rate in perpetuity will be much higher. There is a second constraint that needs to be considered. In keeping with the consistency argument that underlies all growth estimates, it is important that companies reinvest enough to be able to sustain their "stable" growth rates in terminal value. In fact, one simple way of estimating that reinvestment rate is to first estimate a return on capital that a company can generate in stable growth and use it to back into a reinvestment rate:

$$\text{Terminal reinvestment rate} = \text{Stable growth rate/Return on invested capital}$$

Thus, if you generate a return of 12 percent on the capital invested in new projects, you will need to reinvest 25 percent of your after-tax operating income in perpetuity to be able to grow at 3 percent a year.

In fact, *if the return on capital you generate is equal to your cost of capital, the terminal value will not change as growth changes, since growth becomes a neutral variable.* This not only allows you to keep terminal value constrained but also leads to a strong implication. The value added by your growth estimate in stable growth is a function of whether you believe that a firm can maintain its competitive advantages in the long term. If it cannot, its return on capital will drop back to its costs of capital, and the growth rate that you assume will have no effect on value. Thus, the narrative you develop for your company needs a closing part, in which you make judgments about your firm's capacity to sustain excess returns and continue as a growing concern.

Valuation Loose Ends

Once you have estimated cash flows, adjusted for risk in a discount rate, and computed a present value or value for the operating assets, you may think that the bulk of the heavy lifting in valuation is done, but you would be wrong. To get from the operating asset value to the value of equity in a business and from that equity to value of equity per share in a publicly traded company requires judgments on the following:

1. Debt and cash (net debt): In most valuations, the net debt is a minor and trivial detail at the end of the valuation, a number to be netted out from the value of operating assets to get to the value of equity. That does mask estimation issues with one or both of these numbers. With debt, the key question becomes what you would include in it, and the answer is that it should comprise not just the interest-bearing liabilities that you see on a company's balance sheet but also other contractual commitments that the firm faces. Lease commitments, for instance, should be considered as debt and brought into your debt number, making a significant difference in the debt value at retail firms and restaurants, which have substantial operating leases. With cash, you have two details that need to be ironed out. The first is a phenomenon specific to the United States and largely the result of the U.S. corporate tax law. The U.S. tax code requires U.S.-based companies to pay the U.S. corporate tax rate on their foreign income, but only when that income is repatriated to the

United States. U.S. companies, not surprisingly, choose not to bring their cash back to the United States, thus trapping that cash in foreign locales. In late 2015, about $120 billion of Apple's $200 billion cash balance was trapped in its foreign operations, and bringing that cash back to the United States would result in a tax bill of close to $20 billion. When valuing Apple, you have to decide whether you, as equity investors in the company, will ever face this tax bite, and if so, when. The second is in markets where cash balances can be invested in risky securities for which the book value (reported in the financial statements) may be very different from the current value.

2. Cross holdings: It is not uncommon for a company to hold portions of other companies, and as an investor, you partake in these holdings. As a consequence, you have to bring the value of these holdings into your estimated value, and to do this, you first have to understand how the firm accounts for these holdings. With both U.S. and international accounting standards, holdings can broadly be classified into *majority holdings*, for which you own a controlling stake, usually (but not always) more than 50 percent of another business, or *minority holdings*, for which you hold a smaller stake in another business. With majority holdings, you are required to consolidate your financial statements, act as if you fully own the subsidiary, and report operating numbers (revenues, operating income, assets, debt, etc.) accordingly. That requires accountants to estimate the portion of the value of the subsidiary that does not belong to the parent and show it as a liability, which is called minority or noncontrolling interest. With minority holdings, you are generally not required to show any of your holdings in your operating numbers, but you do have to make an adjustment to net income to reflect your share of the earnings in the subsidiary. You often have to show on your balance sheet only the book value of what you have invested in these holdings. Given this confusing mix, it is no surprise that cross holdings are one of the most mangled items in valuation. There is, however, a simple rule that can help you cut through the confusion. If you can, you should value the parent company based on just parent company financials and then value each subsidiary separately (with its own growth, risk, and cash flow characteristics), take your proportionate holding in

each one and add up the values. If you have access to only consolidated financials, you have no choice but to value the portion of the consolidated subsidiary that does not belong to you, using whatever minimal information you have on it and subtracting it out from your consolidated valuation.

3. Stock-based compensation: In the last two decades, many companies have begun compensating their employees with equity in the company, either in the form of restricted shares (with restrictions on trading) or options. Since these are employee compensation, there is *no conceivable argument* for not treating them as operating expenses at the time that they are granted, even if that involves valuing the options using option pricing models. While it took accounting rule makers a while to come to this realization, it is now standard accounting practice in much of the world. Analysts and companies, though, have routinely undercut the process by then adding back these expenses, with reasons ranging from the absurd to the ludicrous. One rationale is that these are noncash expenses, a way for companies to pay in kind or in equity to pump up cash flows. All that has occurred is a skipping of a step, since if these companies had issued the options or restricted stock to the market and then used the cash from the issuance to pay employees, it would have been a cash flow. The other is that these are unusual expenses, strange reasoning in companies where these expenses occur every year. There is a secondary problem that is created, especially from employee options grants in the past. These options, if still outstanding, represent a claim on the equity of the firm and have to be valued and subtracted out from the equity value to get to the value per share. While there are analysts who try to adjust the shares outstanding for these existing options, it is not a good practice, since not only are out-of-the-money options often treated as worthless in this adjustment, but you are ignoring the cash inflow from option exercise and the time value of options when you do this.

Though you may be tempted to deal with these loose ends (cash, cross holdings, and employee options) mechanically, you should try to incorporate their existence and effects into your story, because they represent conscious choices made by the businesses involved. After all, no business is required to borrow money, hold cash, invest in other companies, or grant options to employees. As a simple example, consider a company like Netflix. The company's narrative, if you look at its existing business model, is built on buying the exclusive rights to movies from the content companies, often with multiyear payment commitments, and then seeking out subscribers who pay monthly fees to have access to these movies. The risk to Netflix in this story is that it can be squeezed by the content providers pushing up its broadcasting commitments, whereas it is unable to pass the costs on to the subscribers. That may be an impetus for the company's move toward producing its own content (*House of Cards*, for instance), perhaps as a precursor to changing its story. In the case of Nintendo, a company that holds a cash balance that amounts to almost half the value of the company, the inherent conservatism of its management team, which leads to both the large cash balance and little or no debt, has to be woven into the story that you tell about the company and its resulting value. Finally, if you are valuing a holding company, the subsidiaries that make up the company are not the tail end of the story but the entire one, with your reading of how good the management is in acquiring these subsidiaries becoming the story of the company.

Valuation Refinements

I believe that much of DCF's reputation for rigidity is ill deserved and that most analysts never use its most powerful features. I have used DCFs to value young and old companies, firms in different businesses and countries, and stand-alone assets, and I continue to be pleasantly surprised by how flexible the model is. Here are two features the approach offers that many practitioners are either unaware of or ignore.

1. Currency invariance: The template for DCFs works for any currency and in any interest rate environment, as long as you stay consistent in your assumptions about inflation in your cash flows and discount rates. Put simply, if you are valuing your company in a low-inflation currency, your discount rate will be low, but so will your expected growth rates (since they incorporate the same low inflation). If you switch to a high-inflation currency, both your discount rate and growth rates will increase to reflect inflation.

2. Dynamic discount rates: Most descriptions of the DCF methodology require that you estimate a discount rate upfront for the company but then leave it unchanged through your entire valuation, a practice that is neither sensible nor consistent. As you forecast changes in your company's growth and business mix over time, you should expect your discount rate to change as the company changes. In fact, even if your company's business mix stays static, the mix of debt and equity that it uses can change over time, and as that mix changes, so will the discount rate.

There are many venture capitalists who are dead set against the use of DCF approaches in valuing companies, and their disdain for the approach may reflect their exposure to a rigid version of the model. One reason that I have used a wide range of companies, from young start-ups to declining businesses to illustrate the connection between stories and numbers in this book, is to bring home my belief that the DCF approach is versatile enough to fit almost any valuation need.

Valuation Diagnostics

It is not surprising that when a valuation is done, the focus is entirely on the bottom line—the value you estimate for the business and for its shares, if it is a publicly traded enterprise. However, there is significant information in the output of the valuation that not only may tell you more about the integrity of the valuation but may also provide you with a sense of what you should be keeping track of, if you are an investor in the company:

1. Growth, reinvestment, and investment quality: Earlier in the book, I introduced the valuation triangle, the balance between growth, reinvestment, and risk that makes for a consistent valuation. One simple check of consistency is to aggregate the change in operating income you are projecting for a company over its high-growth phase and divide that change by the reinvestment you are estimating over that same period.

Marginal return on capital = Change in operating income/
Reinvestment

This marginal return on invested capital is a rough measure of how good you think your company's investments will be in the future. If it is too high or too low, and that judgment can be made by comparing it with the company's cost of capital, its historical return on capital, or industry averages, it is a red flag that you should revisit your growth and reinvestment assumptions.

2. Risk and the time value of money: The process of discounting cash flows is the adjustment you make in value to reflect both the time value of money (i.e., you would like to get your cash flows early rather than late) and the operating risk in your company as a going concern. To get a sense of how much you penalize the company for time value and risk, consider adding up the nominal cash flows (with no discounting) and comparing that number to the present value of those cash flows. Even though you may be well aware of the time value of money—one of the fundamental concepts introduced early in a finance class—you may be surprised at how much waiting for a cash flow diminishes its value, especially in a risky or a high-inflation setting.

3. Cash flow value: At the risk of stating the obvious, your early cash flows can be negative and, in fact, should be negative, if you have a young, high-growth company, partly because its earnings are low or negative in the early years and partly because of the reinvestment that will be needed to deliver the high growth. Those negative cash flows, though, play a critical role in capturing the dilution effect, that is, the concern that equity investors have that their ownership will be diluted by future equity issues. Since these future equity issues are made to cover the negative cash flows, *you are capturing the dilution effect by taking the present value of these cash flows into your consolidated value.* Put simply, there is no need to estimate and adjust for future share issuances in your share count in a DCF valuation, because it is already in your value.

4. Negative value for equity: The sum of the present values of your cash flows is the value of your operating assets, and the difference between that number and your net debt is the value of your equity. But what if the operating asset value you obtain is lower than the net debt number you have? Can equity have a negative value? The answer is *no* and *yes*: *no*, because the market price cannot drop below zero, and *yes*, because a company can sometimes continue in existence, even in this diseased state, buoyed by hope that a turnaround can bring up the value of the operating assets. In these cases, equity takes on the characteristics of an option, and investors should treat it as such.

CASE STUDY 9.1: UBER—VALUING
THE URBAN CAR SERVICE COMPANY

Lead-in case studies:

Case Study 6.2: The Ride-Sharing Landscape, June 2014
Case Study 6.3: The Uber Narrative, June 2014
Case Study 8.1: Uber—From Story to Numbers

In chapter 6 I laid out my story for Uber in June 2014, describing it as an urban car service company, and in chapter 8 I connected that story to valuation inputs ranging from revenue growth to cost of capital, all summarized in table 9.1.

These valuation inputs are fed through a valuation model, and table 9.2 summarizes the output. While my estimated value for Uber is approximately $6 billion, note also how the narrative underlies every number in the valuation. It is the story that is driving this valuation, rather than a collection of inputs in a spreadsheet.

Table 9.1
Inputs in Uber Valuation

Input	Assumptions
Total market	The total size of the urban car service company in the base year is $100 billion, growing at 3% per year, pre-Uber. Uber and other ride-sharing companies will attract new users into the business and increase the expected growth rate to 6% per year.
Market share	Uber will reach a 10% market share of the total market, with the market share rising each year to get to this level.
Pre-tax operating margin & taxes	Uber's operating margin will rise from 7% (base year) to 40% by year 10, and Uber's tax rate will drift up from current levels (31%) to the marginal tax rate for the United States (40%).
Reinvestment	Uber will be able to maintain its current low capital–intensity model, generating sales to a capital ratio of 5.
Cost of capital	Uber's cost of capital starts at 12% (the 90th percentile of U.S. companies) in year 1 and drifts down to 10% in year 10 (when it becomes a mature firm).
Likelihood of failure	There is a 10% chance that Uber, given its losses and need for capital, will not make it.

Table 9.2

Uber, the Urban Car Service Company

The story
Uber is an urban car service company, drawing new users into the car service sector. It will enjoy local networking benefits while preserving its current revenue sharing (80/20) and capital intensity (don't own cars or hire drivers) model.

The assumptions

	Base year	Years 1–5 Years 6–10	After year 10	Story link
Total market	100 billion	Grow 6.00% a year	Grow 2.50%	Urban car service + new users
Gross market share	1.50%	1.50% →10.00%	10.00%	Local networking benefits
Revenue share	20.00%	Stays at 20.00%	20.00%	Preserve revenue share
Operating margin	3.33%	3.33% → 40.00%	40.00%	Strong competitive position
Reinvestment	NA	Sales-to-capital ratio of 5.00	Reinvestment rate = 10%	Low capital–intensity model
Cost of capital	NA	12.00% 12.00% → 8.00%	8.00%	90th percentile of U.S. firms
Risk of failure	10% chance of failure (with equity worth zero)			Young company

The cash flows (in $ millions)

	Total market	Market share	Revenues	EBIT $(1-t)^*$	Reinvestment	FCFF[†]
1	$106,000	3.63%	$769	$37	$94	$(57)
2	$112,360	5.22%	$1,173	$85	$81	$4
3	$119,102	6.41%	$1,528	$147	$71	$76
4	$126,248	7.31%	$1,846	$219	$64	$156
5	$133,823	7.98%	$2,137	$301	$58	$243
6	$141,852	8.49%	$2,408	$390	$54	$336
7	$150,363	8.87%	$2,666	$487	$52	$435
8	$159,385	9.15%	$2,916	$591	$50	$541
9	$168,948	9.36%	$3,163	$701	$49	$652
10	$179,085	10.00%	$3,582	$860	$84	$776
Terminal year	$183,562	10.00%	$3,671	$881	$88	$793

The value

Terminal value	$14,418	
PV (terminal value)	$5,175	
PV (CF over the next 10 years)	$1,375	
Value of operating assets =	$6,550	
Probability of failure	10.00%	
Value in case of failure	$—	
Adjusted value for operating assets	$5,895	Venture capitalists priced Uber at $17 billion at the time.

*EBIT $(1-t)$ = (Revenues* Operating Margin) $(1-$ tax rate)
[†] FCFF = Free cash flow to firm

CASE STUDY 9.2: FERRARI—VALUING
THE EXCLUSIVE AUTO CLUB

Lead-in case studies:

Case Study 6.1: The Auto Business, October 2015
Case Study 6.4: The Ferrari Narrative, October 2015
Case Study 7.2: Ferrari, the Exclusive Auto Club
Case Study 8.2: Ferrari—From Story to Numbers

My story for Ferrari in chapter 6 is that it will remain an exclusive auto company, settling for low growth with high margins and low risk. I also looked at an alternative higher-growth story for Ferrari in chapter 7, albeit with lower margins and higher risk. In chapter 8 I connected both stories to valuation inputs, and table 9.3 summarizes those numbers.

Using these inputs, I first valued Ferrari as an exclusive club in table 9.4 and then did a valuation based on the faster-growth narrative in table 9.5. I estimate the value of Ferrari's equity to be €6.3 billion in the former and €6.0 billion in the latter. If you are surprised that the higher-growth story does not deliver a higher value, it is because it is weighed down by the lower operating margins and higher cost of capital.

Table 9.3
Ferrari Valuation Inputs

	My exclusive club	Rev it up
Currency choice	Euros	Euros
Revenue growth	4.00% for next 5 years, dropping to 0.70% in stable growth.	12.00% for next 5 years, dropping to 0.70% in stable growth.
Pre-tax operating margin (and taxes)	Operating margin stays at 18.20% (current level), tax rate of 33.54%.	Operating margin drops to 14.32% over the next 10 years, as a result of lower-price cars and increased marketing costs.
Reinvestment	Sales-to-capital ratio is 1.42, but reinvestment is low, because revenue growth is low.	Sales-to-capital ratio 1.42, but much more reinvestment is needed, since sales increase more.
Cost of capital	Cost of capital is 6.96%, reflecting superrich customers.	Cost of capital is 8.00%, since very (but not super) rich are more affected by economy.

Table 9.4

Ferrari, the Exclusive Club

The story
Ferrari will remain an exclusive club, selling relatively few cars at very high prices and with no advertising, to the superrich, who are unaffected by economic ups and downs.

The assumptions

	Base year	Years 1–5	Years 6–10	After year 10	Story link
Revenues (a)	€2,763	CAGR* = 4.00%	4,00% → 0.70%	CAGR* = 0.70%	Low growth to stay exclusive
Operating margin (b)	18.20%	18.20%		18.20%	High prices + No advertising costs = Current
Tax rate	33.54%	33.54%		33.54%	Stays unchanged
Reinvestment (c)		Sales-to-capital ratio of 1.42		Reinvestment rate = 4.81%	With little growth, little reinvestment
Cost of capital (d)		8.00%	8.00% → 7.50%	7.50%	Lightly affected by macroeconomic forces

The cash flows (in € millions)

	Revenues	Operating margin	EBIT $(1 - t)$[†]	Reinvestment	FCFF[††]
1	€2,876	18.20%	€348	€78	€270
2	€2,988	18.20%	€361	€81	€281
3	€3,108	18.20%	€376	€84	€292
4	€3,232	18.20%	€391	€87	€303
5	€3,362	18.20%	€407	€91	€316
6	€3,474	18.20%	€420	€79	€341
7	€3,567	18.20%	€431	€66	€366
8	€3,639	18.20%	€440	€51	€389
9	€3,689	18.20%	€446	€35	€411
10	€3,715	18.20%	€449	€18	€431
Terminal year	€3,740	18.20%	€452	€22	€431

The value

Terminal value	€6,835
PV (terminal value)	€3,485
PV (CF over the next 10 years)	€2,321
Value of operating assets =	€5,806
−Debt	€623
−Minority interests	€13
+ Cash	€1,141
Value of equity	€6,311

* CAGR = compound annual growth rate
[†] EBIT $(1 - t)$ = (Revenues* Operating Margin) $(1 - \text{tax rate})$
[††] FCFF = Free cash flow to firm

Table 9.5

Ferrari, Rev It Up

The story
Ferrari will go for higher growth with a lower-cost car model, backing up this strategy with more marketing, but becoming more exposed to macroeconomic forces.

The assumptions				
	Base year	Years 1–5	Years 6–10	After year 10
Revenues (a)	€2,763	CAGR* = 12.00%	12.00% → 0.70%	CAGR* = 0.70%
Operating margin (b)	18.20%	18.2% → 14.32%		14.32%
Tax rate	33.54%	33.54%		33.54%
Reinvestment (c)	1.42	Sales-to-capital ratio of 1.42		Reinvestment rate = 4.81%
Cost of capital (d)		8.00%	8.00% → 7.50%	7.50%

The cash flows (in € millions)				
	Revenues	Operating margin	EBIT $(1-t)^\dagger$	Reinvestment	FCFF††
1	€3,095	17.81%	€366	€233	€133
2	€3,466	17.42%	€401	€261	€140
3	€3,881	17.04%	€439	€293	€147
4	€4,348	16.65%	€481	€323	€153
5	€4,869	16.26%	€526	€367	€159
6	€5,344	15.87%	€564	€334	€230
7	€5,743	15.48%	€591	€281	€310
8	€6,043	15.10%	€606	€211	€395
9	€6,222	14.71%	€608	€126	€482
10	€6,266	14.32%	€596	€31	€566
Terminal year	€6,309	14.32%	€600	€35	€565

The value	
Terminal value	€8,315
PV (terminal value)	€3,906
PV (CF over the next 10 years)	€1,631
Value of operating assets =	€5,537
−Debt	€623
−Minority interests	€13
+ Cash	€1,141
Value of equity	€6,041

* CAGR = Compound annual growth rate
† EBIT $(1 - t)$ = (Revenues* Operating Margin) $(1 - \text{tax rate})$
†† FCFF = Free cash flow to firm

CASE STUDY 9.3: AMAZON—VALUING
THE *FIELD OF DREAMS*

Lead-in case studies:

Case Study 6.5: Amazon, the *Field of Dreams* Model, October 2014

Case Study 7.3: Amazon—Alternative Narratives, October 2014

Case Study 8.3: Amazon—From Story to Numbers

With Amazon, my *Field of Dreams* model is built on the presumption that Amazon will continue to focus on revenue growth by following its current strategy of selling products and services at below cost and that it would push toward profitability, though new competitors would keep margins at moderate levels. In chapter 7 I did list two alternative narratives, one a pessimistic one in which Amazon's focus on revenue growth leads it into a wasteland where profits remain a mirage, and the other an optimistic one (at least for investors) in which Amazon's pricing drives much of the competition out of the businesses it is in, allowing it substantial pricing power. Table 9.6 captures the differences in valuation inputs under the three narratives.

In table 9.7, I estimate a value of $175.25 per share in October 2014 for Amazon, using my *Field of Dreams* story, and follow up in table 9.8 with a value per share of $32.72 under the pessimistic scenario and finish with table 9.9 with a value per share of $468.51 under the optimistic scenario.

Table 9.6

Inputs for Valuing Amazon—Alternate Narratives

	My *Field of Dreams* narrative	Pessimistic doomsday story	Optimistic rules the world story
Revenue growth	15.00% for next 5 years, dropping to 2.20% in stable growth.	15.00% for next 5 years, dropping to 2.20% in stable growth.	20.00% for next 5 years, dropping to 2.20% in stable growth.
Pre-tax operating margin	Operating margin rises to 7.38%, the median for retail/media sectors.	Operating margin rises to 2.85%, 25th percentile of retail/media sectors.	Operating margin rises to 12.84%, 75th percentile of retail/media sectors.
Reinvestment	Sales-to-capital ratio stays at current level of 3.68.	Sales-to-capital ratio stays at current level of 3.68.	Sales-to-capital ratio stays at current level of 3.68.
Cost of capital	Cost of capital is 8.39%.	Cost of capital is 8.39%.	Cost of capital is 8.39%.

Table 9.7

Amazon, *Field of Dreams*

The story

Amazon will go for revenue growth in the near term, selling its products and services at close to cost in the media, retail, and cloud computing businesses, and will use its market power to earn higher margins in the future, albeit with new competitors acting as a check.

The assumptions

	Base year	Years 1–5	Years 6–10	After year 10	Story link
Revenues (a)	$85,246	CAGR* = 15.00%	15.00% → 2.20%	2.20%	Focused on revenue growth
Operating margin (b)	0.47%	0.47% → 7.38%		7.38%	Retail + media business average margin
Tax rate	31.80%	31.80%		31.80%	Stays unchanged
Reinvestment (c)		Sales-to-capital ratio of 3.68		Reinvestment rate = 22.00%	Reinvests more efficiently than competitors
Cost of capital (d)		8.39%	8.39% → 8.00%	8.00%	Media + retail + cloud

The cash flows (in $ millions)

	Revenues	Operating margin	EBIT (1—t)[†]	Reinvestment	FCFF[††]
1	$98,033	1.16%	$776	$3,474	$(2,698)
2	$112,738	1.85%	$1,424	$3,995	$(2,572)
3	$129,649	2.54%	$2,248	$4,594	$(2,346)
4	$149,096	3.23%	$3,288	$5,284	$(1,996)
5	$171,460	3.92%	$4,589	$6,076	$(1,487)
6	$192,790	4.62%	$6,069	$5,795	$274
7	$211,837	5.31%	$7,667	$5,175	$2,492
8	$227,344	6.00%	$9,300	$4,213	$5,087
9	$238,166	6.69%	$10,865	$2,940	$7,925
10	$243,405	7.38%	$12,251	$1,424	$10,827
Terminal year	$248,790	7.38%	$12,520	$2,755	$9,766

The value

Terminal value	$168,379	
PV (terminal value)	$76,029	
PV (CF over the next 10 years)	$4,064	
Value of operating assets =	$80,093	
−Debt	$9,202	
+ Cash	$10,252	
Value of equity	$81,143	
Number of shares	463.01	
Value per share	$175.25	Amazon was trading at $287.06 at the time of the valuation

* CAGR = Compound annual growth rate

[†] EBIT (1 – t) = (Revenues* Operating Margin) (1 – tax rate)

[††] FCFF = Free cash flow to firm

Table 9.8
Amazon, *Stockholder Doomsday*

	The story

Amazon will go for revenue growth in the near term, selling its products and services at close to cost in the media, retail, and cloud computing businesses, but will be unable to use its market power to improve operating margins in any of its businesses by much.

			The assumptions		
	Base year	Years 1–5	Years 6–10	After year 10	Link to story
Revenues (a)	$85,246	CAGR* = 15.00%	15.00% → 2.20%	2.20%	Focused on revenue growth
Operating margin (b)	0.47%	0.47% → 2.85%		2.85%	Retail + media business, 25th percentile
Tax rate	31.80%	31.80%		31.80%	Stays unchanged
Reinvestment (c)		Sales-to-capital ratio of 3.68		Reinvestment rate = 22.00%	Reinvests more efficiently than competitors
Cost of capital (d)		8.39%	8.39% → 8.00%	8.00%	Media + retail + cloud

		The cash flows (in $ millions)			
	Revenues	Operating margin	EBIT (1—t)†	Reinvestment	FCFF††
1	$98,033	0.71%	$473	$3,474	$(3,001)
2	$112,738	0.95%	$727	$3,995	$(3,268)
3	$129,649	1.18%	$1,046	$4,594	$(3,548)
4	$149,096	1.42%	$1,446	$5,284	$(3,838)
5	$171,460	1.66%	$1,941	$6,076	$(4,135)
6	$192,790	1.90%	$2,495	$5,795	$(3,300)
7	$211,837	2.14%	$3,086	$5,175	$(2,089)
8	$227,344	2.37%	$3,681	$4,213	$(532)
9	$238,166	2.61%	$4,243	$2,940	$1,302
10	$243,405	2.85%	$4,731	$1,424	$3,308
Terminal year	$248,790	2.85%	$4,835	$2,755	$3,771

	The value	
Terminal value	$65,024	
PV (terminal value)	$29,361	
PV (CF over the next 10 years)	$(15,260)	
Value of operating assets =	$14,101	
−Debt	$9,202	
+ Cash	$10,252	
Value of equity	$15,151	
Number of shares	463.01	
Value per share	$32.72	Amazon was trading at $287.06 at the time of the valuation

* CAGR = compound annual growth rate
† EBIT (1 − t) = (Revenues* Operating Margin) (1 − tax rate)
†† FCFF = Free cash flow to firm

Table 9.9
Amazon, *World Domination*

The story

Amazon will go for revenue growth in the near term, selling at close to cost in the media, retail, and cloud computing businesses, and use its market power to drive out competition and earn very high margins in the future.

The assumptions

	Base year	Years 1–5	Years 6–10	After year 10	Link to story
Revenues (a)	$85,246	CAGR* = 25.00%	25.00% → 2.20%	2.20%	Obsessed with revenue growth
Operating margin (b)	0.47%	0.47% → 12.84%		12.84%	Retail + media business, 75th percentile margin
Tax rate	31.80%	31.80%		31.80%	Stays unchanged
Reinvestment (c)		Sales-to-capital ratio of 3.68		Reinvestment rate = 22.00%	Reinvests more efficiently than competitors
Cost of capital (d)		8.39%	8.39% → 8.00%	8.00%	Media + retail + cloud

The cash flows (in $ millions)

	Revenues	Operating margin	EBIT $(1-t)^\dagger$	Reinvestment	FCFF††
1	$102,295	1.71%	$1,190	$4,632	$(3,441)
2	$122,754	2.94%	$2,464	$5,559	$(3,094)
3	$147,305	4.18%	$4,200	$6,670	$(2,470)
4	$176,766	5.42%	$6,531	$8,004	$(1,473)
5	$212,119	6.65%	$9,627	$9,605	$22
6	$246,992	7.89%	$13,293	$9,475	$3,819
7	$278,804	9.13%	$17,358	$8,643	$8,715
8	$304,789	10.37%	$21,547	$7,060	$14,487
9	$322,345	11.60%	$25,508	$4,770	$20,738
10	$329,436	12.84%	$28,848	$1,927	$26,922
Terminal year	$336,684	12.84%	$29,483	$6,486	$22,997

The value

Terminal value	$396,496
PV (terminal value)	$179,032
PV (CF over the next 10 years)	$28,427
Value of operating assets =	$207,459
−Debt	$9,202
+ Cash	$10,252
Value of equity	$208,510
Number of shares	463.01
Value per share	$450.34

Amazon was trading at $287.06 at the time of the valuation

* CAGR = compound annual growth rate
† EBIT $(1-t)$ = (Revenues* Operating Margin) $(1-$ tax rate)
†† FCFF = Free cash flow to firm

The divergence in values in Amazon across narratives is one reason that the company is often the subject of heated debates among investors, with some contending that those who buy the stock are naïve victims of a con game and others arguing that those who do not invest in it are old fogies who don't understand the new economy.

CASE STUDY 9.4: ALIBABA—THE CHINA STORY

Lead-in case studies:

Case Study 6.6: Alibaba, the China Story, September 2014
Case Study 7.4: Alibaba, the Global Player
Case Study 8.4: Alibaba—From Story to Numbers

In my narrative for Alibaba, I described a company that has not just promised but delivered on the China story. Adapting exceptionally well to the needs and fears of Chinese retailers and consumers, the company dominates online retail traffic in China while delivering solid profits. In my story, Alibaba continues to grow at a rate of 25 percent with the Chinese market, with only limited slippage in the operating margin to 40 percent, but I see it as a China-centric company that will not travel well into other locales. The valuation, summarized in table 9.10, yields a value for Alibaba after its IPO.

Adding on the value of the proceeds from the IPO, anticipated to be $20 billion, the value of equity that I get is $161 billion, translating into an equity value per share of $65.98.

In chapter 7 I outlined an alternative story for Alibaba as a global company able to grow at 40 percent a year for the next five years, more than the 25 percent at which Chinese online retail is growing, by expanding into other countries. In the plausible version of this story, this growth is accompanied by a drop in operating margin to 30 percent and increased investment, captured in a sales-to-capital ratio of 1.50. The resulting value per share is $92.52, and the details are shown in table 9.11.

A few days after this valuation, the bankers set the offering price for Alibaba at $68, but the stock opened at $95 a share. In January 2016, as this book was being written, the stock was back down to $65.

Table 9.10
Alibaba, the China Story

The story
Alibaba will stay China-centric, maintaining its high market share and growing with the Chinese online retail market. Its margins will come down somewhat because of competition, but still stay high.

The assumptions

	Base year	Years 1–5	Years 6–10	After year 10	Link to story
Revenues (a)	$9,268	CAGR* = 25.00%	25% → 2.41%	CAGR* = 2.41%	Grow with Chinese market
Pre-tax operating margin (b)	50.73%	50.73% → 40.00%		40.00%	Increased competition
Tax rate	11.92%	11.92%	11.92% → 25.00%	25.00%	Move to statutory tax rate
Reinvestment (c)	NA	Sales-to-capital ratio of 2.00		Reinvestment rate = 30.13%	Industry average sales/capital
Cost of capital (d)		8.56%	8.56% → 8.00%	8.00%	Advertising + retail risk

The cash flows (in $ millions)

Year	Revenues	Operating margin	EBIT (1—t)[†]	Reinvestment	FCFF[††]
1	$11,585	49.66%	$5,067	$1,158	$3,908
2	$14,481	48.58%	$6,197	$1,448	$4,749
3	$18,101	47.51%	$7,575	$1,810	$5,765
4	$22,626	46.44%	$9,255	$2,263	$6,992
5	$28,283	45.36%	$11,301	$2,828	$8,473
6	$34,075	44.29%	$12,899	$2,896	$10,002
7	$39,515	43.22%	$14,149	$2,720	$11,429
8	$44,038	42.15%	$14,891	$2,261	$12,630
9	$47,089	41.07%	$15,012	$1,525	$13,486
10	$48,224	40.00%	$14,467	$567	$13,900
Terminal year	$49,388	40.00%	$14,816	$4,463	$10,353

The value

Terminal value	$185,205
PV (terminal value)	$82,731
PV (CF over the next 10 years)	$54,660
Value of operating assets =	$137,390
−Debt	$10,068
+ Cash	$9,330
+ IPO proceeds	$20,000
+ Nonoperating assets	$5,087
Value of equity	$161,739
−Value of options	$696
Value of equity in common stock	$161,043
Number of shares	2,440.91
Estimated value /share	$65.98

Alibaba was first priced at $68 and then repriced at $80/share.

* CAGR = Compound annual growth rate
[†] EBIT (1 − t) = (Revenues* Operating Margin) (1 − tax rate)
[††] FCFF = Free cash flow to firm

Table 9.11
Alibaba, the Global Story

		The story			

The story

Alibaba is able to expand into overseas markets, allowing its revenues to grow 40 percent per year for the next five years. Its profit margins will come under pressure as it competes in foreign markets and it will need to reinvest more to grow.

The assumptions

	Base year	Years 1–5	Years 6–10	After year 10	Link to story
Revenues (a)	$9,268	CAGR* = 40.00%	40.00% → 2.41%	CAGR* = 2.41%	Global expansion + China growth
Pre-tax operating margin (b)	50.73%	50.73% → 30.00%		30.00%	Stronger global competition
Tax rate	11.92%	11.92%	11.92% → 25.00%	25.00%	Move to statutory tax rate
Reinvestment (c)	NA	Sales-to-capital ratio of 1.50		Reinvestment rate = 30.13%	More reinvestment globally
Cost of capital (d)		8.56%	8.56% → 8.00%	8.00%	Advertising + retail risk

The cash flows (in $ millions)

	Revenues	Operating margin	EBIT (1—t)[†]	Reinvestment	FCFF[††]
1	$12,975	48.66%	$5,561	$1,158	$3,089
2	$18,165	46.58%	$7,453	$1,448	$3,993
3	$25,431	44.51%	$9,970	$1,810	$5,126
4	$35,604	42.44%	$13,308	$2,263	$6,527
5	$49,846	40.36%	$17,721	$2,828	$8,227
6	$66,036	38.29%	$21,611	$2,896	$10,817
7	$82,522	36.22%	$24,762	$2,720	$13,772
8	$96,918	34.15%	$26,552	$2,261	$16,954
9	$106,540	32.07%	$26,522	$1,525	$20,107
10	$109,108	30.00%	$24,549	$567	$22,838
Terminal year	$111,738	30.00%	$25,141	$7,574	$17,567

The value

Terminal value	$314,262
PV (terminal value)	$139,116
PV (CF over the next 10 years)	$63,071
Value of operating assets =	$202,186
−Debt	$10,068
+ Cash	$9,330
+ IPO Proceeds	$20,000
+ Nonoperating assets	$5,087
Value of equity	$226,535
−Value of options	$696
Value of equity in common stock	$225,839
Number of shares	2,440.91
Estimated value /share	$92.52 Alibaba opened for trading at $92/share.

* CAGR = Compound annual growth rate
[†] EBIT (1 − t) = (Revenues* Operating Margin) (1 − tax rate)
[††] FCFF = Free cash flow to firm

Deconstructing Value

In the last few chapters, I have talked about how a story about a business can be converted into a value. This presupposes that you are in control of the sequence and are doing the valuation. But can you reverse the process? In other words, can you take a DCF valuation, which is all numbers, and back out a story from those numbers? Yes, and there are reasons that you might want to do so. First, once you extract the story from the numbers, you can assess whether it is a story with which you are comfortable. After all, it is not just the numbers that should be driving your investment decision when you are looking at a company, but the story behind the numbers. Second, you can use your backed-out narrative to question the person doing the valuation about the underlying assumptions. One test of whether an analyst is mechanically plugging numbers into models or has a serious story will come out in how he or she responds to your questions.

The process of deconstructing valuations is simple if you use the structure that was developed to convert stories to numbers. Thus, when you see projected revenues for a company in a valuation spreadsheet or model, your questions will have to zero in on what the analyst who did the valuation sees as the total market for the company and the market share that he or she has given the company. That then opens the discussion to the business or businesses that the company operates in and what networking and competitive advantages it brings to these businesses. Figure 9.2 provides some questions, albeit not a comprehensive list, that you may ask about a valuation to understand the story behind it.

Conclusion

Once you have a story for a company and have converted the story into valuation inputs, the process of converting these inputs into value is more mechanical, though some details still need attention. Rather than get lost in the details, though, you will be better served if you use your narrative to decide the specifics on which you want to spend the most time and resources. In my valuation of Amazon, for instance, where it is the future operating margin that is the most contested input in the valuation, I spent more time looking at Amazon's history on this statistic and the differences across companies in both the retail and media sectors than I spent on

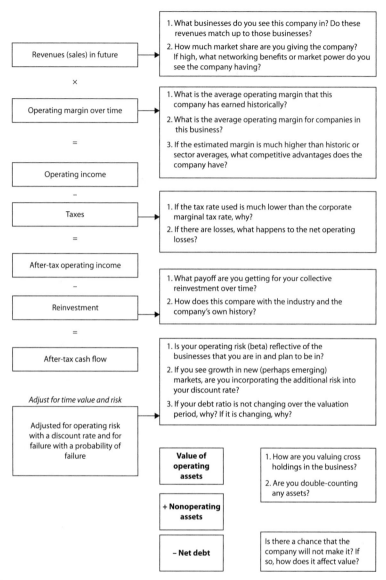

Figure 9.2
Deconstructing a valuation.

assessing cost of capital. With Uber, where the key question is the size of the market that Uber is going after, the part of the story I examined most was the question of whether Uber was just a car service company or something more, and I will come back to it in the next two chapters.

10

Improving and Modifying Your Narrative—The Feedback Loop

If you have followed the template in the last four chapters, you have a story that has now been converted into a valuation. Before you conclude that your job is done, it is worth remembering that your narrative is not the only plausible one and that there might be alternative stories for the same business. Rather than dismiss these alternative narratives as wrong and defend your own, you will be better served if you keep the feedback loop open and consider whether any of these alternative narratives have parts that you may want to borrow or adapt to make your own better. In some cases, these changes may be because others know more about the company being valued and the business it operates in than you do, and their alternative tales may reflect this knowledge. In other cases, these changes may just reflect an admission on your part that your original story was flawed. Whatever the rationale, refusing to change a narrative, just because it is yours, is hubris.

Fighting Hubris

Hubris is a good place to start this chapter, because it lies at the root of so much investing pain. It is natural to feel pride and ownership in a narrative that you, as founder or investor, have developed for a company, and it is almost as natural to feel the urge to not only defend it against criticism but to stay bound to it. Unfortunately, though, investing hell is filled with investors who have defended their "well thought through" stories all the way down into bankruptcy. I have had my own struggles with letting go of my favorite stories, and while I don't have a miracle cure, there are two actions that open me up for change. The first is to tell my story to the groups that are least likely to like that story and allow them to air their disagreements. The second is to be open about the uncertainty that I feel in my own story and how it plays out in the resulting estimates and value.

Get Out of the Echo Chamber

It is easier to tell your story and defend it with groups that think like you do and share your worldview. Consequently, if the story for your company is that of a high-flying tech start-up, telling that story to a group of entrepreneurs and venture capitalists will get heads nodding in agreement and consensus about your superior storytelling abilities. If you try that story out in front of a group of old-time value investors, you will find yourself quickly in the firing line, having to defend almost every part of your story.

While talking to people who don't think like you do is likely to be an uncomfortable experience, you can make it a productive one if you are willing to take the following steps. The first is to be open about tenets in investing and valuation that you think are truths, but are just beliefs. Thus, while growth may always be a "good" in a gathering of venture capitalists, it will be greeted more skeptically in the value investor conferences. To explain why growth is good, you have to then think about how growth affects value, and why growth can sometimes destroy value. That will allow you to explain to the skeptics why their concerns about growth don't hold true, at least in your specific case. The second is that in the process of trying to explain why growth is good to value investors, you may discover that you have perhaps not done your homework or have made an assumption that is either wrong or not well thought through. While your urge will be to cover up your mistakes and move on, you should go back and review your story and perhaps change it.

Face Up to Uncertainty

If you look at each of the valuations that I present in chapter 9, you will notice that they look almost magically precise. The value that I estimate for Amazon, for instance, is $175.25, estimated to the second decimal point. The reality, though, is that this final estimate of value is the end result of estimates that I made along the way, each of which I draw from my story and perhaps back up with data, but still estimates, subject to error. As you get further and further into the number crunching, there will be a point in time where you will start thinking of these estimates as facts and your value estimate as the truth.

The antidote to this false precision is the recognition that your valuation is based on "point estimates"—your base case values for expected growth, margins, and cost of capital—and each of these numbers comes from a probability distribution. Thus, when I estimate revenue growth at Amazon to be 15 percent a year for the next five years, it may be the expected value in a distribution where growth could range from 10 to 20 percent. It is a good idea to be more explicit about this uncertainty that you face, and there are four techniques you can use:

1. What-if analysis: In what-if analysis, you take individual variables in your valuation and vary them, keeping all other inputs fixed. In the Amazon valuation, for instance, I could estimate the value for Amazon for growth rates ranging from 10 to 20 percent. Why do this? The first is to see how much changing a variable affects value and using that knowledge to decide whether you should collect more information about that variable before your investment decision. The second and more cynical reason is to protect yourself from the criticism that will follow if you are wrong. By presenting a range of values, rather than a single best estimate, you can argue that almost everything that happens is as you forecast it to be.

2. Scenario analysis: In scenario analysis, you allow all or many of the variables in your analysis to change across scenarios, and you value your business in each scenario. In its most useless form, the scenarios are defined as best, base, and worst-case scenarios, with the unsurprising results that your business is worth a lot in the best case, nothing or very little in the worst case, and an intermediate amount in the base case. In a more productive form, the scenarios will be built around a key determinant of success, and the analysis will trace out not only what the company will be worth but also how it should act under each scenario. This would be a useful tool in valuing Alibaba, a company that, at least based on

my story, draws its value from growth in China, under different scenarios for growth in the Chinese economy.

3. Decision trees: Decision trees are probabilistic tools designed to evaluate discrete and sequential risks in a business. Thus, they are well suited for evaluating companies that need regulatory approval to operate or pharmaceutical/biotech companies that have to go through multiple stages of the drug approval process. Being forced to examine the sequential events that your company has to go through to get to success makes you think more deeply about weak links in your story. In chapter 2 I looked at Theranos, the company that claimed to have developed a less-intrusive, cheaper blood test that would disrupt the blood-testing business, as an example of a runaway story. It is likely that the problems in the approval process would have come to the surface more quickly if investors had used a decision tree approach to keep track of approval probabilities.

4. Simulations: A simulation is the fullest and richest way of assessing the effect of uncertainty. Unlike a what-if analysis, in which you are restricted to changing only one variable at a time, you can change as many of your input variables as you want, and unlike a scenario analysis, in which you have to break down the future into specific scenarios, simulations allow you to examine a continuum of possibilities. In fact, a version of simulation will even allow you to incorporate decision trees and binding constraints into the simulation; a bank that violates a regulatory capital bound or a debt-laden company that is unable to meet a contractual commitment can be put out of business.

CASE STUDY 10.1:
ALIBABA VALUATION—THE CHINA SCENARIOS

Lead-in case studies:

Case Study 6.6: Alibaba, the China Story, September 2014
Case Study 7.4: Alibaba, the Global Player
Case Study 8.4: Alibaba—From Story to Numbers
Case Study 9.4: Alibaba—The China Story

Table 10.1
Alibaba—Value Under China Growth Scenarios

Scenario	Revenue growth rate	Target operating margin	Cost of capital	Value per share
China growth lower than expected	15.00%	35.00%	9.00%	$40.06
China growth as expected	25.00%	40.00%	8.56%	$65.98
China growth higher than expected	30.00%	50.00%	8.25%	$98.89

In case study 9.4, I valued Alibaba's equity at the time of its IPO in September 2014 at $161 billion and its value per share at $65.98, under the assumption that its revenues would grow 25 percent a year for the next five years and that it would be able to generate a margin of 40 percent. Those assumptions were built on the expectation that the Chinese online retail market would grow at 25 percent a year and that Alibaba would be able to maintain its market share. Consequently, the value rested on my assumption that the Chinese economy would continue to grow, carrying the online retail business with it.

There is the possibility that I was wrong in that assumption. In particular, growth in China could drop off in the coming years, or it is also possible that I have underestimated China's growth potential. In table 10.1 I look at three scenarios built around growth in China and value Alibaba under each one.

The results are not surprising in terms of direction, but the magnitude of the change, a loss of more than a third of value under the China low-growth scenario and an increase of value of almost 50 percent in the high-growth scenario, is an indication of how exposed your narrative is to macroeconomic risk in China.

CASE STUDY 10.2: ALIBABA—A MONTE CARLO SIMULATION

The Alibaba valuation was based on a set of inputs that were estimated with error. While I believe that the expected values for these inputs reflected the company, at least as I saw it in September 2014, it is true that I faced uncertainty in estimating each of the inputs. To capture that uncertainty, I ran a simulation, with probability distributions for the inputs, rather than single expected values. With each input, the expected value from the distributions matched my assumption in my base case, but the probability distribution provides my judgment on the uncertainty that I feel about each input. For example, my estimate for the target operating margin is centered around 40 percent (my base case assumption), but I am assuming that the outcome can lie between 30 and 50 percent, with equal probabilities for each outcome (a uniform distribution). I make similar judgments about revenue growth (with 25 percent as my base case value), the cost of capital (base case value of 8.56 percent), and the sales-to-capital ratio (2.00 in the base case), with different assumptions about the distributions around the base case values for each one. In the simulation I draw from these distributions to estimate Alibaba's value, which I present as a value distribution in figure 10.1.

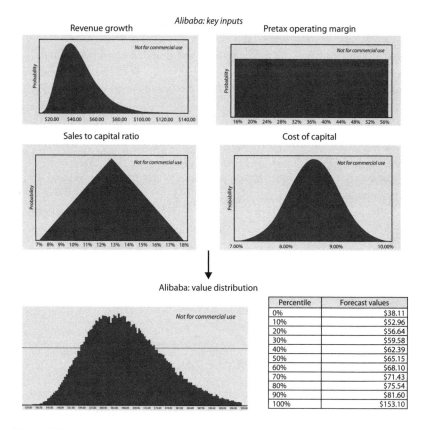

Figure 10.1
Alibaba valuation simulations, September 2014. Mean = $66.45; median = $65.15; lowest value = $38.11; highest value = $153.10.

Note that the mean and median across the 100,000 simulations track closely the base case value of $65.98/share, which should not be surprising, since the expected values of the inputs are the same in both analyses. The additional information is in the percentile distribution of values, with the lowest value being $38.11 a share and the highest one being $153.11. Not only do I get a richer information set to base my decisions on, but I am also reminded of how much error there is in my own estimate. That, in turn, will hopefully make me less likely to label those who disagree with me, in either direction, as wrong and more open to suggestions that I can use to improve my narrative and valuation.

The Pricing Feedback

Once you have a narrative, convert the narrative into numbers, and the numbers into value, you are taking a stand on how much a company is worth. The most immediate feedback that you get is the price that others are willing to pay for the company today. If you are valuing a publicly traded company, that feedback is in real time, since market prices are updated as investors trade. Even with private businesses, you may sometimes have price estimates based on what investors are gauging the company to be worth, though those price estimates will be less frequently updated.

So what? There is nothing more disconcerting than valuing a company and arriving at an estimate that is wildly different from the current price. I know that is why we value companies, i.e., to find market mistakes, but when there is a wide divergence, there are four possible explanations. The first is that you are right and that the market is wrong. The second is that you are wrong and that the market is right. The third is that both you and the market are wrong, because the intrinsic value is an unknowable number. The final possibility is that the pricing and value processes, described and contrasted in chapter 8, have diverged and that the market is pricing companies, whereas you are valuing them. The first explanation suggests either overconfidence or hubris on your part and the second is a total surrender to the market. The third explanation is the one that I start with, since it requires me to accept the possibility that I am wrong in my narrative and, as a consequence, in my value. It then stands to reason that no matter how comfortable I am with my story, I should try to at least gauge what the market is expecting and then compare those expectations to mine, not necessarily with the intent of changing my estimate but as a precursor to doing more research and perhaps making a better decision.

If, after looking at the possibilities, I am still comfortable with my narrative, I conclude that the pricing and value processes have diverged, resulting in a gap between the two. Whether I am willing to put real money on the gap will depend on whether I have faith, first in my own story and resulting value, and the other in the gap closing within my prescribed time horizon.

CASE STUDY 10.3: AMAZON IN OCTOBER 2014— MARKET BREAKEVEN POINTS

Lead-in case studies:

Case Study 6.5: Amazon, the *Field of Dreams* Model, October 2014
Case Study 7.3: Amazon—Alternative Narratives, October 2014
Case Study 8.3: Amazon—From Story to Numbers
Case Study 9.3: Amazon—Valuiong the *Field of Dreams*

In chapter 9 my valuation ($175.25) of Amazon diverged sharply from the market price ($287) at the time. My valuation, though, was driven by my narrative for the company and the revenue growth rate (15 percent for the next five years, leading to revenues of $240 billion in 2024) and operating margin (7.38 percent) that I estimated for the firm. It is clear that investors, or at least those bidding up Amazon's stock price, were more optimistic than I was. To get a measure of how different the market's assumptions were from mine, I estimated the value per share as a function of revenue growth and target operating margins (in ten years) in table 10.2.

Table 10.2
Amazon—Value and Price Breakeven Points

Revenues in 2024 (in billions)	Target pretax operating margin					
	2.50%	5.00%	7.50%	10.00%	12.50%	15.00%
$100	$ 34.36	$ 69.25	$ 104.14	$ 139.03	$ 173.92	$ 208.81
$150	$ 3.75	$ 79.34	$ 127.93	$ 176.52	$ 225.11	$ 273.70
$200	$ 27.20	$ 90.19	$ 153.19	$ 216.18	$ 279.17	$ 342.17
$250	$ 23.76	$ 101.35	$ 178.94	$ 256.52	$ 334.11	$ 411.69
$300	$ 20.29	$ 113.22	$ 206.16	$ 299.10	$ 393.03	$ 484.97
$350	$ 17.02	$ 124.85	$ 232.67	$ 340.50	$ 448.32	$ 556.14
$400	$ 13.90	$ 136.28	$ 258.66	$ 381.03	$ 503.41	$ 625.78

The shaded areas represented values that exceeded the price per share ($287) at the time of the analysis. If investors were pricing Amazon on the basis of intrinsic value, they were clearly expecting Amazon to deliver higher revenues than I was estimating, with much heftier profit margins. At the time of the valuation, my judgment was that these numbers were too high for my tastes and that I would stay with my assessment of value.

In fact, the persistence of Amazon's price climb suggested to me that investors were not valuing Amazon but pricing it and that they were therefore likely to be impervious at least in the near term to fundamentals. That is also why, notwithstanding my assessment that Amazon was overvalued, I did not take the obvious next step and sell short on the stock. Cowardly on my part? Of course, but I think it would have been foolhardy for me to take a position based upon intrinsic value on a pricing stock, if I did not control my time horizon, and in the case of a short sale, I did not.

CASE STUDY 10.4: THE PRICING FEEDBACK— UBER, FERRARI, AMAZON, AND ALIBABA

In chapter 9 I valued Uber, Ferrari, Amazon, and Alibaba and I would be lying if I said that the current pricing of these companies did not influence my valuations.

- With Uber, a nontraded entity, the feedback from the market came in the form of the implied valuations in venture capital investments. My interest in Uber was triggered by a news story that it had been priced at $17 billion in its most recent venture capital round. That news colored my perspective on Uber, and while my valuation on Uber was only $6 billion, I was inclined to give Uber the benefit of the doubt on almost every aspect of my valuation.
- With Ferrari, my valuation was ahead of its IPO, and the IPO delivered a value of about €9 billion, much higher than my estimated value of €6.3 billion (under my exclusive club narrative). I did go back and review my valuation (and story) after the offering, checking to see whether there were parts of the narrative where I could look for higher value, but found no reason to change it.
- With Amazon, the disconnect between my estimated value ($175.25) and the actual price at the time of the analysis ($287.06) was stark and led to some soul-searching for what I might be missing. One reason that I did compute the breakeven points in the last case study was to get a measure of what the market was assuming in its pricing of the stock.

- With Alibaba, my estimated value per share was approximately $66, ahead of its offering. Shortly after I did my value estimation, the bankers set an offering price of $68 for the company, uncomfortably close to my estimated value. Why uncomfortably? Given that bankers price IPOs (rather than value them) to increase the odds that the shares will be bid up on the offering date, I did not view the closeness of my value and offering prices as anything other than pure coincidence. On the offering date, the stock opened at about $95 a share, indicating that investors were much more optimistic than I was about the future of the company.

In each case, the market price did affect my valuation, at least implicitly, and that is almost always going to be the case. When you first start valuing publicly traded companies, the market price will often end up driving your narrative, because you feel safest (even if it is only a perception) when your value is close to the price. As you become more comfortable with both your narratives and your valuation skills, you will become more willing to attach values to companies that are very different from their prices and perhaps even to act on them.

Alternative Narratives

While the pricing of companies provides feedback, it is at the aggregate level (the price of the stock versus your estimated value) rather than on a level that impacts the individual parts of your story. For that more specific feedback, you have to seek out contrary points of view. I don't claim to have the answers on how to do this, but here are a few things that have worked for me in getting that feedback.

1. Make your narrative and valuation transparent: It is difficult to get criticism that you can use to improve your valuation, if you do not reveal the details of your valuation or the story behind the numbers. I have found that the clearer I am about my story and the resulting numbers, the more directed the criticism becomes. Hence, those looking at my Uber valuation can decide which part of my story they disagree with and why, and I can look at their critiques in that context.

2. Have an open forum for people to comment on your valuation: If you claim to welcome criticism, you have to make it easier for people to criticize you, not more difficult. To me, this is one of the

advantages of presenting my valuations online, as I have on my blog for the last few years. Those reviewing the valuation can comment on the valuation, and since I give them the option of remaining anonymous, they can be free in expressing their disagreement. I have also used Google's shared spreadsheets to allow readers to change inputs in my valuation and make their own estimates of value. It is my version of "crowdvaluing," and I can check my narrative against the crowd.

3. Separate the constructive criticism from the noise: It is true that some of the criticism that I get is just noise, people venting because they do not like my conclusions. I have learned, for the most part, to move past these to those criticisms that have heft to them and that I can use to improve my valuation. I have also discovered that there are companies for which investors have such strong feelings that any contrary view will cause a blowback. It is a lesson that I learn and relearn every time that I value Tesla or Amazon.

4. Use the narrative to organize the criticism: Having a clear narrative with parts to it helps me organize the feedback that I get from those who disagree with me. Thus, I can break down disagreements into those about my estimate of the total market, my judgments about market share and operating margins, and my evaluation of risk in a business.

5. Look for the weakest links: If I find particular parts of my narrative are attracting more negative feedback and disagreement than others, it is a signal to me that I have either not been clear about explaining my reasoning or, worse, that I have not fully thought through that part of my story.

6 Think process, not product: When I first started doing valuations, I tended to focus on the bottom line, the ending value. I am still interested in that ending value, but to me the interesting part is the journey that I take to get there.

As a general rule, I find that the more uncertainty there is around a company, the more open I have to be to alternative story lines. There is one final cautionary note that I should add. Listening to others does not require capitulation. I have heard well-reasoned arguments about why a part of my narrative is wrong and have chosen to not make changes to it, because it is still my judgment to make.

CASE STUDY 10.5: UBER—THE GURLEY COUNTERNARRATIVE

Lead-in case studies

Case Study 6.2: The Ride-Sharing Landscape, June 2014
Case Study 6.3: The Uber Narrative, June 2014
Case Study 8.1: Uber—From Story to Numbers
Case Study 9.1: Uber—Valuing the Urban Car Service Company

After my valuation of Uber in June 2014, I received a gracious email from Bill Gurley, an early investor in Uber, telling me that he was planning to post a counter to my Uber valuation and that it would not pull punches. A little while later, I started getting messages from those who had read the post, with some seeking my response and some seeming to view this as the first volley in some valuation battle.[1] The post did provide a very interesting and provocative counternarrative to my urban car service one, and it was interesting to me for several reasons.

1. Like everyone else, I like being right, but I was far more interested in understanding Uber's valuation, and the post provided the vantage point of someone who not only was invested in the company but knew far more about it than I did. Rather than berating me for not getting the new economy or abusing DCF valuation as a tool from the Middle Ages, the post focused on specifics about Uber and the basis for its high value.

2. If it is true that valuation is the bridge between numbers and narrative and that neither the numbers nor the narrative people have an automatic right to the high ground, Bill Gurley's post brought home that message by laying out a detailed and well thought through narrative.

Gurley's narrative lent itself well to a more grounded discussion of Uber as a company and I am grateful to him for providing it. As a teacher, I am constantly on the lookout for "teachable moments," even if they come at my expense.

In my Uber narrative, I viewed Uber as a car service company that would disrupt the existing taxi market (which I estimated to be $100 billion), expanding its growth (by attracting new users) and gaining a significant market share (10 percent). The Gurley Uber narrative was a more expansive one, where he saw Uber's potential market as much larger (drawing in new users) and its networking effects as much stronger, leading to a higher market share. In many ways, this is exactly the discussion I was hoping to have when I first posted on Uber, since it allows me to see how these narratives play out in the numbers. In table 10.3 I contrast the narratives and the resulting values.

Table 10.3

Uber Narratives—Gurley versus Damodaran

	Gurley	Damodaran
Narrative	Uber is a logistics company (moving, delivery, car service), and it will use its networking advantage to gain a dominant market share, while cutting its slice of revenues (to 10%).	Uber will expand the car service market moderately, primarily in urban environments, and use its competitive advantages to get a significant but not dominant market share and maintain its revenue slice at 20%.
Total market	$300 billion, growing at 3% a year	$100 billion, growing at 6% a year
Market share	40.00%	10.00%
Uber's revenue slice	10.00%	20.00%
Value for Uber	$28.7 billion + option value of entering car ownership market ($6 billion+)	$5.9 billion + option value of entering car ownership market ($2–3 billion)

The valuation that I produced for Uber with the Gurley narrative was $28.7 billion, much higher than my estimate of $5.9 billion.

Given that the values delivered by the narratives were so different, the question, if you were an investor, boiled down to which one had a higher probability of being closer to reality and Gurley's had the advantage over mine for at least two reasons. The first is that as a board member and insider, he knew far more about Uber's workings than I did. Not only were his starting numbers (on revenues, operating income, and other details) far more precise than mine, but he had access to how Uber was performing in its test markets (with the new users that he lists). The second is that as an investor in Uber, he had skin in the game and more at stake than I did and should therefore be given more credence. The third is that he not only had experience investing in young companies but had been right on many of his investments.

Does that mean that I was abandoning my narrative and the valuation that goes with it? No, or at least not right then, and there were three reasons why. First, it is difficult, if not impossible, for someone on the inside not to believe the best about the company that he or she invests in, the managers he or she listens to, and the products that it offers. Second, an investor in a company, especially one without an easy exit route, is more attached to his or her narrative than someone who has little to lose (other than pride) from abandoning or altering narratives. Third, as Kahneman notes in his book on investor psychology, experience is not a very good teacher in investing and markets.[2] As human beings, we often extract the wrong lessons from past successes, don't learn enough from our failures, and sometimes delude ourselves into remembering things that never happened. I am not suggesting that Bill Gurley was guilty of any of these sins, but I am, by nature, a cautious convert, and I waited to buy into his narrative, compelling though it may be.

The Gurley narrative for Uber made a good case that the convenience and economics of Uber will expand the car service market initially to include light users and nonusers (suburban users, rental car users, aged parents, and young children), but it did highlighted three requirements for Uber's success:

1. Reason to switch: Uber has to provide users with good reasons to switch from their existing services to Uber. For taxi services, the benefits from using Uber are documented well in the Gurley narrative. Uber is more convenient (an app click away), more dependable, often safer (because of the payment system), and sometimes cheaper than taxi service. However, the trade-off gets murkier as you look past taxi services. Since mass transit will continue to be cheaper than Uber, it is comfort and convenience that will be the reasons for switching. With car rentals, Uber may be cheaper and more convenient in some senses (you don't have to worry about picking up a rental car, parking it, or having it break down) and less convenient in others (especially if you have multiple short trips to make). With suburban car service, the problem that Uber may face is that a car is usually more than just a transportation device. Any parent who has driven his or her kids to school will attest that in addition to being a driver, he or she has to play the roles of personal assistant, private investigator, therapist, and mind reader.

2. Overcome inertia: Even when a new way of doing things offers significant benefits, it is difficult to overcome the unwillingness of human beings to change the way they act, with that inertia increasing with how set they are in their ways. It should come as little surprise that Uber was initially most successful with young people, not yet set in their ways, and that it was slower to make inroads with older users. That inertia will be an even stronger force to overcome as you move beyond the car service market. The articles that point to young people owning fewer cars are indicative of larger changes in society, but I am not sure they can be taken as an indication of a sea change in car ownership behavior. After all, there has been almost as much written on how many young people are moving back in with their parents, and both phenomena may be the results of a more difficult economic environment for young people, who come out of college with massive student loans and few job prospects.

3. Fight off the status quo: The taxi cab empire, hobbled and inefficient though it may be, will fight back, since there are significant economic interests at stake. As both Uber and Lyft have discovered, taxi service providers can use

regulations and other restrictions to impede the new entrants into their businesses. Those fights will get more intense as car rental and car ownership businesses get targeted.

One way to contrast my narrative with Bill Gurley's is to think in terms of the possible/plausible/probable distinction that I laid out in chapter 7. In figure 10.2 I display how the two narratives vary on this classification.

The second part of the Gurley Uber narrative rests on the company having network benefits that allow it to capture a dominant market share. As Bill Gurley noted, a networking effect shows up any time you, as a user of a product or service, benefit from other people using the same product and service. If the networking effect is strong enough, it can lead to a dominant market share for the company that creates it and potentially to a "winner-take-all" scenario. The arguments presented in his post for the networking effects—pick-up times, coverage density, and utilization—all seem to me to point more to a local networking effect rather than a global networking one. In other words, I could see why the largest car service provider in New York may be able to leverage these advantages to get a dominant market share in New York, but these advantages will not be of much use to it in Miami, if it is not the dominant player there. There are global networking advantages, such as stored data that can be accessed by users in a new city and partnerships with credit card, airline, and car companies, but they are weaker. In fact, if the local networking advantages dominate, this market could very quickly devolve into a city-by-city trench warfare among the different

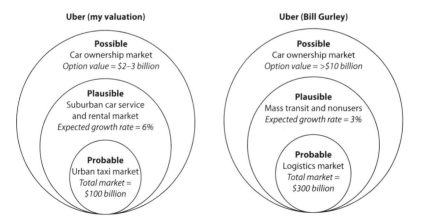

Figure 10.2
Probable, plausible, and possible—Damodaran narrative versus Gurley narrative.

players, with different winners in different markets. Thus, it is possible that Uber will become the dominant car service company in San Francisco, Lyft in Chicago, and a yet-to-be-created company in London. For the Gurley Uber narrative to hold, the global networking advantages had to move front and center.

CASE STUDY 10.6: FERRARI—FEEDBACK FROM A DUTY-FREE CATALOG

My final case study is a brief one but is meant to illustrate how feedback can come from unusual places. A few weeks after I valued Ferrari for its IPO and arrived at a value of €6.3 billion, well below the €9 billion that it went public at, I was on a flight to Europe and, in a moment of boredom, I leafed through the pages of the duty-free magazine on the plane. My eye was drawn to at least two of the products in the magazine—a Ferrari watch and Ferrari pen.

I was uninterested in buying either of them, but it served as a reminder to me that Ferrari has a powerful brand name that stretches beyond automobiles into other luxury products. That led me to consider the possibility that my narrative of Ferrari as an exclusive auto company could be displaced by an alternate narrative of Ferrari as a luxury brand name company that happens to make automobiles. Note that the value you would attach to Ferrari under the latter narrative may be much larger, since it will expand the potential market beyond cars to electronics, clothes. and perhaps even shoes.

Conclusion

I like telling stories about companies, but I do sometimes get too attached to my stories. This chapter is just as much about how I try to confront that weakness as it is about valuation. In particular, I have found that being more open about my valuation assumptions and narratives and having a forum where I can share these valuations has allowed me to get some very valuable feedback, especially from those who disagree with me. It still remains up to me to decide how I respond to that feedback, but I have learned, sometimes the hard way, that being open to changing your narrative is not a sign of weakness but of strength.

11

Narrative Alterations—
The Real World Intrudes

In business, few things ever happen the way that you expect them to and it is a given that you are going to be surprised, sometimes in good ways and sometimes in bad. In chapter 6 I talked about grounding narratives in the real world, but if the real world changes, your narrative, to stay realistic, has to change as well. In this chapter I start with a look at the causes of narrative changes, which can range from the qualitative to the quantitative and from big macroeconomic/political news stories to earnings reports at companies. I then look at classifying narrative alterations, from shifts, where the story requires tweaking or modifying in specifics but not in structure; to changes, where the story structure is altered; to breaks, where a story comes to an abrupt stop; and I close by examining the value consequences of these alterations to narratives.

Why Narratives Alter

In the last chapter I stressed the importance of using feedback to improve and change your narrative for a business. In this chapter I expand on that notion, but the changes I address occur in response to new information you receive about the company, the sector or businesses it operates in, or the overall economy or the country in which it is incorporated or operates.

If the only constant in business is change, and the pace of change is increasing with technology and globalization, it stands to reason that no narrative can stay unchanged for a long period. It is prudent to respond to new developments and information by revisiting your narrative and evaluating whether any parts of it may need to be changed. The news itself can take different forms and can come from many sources:

1. Qualitative versus quantitative: The news can be quantitative, ranging from the surprises in earnings reports to government reports on inflation and economic growth. It can also be qualitative, some examples being a change in top management, a legal judgment for or against the firm, or the announcement that an activist investor has taken a position in the company.

2. Inside versus outside: The information can sometimes be from the company in the form of either a required financial disclosure or as a corporate announcement (of an acquisition, divestiture, or a buyback) and sometimes from external sources (financial news, equity research analysts following the company, or regulatory authorities). In some cases it may even be from a competitor, with the information that you get changing the way you think about the market and competitive dynamics.

3. Micro versus macro: Much of the information that you get is at the micro level, that is, it is about the company, its competitors, or the sector. Some of the news that you get will be about macroeconomic factors, that is, shifts in interest rates, exchange rates, or inflation can alter your story. To the extent that your company is exposed substantially to these macroeconomic variables, they may cause significant alterations in your narrative.

Suffice it to say that there is no narrative that is impervious to news, and it therefore follows that the intrinsic values of companies (which reflect these narratives) will also change over time, sometimes by large amounts. The view promoted by some old-time value investors that intrinsic valuation is timeless and constant is not only wrong but can be dangerous to portfolio health.

Classifying and Incorporating Narrative Alterations

One obvious way to think of classifying narrative alterations is to think in terms of the bottom line, that is, the value of the business, and break down narrative alterations into good news (increasing value) and bad news (decreasing value). Unless the news that you get is unambiguously better than expected or consistently worse than expected for a company, this classification is not easy to make. With most companies, though, the push and pull of good and bad news will mean that you will not have a measure of the effect on value until you work through the entire narrative and revalue the company. With that in mind, I propose that you think of narrative alterations in terms of how new information changes your overall story, even if some of the changes are very positive and others are clearly negative. Based on this classification, you can classify narrative alterations into narrative breaks, narrative changes, and narrative shifts, with the first representing a complete breakdown of your story and the last requiring a tweaking of your story.

Narrative Breaks

Any number of events can cause a story to come to an abrupt end, and many of them have negative connotations:

1. Natural or man-made disasters: A promising and profitable business story can be brought to an abrupt end by a natural disaster or a terrorist attack. In November 2015, for instance, the Sahafi Hotel, a luxury hotel in Mogadishu, was targeted and bombed by terrorists. It is unlikely that insurance will allow this hotel in an emerging market to be made whole again, and while this may be premature, there is a chance the Sahafi Hotel will not reopen its doors. As an owner or an investor in the company, your value loss may be permanent.

2. Legal or regulatory action: You may be a business awaiting a legal judgment or a regulatory decision that, if it goes against you, can be catastrophic enough to end your narrative. A small pharmaceutical or biotechnology firm with a single (potentially blockbuster) drug wending its way through the approval process can find itself at the end of its story if the FDA rules against it. As an illustration, consider Aveo Pharmaceuticals, a Boston-based biotech company that spent seven years developing a drug to treat kidney cancer and whose market capitalization reached a billion dollars in 2013. After setbacks in clinical trials and questions about the trial design, the FDA rejected the drug, leading to a 70 percent drop in value and the laying off of 62 percent of the company's employees.

3. Failure to make contractual payments: A firm that is required to make contractual payments will find its business model at risk if it fails to meet its obligation. That is obviously the case when you have a bank loan or corporate bonds outstanding, but it can extend to cover lease obligations for retailers and even player contract payments for a sports franchise. In late 2015 and early 2016, as commodity prices plunged and concern about distress climbed, equity values at highly levered commodity companies collapsed.

4. Government expropriation: While expropriation by the government is less common than a few decades ago, there are still parts of the world where a business can be taken over without the owners receiving fair compensation. When the Argentine government nationalized the Argentine oil company YPF in 2011, investors in the company woke up overnight to a diminished value.

5. Capital squeeze: Many ongoing businesses need capital not just for expansion but for day-to-day operations, and a market crisis that shuts down access to capital could cause these businesses to fold. While Greece, Argentina, and the Ukraine may all come to mind when you think of this phenomenon, this problem is not restricted to emerging markets, as we saw in 2008, when developed markets exhibited the same behavior.

6. Acquisition: In perhaps one of the few instances of an unexpected narrative end that is good news, a company can be acquired and become part of a much larger entity. Thus, when Apple acquired Beats, the headphone/music company, the story of Beats ended as it was swallowed up into the much larger narrative of Apple as a company.

As you look at this list, you can see the risk of a narrative break will vary across companies as a function of a number of factors. The first is that *exposure to discrete and catastrophic risks* is more likely to create a narrative break than exposure to continuous risk. Thus, a large currency devaluation in a fixed-exchange rate currency is more likely to create a game-ending shock than day-to-day movements in floating exchange rates. The second is a related point: companies with risks that can be insured or hedged are more protected than companies with *risks that cannot be protected against*. The third is that the events listed above will be more likely to tip you into a narrative break if you are a *small company with a limited financial buffer* than a larger one with more of a cushion. Finally, if you have *more access to capital*, you are less likely to have shut down your business in the event of a large event. That is perhaps why these narrative breaks are more common in private businesses (with fewer sources of capital) than in their publicly traded counterparts, and emerging market companies more frequently shutter their businesses in the face of unexpected shocks than do developed market companies.

CASE STUDY 11.1: NARRATIVE BREAKS

At the start of 2014, a company called Aereo claimed to have found a legal way to broadcast cable channels on handheld devices, without users having to pay cable fees. While the response from most people was disbelief, that did not stop investors from valuing the company at $800 million in early 2014. In the summer of 2014, the U.S. Supreme Court, which was called to rule on the legality of Aereo's streaming, ruled against it. Overnight, the value of the business dropped toward zero, and a few months later, the company folded.

A more perverse example is Ashley Madison, an online service that facilitates cheating on spouses via online connections. Without passing judgment on the morality of this business model, the company had no shortage of investors and was looking forward to an imminent initial public offering, where it planned to raise $200 million from the market. Those plans came crashing down to earth when a computer hacker got into Ashley Madison's website and released a partial list of its customers, not good news in a site dedicated to cheating. While the company was not put out of business, it was mortally wounded, and its valuation crashed in the aftermath of this news story.

Narrative Changes

In a narrative change, a part or many parts of your story are changed significantly by real-world developments. These changes can come from different sources and have positive or negative effects, but one way to organize them is to use the narrative framework that we developed in chapter 8 (see figure 11.1).

When you make these changes, though, recognize that you will have to explain what parts of the story you have changed and why, and also be ready for criticism from two sources:

- The value scolds: Coming from a belief system that intrinsic value is a stable, perhaps even constant number and that big changes in it are an indication of weakness, value purists will pounce on your changes and

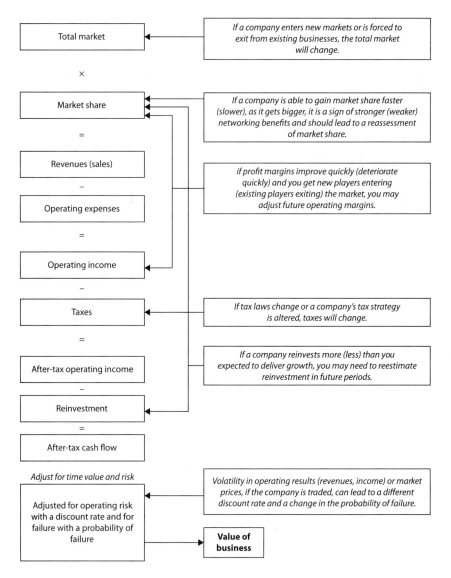

Figure 11.1
New stories and narrative changes.

argue that this is more a sign that your original valuation was flawed than a sensible adjustment to new information. My response to critics who ask me how my valuations can change so much over short periods is to quote John Maynard Keynes, who is rumored to have said: "When the facts change, I change my mind. What do you do, sir?"

- The hindsight gurus: There will be another group of critics who will take you to task for not having the foresight to see the changes that you have made coming at the time of your original valuation. My defense with this group is to compliment them on their capacity to forecast the future, to accept meekly my inability to match them on this skill, and to invite them to look in their crystal balls and tell me what they see coming in the next few years.

It is true that some companies are more exposed to narrative changes than others. In particular, companies that are early in their life cycle will see bigger changes than mature companies, a point I will return to in chapter 14, when I talk about the life cycle effect on narratives and numbers.

CASE STUDY 11.2: UBER—NEWS AND VALUE, SEPTEMBER 2015

In chapter 9 I valued Uber at $6 billion in June 2014 and found it to be worth significantly less than the investor pricing of $17 billion. In the time period between June 2014 and September 2015, each week brought more stories about Uber, with some containing good news for those who believed that the company was on a glide path to a $100 billion IPO and some containing bad news that evoked predictions of catastrophe from Uber doubters. For me, the test with each news story was to see how that story affected my narrative for Uber and, by extension, my estimate of its value. In keeping with this perspective, I broke down the news stories based upon narrative parts and valuation inputs.

1. The total market: The news on the car service market was mostly positive, indicating that the market was much broader, growing faster, and more global than I had thought a year prior.

    a. Not just urban and much bigger: While car service remained most popular in the urban areas, it made inroads into exurbia and suburbia. A presentation to potential investors in the company put Uber's gross billings for 2015 at $10.84 billion. It is true that this was an unofficial number and may have had some hype built into it, but even if that number overestimated revenues by 20 or 25 percent, it represented a jump of 400 percent from 2014 levels.

    b. Drawing in new customers: One reason for the increase in the car service market was that it was drawing in customers who would never have taken a taxicab or a limo service in the first place. In San Francisco, for instance, the city where Uber was born, it was estimated that ride-sharing companies had tripled the size of the taxicab and car service market.

c. With more diverse offerings: The other reason for the jump in the size of the ride-sharing market is that it had morphed to include alternatives that expanded choices, reduced costs (car-pooling services), and increased flexibility.

d. And going global: The biggest stories on ride sharing came out of Asia, as the ride-sharing market expanded rapidly in that part of the world, especially in India and China. That should really have come as no surprise, since these countries offered the trifecta for ride-sharing opportunities: large urban populations with limited car ownership and poorly developed mass transit systems.

The bad news on the car service market front came mostly in the form of taxi driver strikes, regulatory bans, and operating restrictions. Even that bad news, though, contained seeds of good news, since the status quo crowd would not have been trying so hard to stop the upstarts if ride-sharing was not taking business away from taxicabs. The attempts by taxi operators, regulators, and politicians to stop the ride-sharing services reeked of desperation, and the markets seemed to reflect that. Not only did the revenues collected by taxicabs in New York City drop significantly between 2013 and 2015, but so did the price of cab medallions, which lost almost 40 percent of their value (roughly $5 billion in the aggregate) in that two-year period.

In my June 2014 valuation I had noted the possibility that Uber could move into other businesses. The good news between June 2014 and September 2015 was that it delivered on this promise, offering logistics services in Hong Kong and New York and food-delivery service in Los Angeles. The bad news was that it was slow going, partly because these were smaller businesses than ride sharing and partly because the competition was more efficient than the car service business. However, these new businesses moved from just being possible to plausible, thus expanding the total market.

Bottom line: The total market for Uber is bigger than the urban car service market that I visualized in June 2014, and Uber will attract new customers and expand in new markets (with Asia becoming the focus), and perhaps even into new businesses.

2. Networking and competitive advantages: The news on this front was mixed. The good news was that the ride-sharing companies increased the cost of entry into the market with tactics such as paying large amounts to drivers as sweeteners for signing up. In the United States, Uber and Lyft became the biggest players, and some of the competitors from the previous year had either faded away or were unable to keep up with these two. Outside the United States, the good news for Uber was that it was not only in the mix almost everywhere in

the world, but that Lyft had, at least for the moment, decided to stay focused on the United States. The bad news for Uber was that the competition was intense, especially in Asia, and it was fighting against domestic ride-sharing companies that dominated these markets: Ola in India, Didi Kuaidi in China, and GrabTaxi in Southeast Asia. Some of the domestic company dominance could be attributed to these companies being first movers with better understanding of local markets, but some of it also reflected the tilt in these markets (created by local investors, regulation, and politics) toward local players. There was even talk that these competitors would band together to create a "not-Uber" network, and that story got backing when Didi Kuaidi and Lyft announced a formal partnership. All of these ride-sharing companies were able to access capital at sky-high valuations, reducing the significant cash advantage that Uber had earlier in the process. As competition picks up, one of the key numbers that will be under pressure is the sharing of the gross billing, set historically at 80 percent for the driver and 20 percent for the ride-sharing business. In many U.S. cities, Lyft was already offering drivers the opportunity to keep all of their earnings if they drove more than 40 hours a week. While the threat of mutually assured destruction had kept both companies from directly challenging the 80/20 sharing rule, it is only a matter of time before that changes.

3. Cost structure: This is the area where mostly bad news was delivered. Some of the pain came from within the ride-sharing business, as companies offered larger and larger upfront payments to drivers to get them to switch from competitors, pushing up this component of costs. Much of the cost pressure, though, came from outside:

   a. Drivers as partial employees: Early in the summer of 2015, the California Labor Commission decided that Uber drivers were employees of the company, not independent contractors. That ruling was further affirmed by a court decision that Uber drivers could sue the company in a class action suit, and it looked likely that there would be other jurisdictions where this fight would continue. It appeared almost inevitable that at the end of the process, drivers for ride-sharing companies would be treated perhaps not as employees but at least as semiemployees, entitled to some (if not all) of the benefits of employees (leading to higher costs for ride-sharing companies).

   b. The insurance blind spot: Ride-sharing companies in their nascent years have been able to exploit the holes in auto insurance contracting, often just having to add supplemental insurance to the insurance their drivers already have. As both regulators/legislators and insurance companies tried to fix this gap, it looked likely that drivers for ride-sharing companies would soon have to buy more expensive insurance and that ride-sharing companies would have to bear a portion of that cost.

c. Fighting the empire is not cheap: Groups vested in the status quo (the taxi business and its regulators) were fighting back in many cities around the world. That fight was expensive as the amount of money spent on lobbying and legal fees increased and new fronts opened up.

The evidence that costs were running far ahead of revenues again came from leaked documents from the ride-sharing companies. One showed that Uber was a money loser in the previous two years and that the contribution margins (the profits after covering just variable costs) by city not only revealed big differences across cities but were uniformly low (ranging from a high of 11.1 percent in Stockholm and Johannesburg to 3.5 percent in Seattle).

Bottom line: The costs of running a ride-sharing business are high, and while some of these costs will drop as business scales up, the operating margins are likely to be smaller than I anticipated just over a year ago.

4. Capital intensity and risk: The business model that I assumed for my initial Uber valuation was minimalist in its capital requirements, since Uber not only did not own the cars in their car service but invested little in corporate offices or infrastructure. That translated into a high sales-to-capital ratio, with $1 in capital generating $5 in additional revenues. While that basic business model had not changed by September 2015, ride-sharing companies were recognizing that one of the downsides of this low–capital intensity model was that it increased competition on other fronts. Thus, the high costs that Uber and Lyft were paying to sign up drivers could be viewed as a consequence of the business models they had adopted, in which drivers were free agents without contracts. In September 2015 there was no sign that any of the ride-sharing companies were interested in altering the dynamics of this model by either upping their investment in infrastructure or in the cars themselves, but there was a news story about Uber hiring away the robotics faculty at Carnegie Mellon, suggestive of change to come.

Bottom line: Ride-sharing companies will continue with the low–capital intensity model for the moment, but the search for a competitive edge may result in a more capital-intensive model, requiring more investment to deliver sustainable growth.

5. Management culture: Though not a direct input into valuation, it is unquestionable that when investing in a young business, you should be aware of the management culture in that business. With Uber, the news stories about its management team and the responses to these stories would have reflected your priors on the company. If you were predisposed to like the company, you would have viewed Uber's management team as confident in its attacks on new markets, aggressive in defending its turf, and creative in its counterattacks. If you did not like the company, the very same actions would be viewed as indicative of the

arrogance of the company, its challenging a status quo would signal its unwill-ingness to play by the rules, and its counterattacks would be viewed as overkill.

Bottom line: There seems no reason to believe that Uber will become less aggres-sive in the future. The question of whether this will hurt them as they scale up remains unresolved.

In summary, a great deal had changed between June 2014 and September 2015, partly because of real changes in the ride-sharing market during the period and partly because I had to fill in gaps in my knowledge about the market. In table 11.1 I compare the inputs that I used to value Uber in June 2014 with my estimates in September 2015.

Table 11.1
Input Changes from News Stories—Uber

Input	June 2014	September 2015	Rationale
Total market	$100 billion; Urban car service	$230 billion; Logistics	Market is broader, bigger, and more global than I thought it would be. Uber's entry into delivery and moving businesses is now plausible, perhaps even probable.
Growth in market	Increase market size by 34.00%; CAGR* of 6.00%.	Double market size; CAGR of 10.39%.	New customers being drawn to car sharing, with more diverse offerings.
Market share	10.00% (local networking)	25.00% (weak global networking)	Higher cost of entry will reduce competitors, but remaining competitors have access to capital and, in Asia, the hometown advantage.
Slice of gross receipts	20.00% (left at status quo)	15.00%	Increased competition will reduce car service company slice.
Operating margin	40.00% (low-cost model)	25.00% (partial employee model)	Drivers will become partial employees, with higher insurance and regulatory costs.
Cost of capital	12.00% (ninth decile of U.S. companies)	10.00% (75th percentile of U.S. companies)	Business model in place and substantial revenues.
Probability of failure	10.00%	0.00%	Enough cash on hand to fend off threats to survival.

* CAGR = Compound annual growth rate

Table 11.2
Uber, The Global Logistics Company

The story

Uber is a logistics company, doubling the market size by drawing in new users. It will enjoy weak global networking benefits while seeing its slice of revenues slip (85/15), higher costs (with drivers as partial employees), and low capital intensity.

The assumptions

	Base year	Years 1–5	Years 6–10	After year 10	Story link
Total market	$230 billion	Grow 10.39% a year		Grow 2.25%	Logistics + new users
Gross market share	4.71%	4.71% → 25.00%		25.00%	weak global networking
Revenue share	20.00%	20.00% →15.00%		15.00%	Lower revenue share
Pretax operating margin	−23.06%	−23.06% → 25.00%		25.00%	Semi-strong competitive position
Reinvestment	NA	Sales to capital ratio of 5.00		Reinvestment rate = 9.00%	Low capital intensity model
Cost of capital	NA	10.00%	10.00% → 8.00%	8.00%	At 75th percentile of U.S. firms
Risk of failure	No chance of failure (with equity worth zero)				Cash on hand + capital access

The cash flows ($ millions)

	Total market	Market share	Revenues	EBIT (1–t)*	Reinvestment	FCFF†
1	$253,897	6.74%	$3,338	$(420)	$234	$(654)
2	$280,277	8.77%	$4,670	$(427)	$267	$(694)
3	$309,398	10.80%	$6,181	$(358)	$302	$(660)
4	$341,544	12.83%	$7,886	$(200)	$341	$(541)
5	$377,031	14.86%	$9,802	$62	$383	$(322)
6	$416,204	16.89%	$11,947	$442	$429	$13
7	$459,448	18.91%	$14,338	$956	$478	$478
8	$507,184	20.94%	$16,995	$1,621	$531	$1,090
9	$559,881	22.97%	$19,935	$2,455	$588	$1,868
10	$618,052	25.00%	$23,177	$3,477	$648	$2,828
Terminal year	$631,959	25.00%	$23,698	$3,555	$320	$3,234

The value

Terminal value	$56,258	
PV (terminal value)	$22,914	
PV (CF over next 10 years)	$515	
Value of operating assets =	$23,429	
Probability of failure	0%	
Value in case of failure	$-	
Adjusted value for operating assets	$23,429	Venture capitalists priced Uber at about $51 billion at the time of the valuation.

* EBIT (1 − t) = (Revenues* Operating Margin) (1 minus tax rate)
† FCFF = Free cash flow to firm

In table 11.2 I summarize Uber's valuation in September 2015 and estimate a value of $23.4 billion. Note that this value is weighed down by the negative cash flows in the first 5 years (the "cash burn") but the cash flows turn around in the later years to deliver a terminal value high enough to more than compensate.

I was wrong about Uber's value in June 2014, when my estimate of $6 billion was below the $17 billion assessment by venture capitalists. Correcting for both my cramped vision and the changes that had occurred since June 2014, produced my new estimated value of $23.4 billion in September 2015 (as shown in Table 11.2). Even though my estimated value for Uber increased from June 2014 to September 2015, the investor pricing took the company from $17 billion in June 2014 to $51 billion in September 2015. Talk about a moving target!

Narrative Shifts (Tweaks)

If all or most news stories caused narrative breaks or changes, our valuations would be in a constant state of motion and investing would become a chaotic and risky endeavor. That is what happens during a market crisis, and it is one reason why periods like the last quarter of 2008 are so harrowing for investors. Luckily, this is the exception rather than the rule, and information has only a marginal impact on narratives and on value for more mature companies in more settled markets. Again, you can use the narrative framework to illustrate these small shifts in stories from period to period. Specifically, you can trace how a news story changes the total market for a company, even if all the company does is stay in its existing business model. Alternatively, you may be called upon to tweak the market share, profit margins, or risk characteristics of a company as news stories about the company emerge.

If you invest primarily in mature companies, with established business models, this is perhaps the state of play for you, and your intrinsic value will follow the smooth path that value scolds assume is a universal one. Is this stability good or bad for investors? While at first sight it seems like a blessing to have stable stories and values, there is a downside, at least from an investing standpoint. The market prices for these stocks will also reflect this stability in story line and will be less likely to wander away from values. In the language of value and price, the gap between price and value will be smaller at these companies. Since investors make money from exploiting the gap, it stands to reason that you will find fewer and smaller market mistakes with stable companies than with the younger and more unstable companies that are exposed to narrative breaks and changes. That is the reason why I prefer to spend my time and resources valuing companies on what I term the "dark side," where there is significant uncertainty about how narratives will evolve in the future. I know that this contradicts traditional value investing advice, which is to stay with the familiar and the comfortable, but that approach also offers far less upside to investors.

CASE STUDY 11.3: APPLE—THE MEH CHRONICLES, FEBRUARY 2015

I have valued Apple multiple times over the last four decades, but my current sequence of valuations had its start in 2011, when I valued Apple after it became the largest market-capitalization company in the world. Every three months after that valuation, I revalued Apple to reflect what I had learned about the company and in

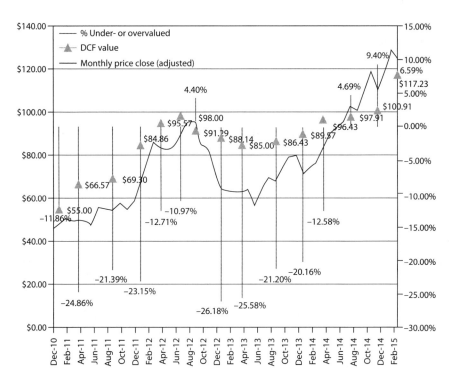

Figure 11.2
Apple price and value, 2011–2015.

comparison to the stock price. Figure 11.2 chronicles my estimates of value for Apple and stock price movements starting in 2011 and going through February 2015.

Note that while stock prices ranged from $45 to more than $120 over this period, my value estimates had a much tighter range, reflecting my largely unchanged story line for the company over the period. Starting in 2011, my narrative for Apple had been that it was a mature company, with limited growth potential (revenue growth rate of less than 5 percent) and sustained profitability, albeit with downward pressure on margins as its core businesses (especially smartphones) become more competitive. I allowed for only a small probability that the company would introduce another disruptive product to follow up its trifecta from the prior decade (the iPod, the iPhone, and the iPad), partly because of its large market cap and partly because I thought it had used up its disruption magic over recent years.

Looking at the earnings reports and news stories from the company between 2011 and 2015 in table 11.3, you can perhaps see why my basic story did not change much over the period. For much of the time period, Apple matched or beat revenue and earnings estimates, albeit by small amounts, but the market was unimpressed, with stock prices down on six of the nine postreport days and seven of the nine postreport weeks.

Note that after controlling for the quarterly variations, revenues were flat or only had mild growth, and operating margins were on a mild downward trend. With Apple, the other focus in the earnings reports was on iPhone and iPad sales, and table 11.4 reports on the unit sales that Apple reported each quarter, with the growth rates over the same quarter's sales in the prior year. In the last two columns, I report Apple's global market share in the smartphone and tablet markets, by quarter.

Table 11.3
Revenues, Operating Income and Price Reaction

	Revenues (in millions)			Operating income/ margin		Price reaction	
Report date	Actual	Estimate	Percent surprise	Income	Margin	1 day after	1 week after
7/24/12	$35,020	$37,250	−5.99%	$11,573	33.05%	−4.32%	−11.12%
10/23/12	$35,966	$35,816	0.42%	$10,944	30.43%	−0.91%	−3.10%
1/30/13	$54,512	$54,868	−0.65%	$17,210	31.57%	−12.35%	−3.89%
5/1/13	$43,603	$42,298	3.09%	$12,558	28.80%	−0.16%	0.50%
7/24/13	$35,323	$35,093	0.66%	$9,201	26.05%	5.14%	−2.65%
10/30/13	$37,472	$36,839	1.72%	$10,030	26.77%	−2.49%	−1.85%
1/29/14	$57,594	$57,476	0.21%	$17,463	30.32%	−7.99%	−0.83%
4/23/14	$45,646	$43,531	4.86%	$13,593	29.78%	8.20%	4.17%
7/23/14	$37,432	$37,929	−1.31%	$10,282	27.47%	2.61%	−1.41%

Table 11.4

Apple's Smartphone and Device Sales

	iPhone (in millions)		iPad (in millions)		Global market share	
Report date	Units sold	Year-over-year growth rate	Units sold	Year-over-year growth rate	Smartphone	Tablet
7/24/12	26.00	28.1%	17.00	83.8%	16.6%	60.3%
10/23/12	26.90	57.3%	14.00	26.1%	14.4%	40.2%
1/30/13	47.80	29.2%	22.90	48.7%	20.9%	38.2%
5/1/13	37.40	6.6%	19.50	65.3%	17.1%	40.2%
7/24/13	31.20	20.0%	14.60	−14.1%	13.2%	33.1%
10/30/13	33.80	25.7%	14.10	0.7%	12.9%	29.8%
1/29/14	51.00	6.7%	26.00	13.5%	17.6%	33.2%
4/23/14	43.70	16.8%	16.40	−15.9%	15.2%	32.5%
7/23/14	35.20	12.8%	13.30	−8.9%	NA	NA

While the market fixation with Apple's iPhone and iPad sales may be disconcerting to some, it made sense for two reasons. First, it reflected the fact that Apple derived most of its revenues from smartphones/tablets and that the growth in unit sales and change in market share became a proxy for future revenue growth. Second, Apple's earnings were being sustained by its impressive profit margins in the smartphone and tablet businesses, and looking at how well Apple was doing in these markets became a stand-in for how sustainable the company's margins (and earnings) would be in the future. Each quarter, there were rumors of another Apple disruption in the works, but each time the promises of an iCar or an iTV did not pan out, and investor expectations that Apple would pull another rabbit out of its hat eased.

The price behavior of Apple in the quarters starting in the middle of 2014 going through February 2015 reflected this period of stability, temporary though it may be for Apple, when investor expectations had moderated and the company was being measured for what it really was: an extraordinarily profitable company with the most valuable franchise in the world: the iPhone. It seemed to have stabilized its position in the smartphone world and was seeing its tablet market shrink, while its personal computer business was being treated as a ancillary business. Investors and analysts were treating it as a mature company that was being powered by the iPhone money machine, for which margins were declining only gradually. Since that is the narrative that I had been using all along in my valuations, I saw little change in my assessment of intrinsic value for Apple. Allowing for the stock split, the value per share that I assessed in February 2015 with the information in the new earnings report incorporated into my estimates was $96.55, almost unchanged from my estimate of $96.43 in April 2014.

Conclusion

It is natural to want to hold onto your narrative and to keep it unchanged, even in the face of contradictions. Rather than let hubris keep you wedded to your old story, you should think about how your narrative is altered by events, small and large. In this chapter I started by looking at classifying narrative alterations into breaks, changes, and shifts and the resulting effects on value. In particular, narrative breaks represent an end to a story that might have had promise at some stage, but no more. Narrative changes make significant modifications to the story that you have for a company, and with those changes can come large changes in value. Narrative shifts are much smaller alterations that nevertheless will show up as increases or decreases in value. Admitting you were wrong on a narrative (and the resulting value) is never easy, but it gets easier each time you do it. Who knows? One day, you may actually enjoy admitting your mistakes! I have not reached that level of serenity yet, but I keep trying.

12

News and Narratives

In the last chapter I looked at how the real world delivers surprises that alter narratives and affect value. In this chapter I will continue that discussion by looking at how corporate news announcements may (or may not) affect narratives and value, starting with earnings reports, perhaps the most ubiquitous and widely followed of these news stories, and then moving on to more infrequent but often more consequential announcements about new investments, financing (borrowing or new stock issues), and plans to return cash (dividends or stock buybacks) that can change your stories, and value.

The Information Effect

You don't have to be a believer in efficient markets to accept the proposition that markets move on news. Stock prices are driven up and down by new information, and the only debatable issue is whether the price changes that you see are consistent with the news, both in terms of direction (good or bad) and in magnitude. Not surprisingly, news stories also have an effect on narratives, and as noted in the last chapter, they can alter the trajectory radically in some cases, change it marginally in others, and end it in extreme cases.

In this chapter I focus on how corporate news releases affect their narratives, starting with earnings reports, released quarterly in some parts of the world (including the United States) and semiannually or annually in others. I then look at more infrequent announcements that companies make about their investment decisions (acquisitions, in particular), financing (to add to or pay down debt), and dividends (initiated or suspended, increased or decreased, and defined broadly to also include buybacks) to see how these can change the story you tell about a company. The final section focuses on what is loosely categorized as corporate governance news and, in particular, how a corporate scandal can alter perceptions about a company (and its narrative) and why having a change in the investor base (especially the entry or exit of activist investors) can change the story for a company. As you go through the chapter, it is worth emphasizing that having the company as the source of your news is both a plus and a minus. The plus is that the company has access to information that most investors otherwise would not have. The minus is that the company is a biased source, especially when it is in the midst of a crisis.

Earnings Reports and Narratives

Each quarter, U.S. companies, in particular, go through a ritual called the earnings season, when they report their quarterly earnings. These announcements are among the most analyzed and awaited news stories about companies. Sell-side equity research analysts spend a considerable portion of their time estimating what the earnings will be, and the company's top managers spend just as much time trying to get expectations under control. When the earnings report comes out, the announced earnings per share is measured against expectations and is classified as positive if it beats expectations and negative if it does not meet expectations.

Much of what happens in the period around the earnings report involves the pricing process. The price reaction to an earnings report is usually consistent with the surprise contained within it, with positive or negative surprises evoking positive or negative price reactions. As a consequence, companies have increasingly turned to using the discretion that is granted to them in the accounting for income and expenses to "manage" earnings and to beat expectations, and there is some evidence that

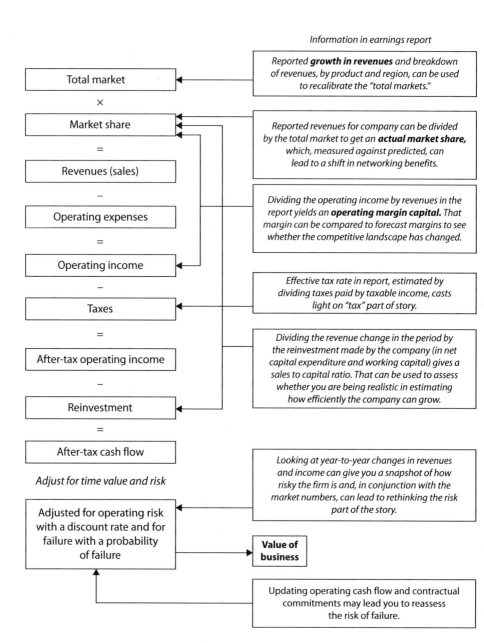

Figure 12.1
Earnings reports and narratives.

as companies have learned to play the earnings game, market reactions to earnings reports have also become more complex. Thus, when a company consistently manages to beat earnings per share expectations by five cents per share every quarter, at some point in time the market raises the bar for measuring earnings surprises to five cents above the analyst expectations.

If you are an investor, uninterested in playing the pricing game and more concerned with value, you will look at earnings reports very differently than traders would. Rather than focus on whether the reported earnings per share meet or beat expectations, you will scan these reports for information that could change your narrative about the company and, by extension, its value. Figure 12.1 outlines how you can use the narrative framework to change your story to reflect the information from the earnings report.

As you can see, this assessment may cause you to have a very different reaction to a given earnings report than traders, who are more focused on earnings surprises. An earnings release that reports higher than expected earnings per share (good news on the pricing front) can cause negative changes in your narrative, leading you to reduce the value of the firm just as price increases. Conversely, an earnings report that reports worse-than-expected earnings can change your story in positive ways, again causing a deviation between price and value movement.

CASE STUDY 12.1: EARNINGS REPORTS AND NARRATIVE
CHANGES—FACEBOOK IN AUGUST 2014

I valued Facebook just before its IPO in February 2012 at about $27/share and argued that the stock was being overpriced at $38 for the offering. The tepid response to the offering price made me look right, but for all the wrong reasons. The botched IPO was not because the stock was overpriced or because the market attached a lower value to the stock but largely due to the hubris of Facebook's investment bankers, who seemed to not only think that the stock would sell itself but actively worked against setting a narrative for the company. My initial valuation, though it looked conservative in hindsight, was based upon the belief that Facebook would be as successful as Google in its growth in the online advertising business, while maintaining its sky-high profit margins. Table 12.1 shows the valuation, with the story embedded in it, at the time of the IPO.

Table 12.1
Facebook, the Google Wannabe

			The story		

Facebook is a social media company that will use its giant user base to become an online advertising success story, almost as big as Google. Its growth path and profitability will resemble Google in its early years.

The assumptions

	Base year	Years 1–5	Years 6–10	After year 10	Link to story
Revenues (a)	$3,711	CAGR* = 40.00%	40.00% → 2.00%	CAGR* = 2.00%	Grow like Google
Pretax operating margin (b)	45.68%	45.68% → 35.00%		35.00%	Competitive pressures
Tax rate	40.00%	40.00%		40.00%	Leave unchanged
Reinvestment (c)	NA	Sales-to-capital ratio of 1.50		Reinvestment rate = 10.00%	Industry average sales/capital
Cost of capital (d)		11.07%	11.07% → 8.00%	8.00%	Online advertising business risk

The cash flows (in $ millions)

	Revenues	Operating margin	EBIT (1-t)†	Reinvestment	FCFF†
1	$5,195	44.61%	$1,391	$990	$401
2	$7,274	43.54%	$1,900	$1,385	$515
3	$10,183	42.47%	$2,595	$1,940	$655
4	$14,256	41.41%	$3,542	$2,715	$826
5	$19,959	40.34%	$4,830	$3,802	$1,029
6	$26,425	39.27%	$6,226	$4,311	$1,915
7	$32,979	28.20%	$7,559	$4,369	$3,190
8	$38,651	37.14%	$8,612	$3,782	$4,830
9	$42,362	36.07%	$9,167	$2,474	$6,694
10	$43,209	35.00%	$9,074	$565	$9,509
Terminal year	$44,073	35.00%	$9,255	$926	$8,330

The value

Terminal value	$138,830	
PV (terminal value)	$52,832	
PV (CF over the next 10 years)	$13,135	
Value of operating assets =	$65,967	
−Debt	$1,215	
+ Cash	$1,512	
Value of equity	$66,284	
−Value of options	$3,088	
Value of equity in common stock	$63,175	
Number of shares	2,330.90	
Estimated value/share	$27.07	The offering price was set at $38/share.

*CAGR = Compound annual growth rate
† EBIT (1 − t) = (Revenues* Operating Margin) (1 − tax rate)
†† FCFF = Free cash flow to firm

Table 12.2
Facebook Earnings Reports, 2012 to 2014

	Revenues (in millions)			Operating income in millions/margin		Earnings per share (EPS)	Price reaction
Report date	Actual	Estimate	% Surprise	Income	Margin	% Surprise	Week after
7/26/12	$1,184	$1,157	2.33%	($743.00)	−62.75%	54.02%	−25.35%
10/23/12	$1,262	$1,226	2.94%	$377.00	29.87%	−137.74%	8.77%
1/30/13	$1,585	$1,523	4.07%	$523.00	33.00%	25.00%	−7.01%
5/1/13	$1,458	$1,440	1.25%	$373.00	25.58%	16.88%	−1.13%
7/24/13	$1,813	$1,618	12.05%	$562.00	31.00%	47.73%	38.82%
10/30/13	$2,016	$1,910	5.55%	$736.00	36.51%	36.00%	0.22%
1/29/14	$2,585	$2,354	9.81%	$1,133.00	43.83%	1.01%	16.18%
4/23/14	$2,502	$2,356	6.20%	$1,075.00	42.97%	47.06%	−2.57%
7/23/14	$2,910	$2,809	3.60%	$1,390.00	47.77%	22.45%	4.75%

Looking at Facebook's nine earnings reports between its IPO in 2012 and late 2014, the market reaction shifted significantly over the period, as evidenced in table 12.2.

The botched public offering colored the market response to the very first earnings report, with the stock down almost 25 percent. In fact, I revalued Facebook after this report, when the stock price plunged below $20, and argued that there was nothing in the report that changed my initial narrative and that the company looked undervalued to me. I was lucky enough to catch it at its low point, since the company turned the corner with the market by the next quarter and the stock price more than doubled over the following year. I revisited the valuation after the August 2013 earnings report and with narrative changes came up with $38/share, leaving me with the conclusion that the stock was fully priced at $45 and that it was prudent to sell. Looking at the earnings numbers across the quarters, it is clear that Facebook mastered the analyst expectations game, delivering better than expected numbers for both revenues and earnings per share for each of the last seven quarters.

With Facebook, the market also paid attention to the size and growth of its user base and the company's success at growing its mobile revenues. In table 12.3 I list these numbers and Facebook's invested capital each quarter (computed by adding the book values of debt and equity and netting out cash) and a measure of capital efficiency (sales as a proportion of invested capital) from the IPO to August 2014.

Table 12.3
The Changing Look of Facebook

Report date	Active users	Mobile active users	Percent of revenue from mobile	Net income	Capital	Trailing 12 month sales/capital
7/26/12	955	543	NR	($157)	$3,515	1.23
10/23/12	1010	604	NR	($59)	$4,252	1.09
1/30/13	1060	680	23.00%	$64	$4,120	1.24
5/1/13	1100	751	30.00%	$219	$4,272	1.28
7/24/13	1150	819	41.00%	($152)	$3,948	1.55
10/30/13	1190	874	49.00%	$425	$4,007	1.71
1/29/14	1230	945	53.00%	$523	$4,258	1.85
4/23/14	1280	1010	59.00%	$642	$4,299	2.07
7/23/14	1320	1070	62.00%	$791	$4,543	2.20

This table captures the heart of the Facebook success story during this period: a continued growth rate in a user base that was already immense, a dramatic surge in both online users and advertising, and improved capital efficiency (note the increasing sales-to-capital ratio). The August 2014 earnings report provided more of the same: continued user growth, increased revenues from mobile advertising, and improved profitability. Looking at that report, I had to conclude that *I had been wrong* about Facebook's narrative, for the following reasons:

1. While my initial reaction to Facebook's *success on the mobile front* was that it needed to accomplish such growth to sustain its narrative as a successful online advertising company, the rate at which Facebook grew in the mobile market was staggering. In fact, given its results through August 2014, I saw a very real possibility that Facebook would supplant Google as the online advertising king and continue to maintain its profitability. That is a *narrative shift*, which will translate into a larger market share of the online advertising market, higher revenue growth, and perhaps more sustainable operating margins (than I had forecast).

2. The *inexorable growth in the user base*, astonishing in light of the size of the existing base, was also surprising. It is Facebook's biggest asset and a platform they could use to enter new markets and sell new products/services. Between 2012 and 2014, Facebook showed a willingness to spend large amounts of money on acquiring the pieces it needed to keep increasing its user base and to profit from it. The downside of this strategy is that growth has been costly, but the upside is that Facebook positioned itself to monetize its user

base. While the revenue breakdown did not reflect this business expansion yet, I thought that Facebook was *better positioned for a narrative change* in August 2014 than it was a year or two prior.

My updated valuation for Facebook in August 2014 reflected these adjustments. Incorporating a higher revenue target ($100 billion, rather than $60 billion) and more sustained margins (40 percent instead of 35 percent), I valued the company's operating assets at $132 billion, a little more than double my estimate of $65 billion at the time of its IPO and the stock at almost $70/share. Did I have regrets about selling the shares at $45? For a brief moment, yes, but then again, I considered it a reminder of why it is so important that I keep feedback loops open and listen to those who disagree with me on my valuations.

Other Corporate News Stories

In addition to earnings reports, companies make news for other reasons, some good and some bad. While these announcements are not as frequent as earnings announcements, they often contain news that has bigger consequences for value. Broadly speaking, almost all corporate announcements of consequence can be categorized into news about investments (adding new assets, divesting old ones, or updating existing ones), financing (raising new financing or paying down old financing), and dividends (decreasing or increasing cash returned to investors in dividends or buybacks).

Investment News

The best way to frame investment announcements is to structure them around a balance sheet and think about these announcements as a restructuring of the asset side of the balance (figure 12.2).

Viewed from this perspective, companies can either add new assets (by taking on new projects or acquisitions) to the balance sheet or they can remove existing investments (by shutting them down, liquidating, or divesting). They can also provide information about ongoing investments that may lead to a reassessment of their values. In sum, they can reinforce or change an existing narrative for a company.

With new investments and divestitures of existing assets, you have to trace through the effect that these actions will have on the narrative for

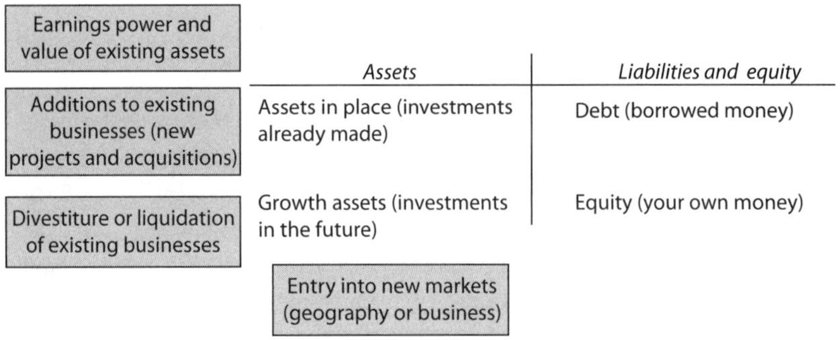

Earnings power and value of existing assets		
	Assets	Liabilities and equity
Additions to existing businesses (new projects and acquisitions)	Assets in place (investments already made)	Debt (borrowed money)
Divestiture or liquidation of existing businesses	Growth assets (investments in the future)	Equity (your own money)
	Entry into new markets (geography or business)	

Figure 12.2
Investment news, narratives, and value.

the company and hence its value. Thus, the announcement by Tesla that it would build a new battery factory, costing almost $5 billion, changed my story for the company from one that was built around it being a luxury auto company to one that incorporated an energy business. In the same vein, the news from GE that it would sell off GE Capital, its financing arm, in 2015, altered the story you would tell about the company by removing one if its biggest business pieces.

Acquisitions are among the biggest investment decisions that companies make, for two reasons. One is magnitude, since they tend to be much bigger (in terms of money spent) than internal investments. The other is that companies tend to do acquisitions for a wider range of reasons, and an acquisition can dramatically change the narrative arc in both good and bad ways. For instance, the acquisition of Jaguar Land Rover, a global luxury automaker, by Tata Motors, an Indian mass automaker, in 2009, changed the story that you would tell about the latter. Figure 12.3 provides some of the possible story lines that emerge from acquisitions tied to different parts of the narrative process.

Note that almost every change that is listed in this figure tilts positive, which may lead you to the inexorable conclusion that acquisitions will always increase value. The reason that you should be cautious in this conclusion is that the effect of an acquisition on the acquiring company's stockholders will be the net of the price paid for the acquisition. Thus, notwithstanding the potential for an acquisition to change the narrative (and value) in positive ways, the stockholders in the acquiring firm will be worse off if the price paid is too high.

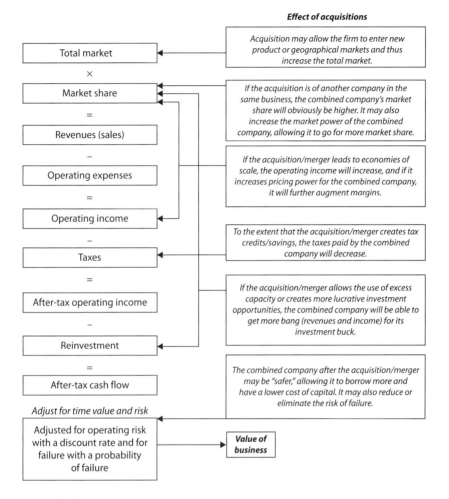

Figure 12.3
Acquisition effects on narratives and numbers.

CASE STUDY 12.2: AB INBEV AND SABMILLER—
THE CONSOLIDATION STORY

On September 15, 2015, AB InBev, the largest beer-manufacturing company in the world announced its intent to buy SABMiller, the second-largest brewery globally, and the market's initial reaction was positive, with the stock prices of both AB InBev and SABMiller increasing on the story. Figure 12.4 captures the key details of the deal, including the rationale and consequences.

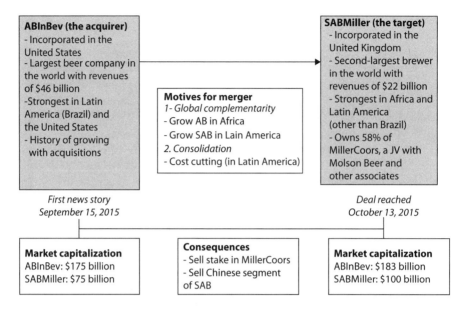

Figure 12.4
The AB InBev–SABMiller deal.

As an investor in AB InBev, consider the effect this deal would have had on your narrative for the company. The company had built a reputation for aggressive growth, unmatched efficiency, and its capacity to wring cost cuts in a mature business, as manifested in its acquisition and turnaround of Grupo Modelo, a Mexican brewery. It was also run by a Brazil-based private equity group (3G) known for their skills at allocating capital. While the SABMiller deal was of much greater magnitude than prior acquisitions, it did fit into that pattern of AB InBev's cost-cutting and efficiency.

In table 12.4, I summarize how bringing the AB InBev efficiency model to SABMiller would change the value of the combined company and the resulting value of synergy.

Assuming that AB InBev would be able to bring its cost-cutting skills to SABMiller, I increased the operating margin for the combined company from 28.27 percent to 30 percent (translating into annual cost reductions of approximately $1.3 billion), and this in turn pushed up the after-tax return on capital that the company will be able to make on new investments from 11.68 to 12 percent. A higher reinvestment rate (50 percent, up from 43.58 percent) added in the possibility that the combined company would also be able to find more investment opportunities in its combined markets,

Table 12.4

Valuing Synergy in the AB InBev–SABMiller Deal

	AB InBev	SABMiller	Combined firm (no synergy)	Combined firm (synergy)	Actions
Cost of equity	8.93%	9.37%	9.12%	9.12%	
After-tax cost of debt	2.10%	2.24%	2.10%	2.10%	
Cost of capital	7.33%	8.03%	7.51%	7.51%	No changes expected
Operating margin	32.28%	19.97%	28.27%	(30.00%)	Cost-cutting and economies of scale
After-tax return on capital	12.10%	12.64%	11.68%	(12.00%)	Cost-cutting also improves return on capital
Reinvestment rate	50.99%	33.29%	43.58%	(50.00%)	More aggressive reinvestment in shared markets
Expected growth rate	6.17%	4.21%	5.09%	(6.00%)	Higher growth because of reinvestment
Value of firm					
PV of FCFF in high growth	$28,733	$9,806	$38,539	$39,151	
Terminal value	$260,982	$58,736	$319,717	$340,175	
Value of operating assets	$211,953	$50,065	$262,018	$276,610	Value of Synergy = $14,591.76

increasing the expected growth rate from 5.09 to 6 percent. While these changes are small in percentage terms, it is worth remembering that when the largest brewery in the world buys the second-largest brewery, it is difficult to post dramatic changes in percentage market share or growth. I estimated the value of synergy in this deal at $14.6 billion, assuming it would be delivered instantaneously.

It is worth noting that AB InBev paid a premium of almost $30 billion to acquire SABMiller, and that brings home the point I made earlier about how the price you pay is what determines value creation and destruction. If my assessment of deal synergy is on target, this deal created about $14.6 billion in value for AB InBev's stockholders, but paying $30 billion for SABMiller made these stockholders worse off (by approximately $15.4 billion). If this deal does turn out to be value destroying, it will also lay siege to another part of AB InBev's narrative: 3G's reputation for shrewd capital allocation.

Assets	Liabilities and equity
Assets in place (investments already made)	Debt (borrowed money)
Growth assets (investments in the future)	Equity (your own money)

Increase debt in capital
Pluses: Increases tax benefits of debt and signals confidence in stability of future earnings
Minuses: Increases chances of distress and may signal less growth in future

Decrease debt in capital
Pluses: Reduces distress cost and likelihood
Minuses: Lose tax benefits and signal lack of confidence in future earnings

Figure 12.5
Financing decisions and value.

Financing News

When a company announces its intent to borrow more money or pay off debt, it is setting in motion actions that can alter your narrative for that company, both directly or indirectly.

Consider first the decision to borrow more money, which changes your narrative in both good and bad ways if you are an investor (figure 12.5). On the plus side, it allows the company to exploit the debt tilt in the tax code and increase the value of the business by the value of tax savings from debt. On the minus side, not only does it increase the chances of default (failure) but may also open the door to operating backlash if the company is perceived to be in financial trouble and customers hold back on buying its products. Consequently, a debt-increasing action by a firm can ripple through your story, altering the potential for growth and increasing the tax benefit component of value, while also altering the risk of the investment. The net effect can be either positive or negative.

A decision to reduce debt also affects your narrative. Not only does it reduce the potential for tax savings from interest expenses, but it can also be viewed by some investors (fairly or unfairly) as a signal that the management of the company feels less secure about future earnings and cash flows. It may be the precursor to other actions that the firm may take to make itself a business with a less risky story for investors.

CASE STUDY 12.3: APPLE'S DEBT DECISION

In April 2013 Apple announced its first bond issue, raising $17 billion from the market. Given its market capitalization at the time, which was more than $500 billion, the bond issue by itself was too small to have much of an impact on the value of the company. However, the decision to borrow in the bond market did have the potential to change the company narrative in ways that could create larger effects on value.

For those investors whose story of Apple had been based on the assumption that the management of the company, based on its history and culture, would never borrow money, the news that the company would borrow money was good news, insofar as it allowed the company to capture some of the tax benefits it was leaving on the table. At the same time, it was potentially bad news for the investors in the company, who were convinced that Apple could revert to its high-growth path from the previous decade with an endless stream of new products, since the debt issue suggested that managers did not share their optimism. Not surprisingly, the debt issue ended up being a wash in the financial markets, with Apple's stock price barely budging on the announcement.

Dividends, Buybacks, and Cash Balances

Investors invest in businesses to generate returns, and cash returned to stockholders in the form of dividends and buybacks represents the harvesting of these investments. Thus, when companies announce changes in both the amount of cash they return to stockholders and the manner in which that cash is returned, it can lead to a reassessment of the stories that govern their value (figure 12.6).

If a company decides to return more cash than it has historically, it can be either good or bad news for your narrative for the company, depending on your initial framing of the company. Thus, if your initial view of the company is that it is a high-growth business with significant investment opportunities, an initiation or increase in dividends may lead you to negatively reassess the growth potential portion of your story (and your value). If your initial perspective on the company is that it is in a mature business with few investment opportunities and that the existing management is not only holding back cash unnecessarily but also may waste that cash (by taking bad investments), a decision by the firm to

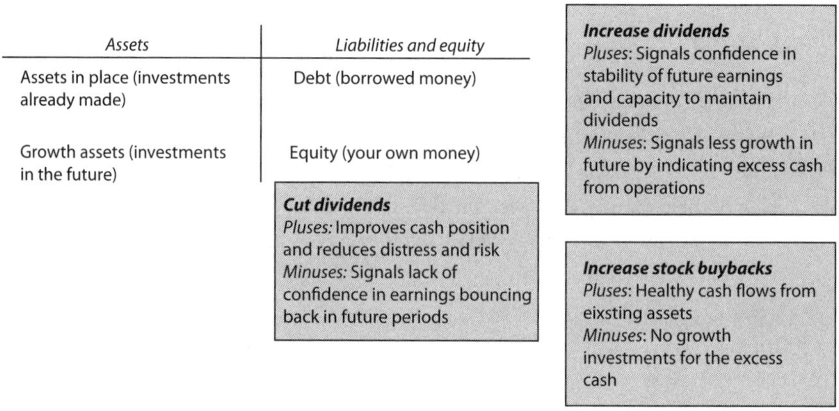

Assets	Liabilities and equity
Assets in place (investments already made)	Debt (borrowed money)
Growth assets (investments in the future)	Equity (your own money)

Increase dividends
Pluses: Signals confidence in stability of future earnings and capacity to maintain dividends
Minuses: Signals less growth in future by indicating excess cash from operations

Cut dividends
Pluses: Improves cash position and reduces distress and risk
Minuses: Signals lack of confidence in earnings bouncing back in future periods

Increase stock buybacks
Pluses: Healthy cash flows from eixsting assets
Minuses: No growth investments for the excess cash

Figure 12.6
Dividend decisions and value.

increase cash returned may be an indication that the management has come to its senses, thus making your narrative more positive (and your value higher).

There are two ways of returning cash to investors, the first being dividends and the second being stock buybacks. When companies alter their conventional patterns of returning cash, there may be information in their actions that can affect your story and value. When a company that has historically paid only dividends initiates a stock buyback, you should consider the possibility that the firm feels less secure about future growth than previously. After all, one of the biggest benefits of buybacks, relative to dividends, is that you gain more flexibility in how much cash you return, and when. Conversely, when a firm that historically has returned cash only in the form of buybacks decides to switch back to dividends, there are storytelling implications that the firm perceives its earnings stream as less volatile than it was.

CASE STUDY 12.4: SLOW-MOTION STORY CHANGES—IBM'S BUYBACK DECADE

For much of the twentieth century, IBM was one of the great growth companies in the world, able to post double-digit growth as the leading mainframe computing company in the world. The growth of personal computers in the 1980s put a damper on IBM's growth, and the company had a fall from grace in the latter part

Table 12.5

IBM's Operating and Share Count History

Year	Revenues	Net income	Dividends	Buybacks	Cash return	Cash return/net income	# Shares
2005	$91,134	$7,934	$1,250	$8,972	$10,222	128.84%	1,600.6
2006	$91,423	$9,492	$1,683	$9,769	$11,452	120.65%	1,530.8
2007	$98,785	$10,418	$2,147	$22,951	$25,098	240.91%	1,433.9
2008	$103,630	$12,334	$2,585	$14,352	$16,937	137.32%	1,369.4
2009	$95,758	$13,425	$2,860	$10,481	$13,341	99.37%	1,327.2
2010	$99,870	$14,833	$3,177	$19,149	$22,326	150.52%	1,268.8
2011	$106,916	$15,855	$3,473	$17,499	$20,972	132.27%	1,197.0
2012	$102,874	$16,604	$3,773	$13,535	$17,308	104.24%	1,142.5
2013	$98,368	$16,483	$4,058	$14,933	$18,991	115.22%	1,094.5
2014	$92,793	$12,022	$4,265	$14,388	$18,653	155.16%	1,004.3
2015 (LTM)	$83,795	$14,210	$4,725	$4,409	$9,134	64.28%	984.0
Aggregate	$1,065,346	$143,610	$33,996	$150,438	$184,434	128.43%	

of the decade. In an often-told comeback story, Lou Gerstner presided over the reinvention of IBM as a business services company in the 1990s, as the company rode the tech boom to growth again. After the tech bubble burst in the early part of the last decade, IBM found itself fighting for market share yet again.

While the narratives on IBM have spanned the spectrum, the company has behaved in a consistent fashion for much of the last decade, choosing to return most of its earnings in the form of dividends and buybacks. In table 12.5, I summarize the earnings and cash return numbers for IBM and the shares outstanding in the company.

During this period, the cash returned, in the aggregate, amounted to 128.43 percent of earnings, with buybacks representing the bulk of the cash returned. While IBM did report growth in net income over this period, that growth was accompanied by declining revenues and a sharp decline in shares outstanding.

While there are many who have criticized IBM for returning too much cash, there is an alternative story line that is consistent with the company's behavior. Faced with a declining business and fewer investment opportunities, the company has adopted a strategy of partially liquidating itself each year, with the intent of making itself a smaller business. If you are an investor in IBM and you are investing in the expectation that it will revert to being a growing company, you are fighting not only the facts on the ground but a company that is not behaving in accordance with your story. Rather than blame the company for not adapting to your story (of high growth with reinvestment), would it not make more sense to adapt your story to the company's behavior? With IBM, that would mean changing your story about the company to one of low or even negative growth over time, as the company becomes a smaller, leaner, and hopefully more profitable enterprise.

Corporate Governance Stories

The top management of a business plays a key role in setting, maintaining, and changing its narrative, and news stories about managers, good or bad, can have effects on narrative and value. In this section, we start with stories of misconduct and scandal about companies and how these can have significant effects on their values. We then move on to looking at how the entry or exit of a key investor or investor group can sometimes cause you to reassess your narrative for a firm (and its value).

Corporate Scandal and Misconduct

Companies sometimes get in the news for the wrong reasons, with stories about corporate or managerial misconduct, a failure to disclose material information, or stories of managerial incompetence. These stories have consequences at many levels. The first is that they cause a distraction, as the managers of a company that has been accused of misconduct spend a significant portion of their time doing damage control, thus delaying and deferring investment and operating decisions. The second is that these actions can result in fines and fees if the misconduct crosses the threshold of illegality. The third is that they can sometimes put the company in legal jeopardy, as aggrieved customers, shareholders, and suppliers sue the company for damages.

While all of the above can result in significant costs and value, there can be even more lasting damage if the corporate narrative changes as a consequence of the misconduct. This is due to several reasons. The first is that the scandal can unalterably change the reputation of the company, and to the extent that its narrative was built on that reputation, its story as well. Thus, the news in 2015 that Volkswagen, a company that built its reputation on German efficiency and reliability, had cheated on emissions controls for its diesel cars in the United States could have altered your story line for the company and had large consequences for value. The second is that a key component or components of the company's business model may have been built on questionable business practices, which once exposed, can no longer be continued. The third is that large scandals often result in management turnover, with the new management perhaps bringing a different perspective to the company.

CASE STUDY 12.5: VALEANT'S DRUG BUSINESS MODEL AT RISK?

Lead-in Case Study 5.1: The Pharmaceutical Business—R&D and Profitability, November 2015

In an assessment of pharmaceutical companies in chapter 5, I argued that the conventional business model for these companies, built around R&D, had deteriorated. While pharmaceutical companies have been able to maintain hefty profit margins for the last decade, the payoff to R&D has been steadily declining, with little or no revenue growth coming from the pipeline. Investors have responded accordingly, scaling down the pricing of these companies, which has manifested in lower multiples of revenues and earnings.

It is in the context of this history that you have to consider the rise of Valeant, a Canadian pharmaceutical company that went from obscurity in 2009 to the very top of the ranks in 2015. In figure 12.7, I graph the meteoric increase in revenues and operating income at the company in the time period between 2009 and 2015.

So, how did Valeant pull off this feat of growing in a sector where others were struggling? As shown in table 12.6, it took a path that was very different from other pharmaceutical companies, investing less in R&D than the typical drug company but investing far more in acquisitions and using those acquisitions to deliver not only high revenue growth but also high margins and earnings per share growth. The combination made Valeant a favorite of value investors and took its market capitalization to over $100 billion. In September 2015 Valeant's business model came under assault for two reasons:

1. The price increases in the drugs that the company acquired as a result of its acquisitions drew the attention and ire of politicians, health-care professionals, and insurance companies.

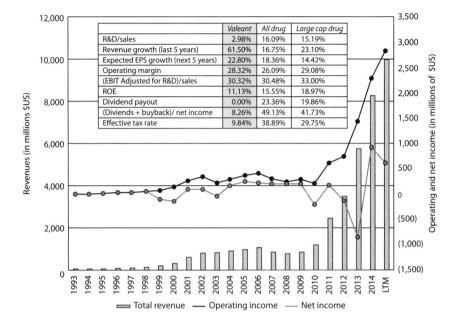

Figure 12.7
Valeant's operating history.

2. The company's relationship to Philidor, an online pharmacy, came under scrutiny. Some argued that Philidor was being used by Valeant to pass through its high drug prices to the patients, insurance companies, and the government.

Table 12.6
Valeant versus Sector

	Valeant	All drug companies	Large drug companies
R&D/sales	2.98%	16.09%	15.19%
Revenue growth (last 5 years)	61.50%	16.75%	23.10%
Expected EPS growth (next 5 years)	22.80%	18.36%	14.42%
Operating margin	28.32%	26.09%	29.08%
(EBIT adjusted for R&D)/sales	30.32%	30.48%	33.00%
Return on equity	11.13%	15.55%	18.97%
Dividend payout	0.00%	23.36%	19.86%
(Dividends + buyback)/net income	8.26%	49.13%	41.73%
Effective tax rate	9.84%	38.89%	29.75%

After initially attempting to defend itself as guiltless, Valeant cuts its cord to Philidor, but the damage had been done.

The spotlight on Valeant as a result of this crisis put at risk two pieces of its historically successful narrative: using acquisitions instead of R&D to grow and the repricing of old drugs as the basis for high profit margins. Analysts who had taken its financial statements at face value became more questioning of the acquisition debris in their financials, making it more difficult to continue on that path. The pricing hikes were not unique to Valeant, but being tagged in this crisis made it more difficult for them to continue increasing prices, at least for the near term. The company lost 70 percent of its value in the weeks following the scandal, perhaps reflecting the market's view that if Valeant was forced to follow a more conventional path of investing in R&D and measured price increases, it would resemble other pharmaceutical firms in both its operating results and pricing.

Investor Composition

You would expect shareholders, as owners of publicly traded firms, to have a say in corporate narratives, but in most publicly traded firms in the world, they do not. One reason is that in big publicly traded firms, with thousands of shareholders, the splintering of shareholding means that most investors have only small stakes in the company, making their influence minimal. Even those shareholders who own larger stakes in companies, generally institutional investors, are passive investors with little or no interest in challenging existing business models, even if they disagree with them. There are, however, two groups of investors who have the potential to change business models (and the stories about businesses), and the entry of either into a company can cause narrative changes.

- *Activist investors*, armed with capital and willing to fight over the long haul, target mature companies that they believe are investing badly or too much in bad businesses. They generally push these companies to invest less, borrow more, and return more cash to stockholders, and by doing so, they offer a counternarrative to managers who may be more intent on preserving the status quo. The appearance of a Carl Icahn or a Nelson Peltz, both well-known activist investors, in the investor ranks of a publicly traded company may be a signal that you should reassess the story you are telling about that company and, by extension, its value.

- *Strategic investors* are those who invest in a company in the hope of using the investment to further other interests. In many cases strategic investors are other companies that have chosen to invest in your company because they believe they can generate side benefits from the investment. To the extent that the strategic investor has deep pockets and a different endgame, it is possible that the entry of that investor will change your corporate narrative. For example, the news story that General Motors had made a $500 million investment in Lyft, the ride-sharing company, could not only change the risk portion of your story (by making it less likely that Lyft will fail) but also the business portion of the story (by increasing the likelihood that Lyft will move from a pure ride-sharing business to one that has a driverless or electric car component).

Conclusion

A corporate story is not a timeless classic. It is a constantly changing, ever-shifting narrative that will be affected by news about the company, starting with earnings reports and financial filings but also extending to include corporate announcements about investment, financing, and dividend policy. The extent to which these announcements affect narrative and value will vary across the announcements and can change them in positive or negative ways. The market reaction to these announcements is more of a pricing game, and it is conceivable that a news story can cause large price changes without much change in value or large value changes with little price effect. To the extent that top managers in the company play a role in setting its narrative, news that is about them will also affect both value and price.

13

Go Big—The Macro Story

In the chapters leading up to this one, I have focused primarily on individual companies and talked about how stories about these companies drive their valuations. In some cases, though, it is stories about the economy, interest rates, or commodities that drive the valuations of individual companies. In this chapter I focus on these big stories, breaking them down into stories that relate to variables like interest rates and inflation that affect all companies, some that are built on the effects of political and commodity price movements that affect a significant subset of companies, and a few that try to take advantage of lifestyle trends.

Macro Versus Micro Stories

In a micro story you start with a company, and while you consider the market and the competitive landscape in constructing your story, it is the company that is your focus. While that may be the appropriate point of view for many companies, it may not work in businesses in which what happens to your investment is driven primarily by macro variables over which you have little or no control. That is clearly the case with mature commodity companies, where the commodity price path determines the future earnings and the company's influences are at the margins. It is also often true for cyclical companies, for which the course of the economy will drive the profitability and cash flows in future years. Finally, in some risky emerging markets, the story line for a company is less determined by what happens in the corporate boardrooms and executive suites and more by political and economic developments in the country.

I must confess that I am far more uncomfortable telling macro stories than micro ones, for two reasons. The first is that I feel less in control, since macro variables are driven by forces that are both complicated and global; small changes in one part of the world can cause unexpected shifts in these variables. The second is that I know that my macro forecasting skills leave much to be desired. Consequently, any macro forecasts I build into my story line, even accidentally, can be problematic.

Not all analysts share my dislike for macro models. Some actively pursue them, because the payoff to getting macro bets right is huge; if you can forecast oil prices or interest rates well, your pathway to profitability will be quick and painless. In recent years a new strand of macro investing has become more common, in which investors forecast lifestyle trends and try to invest in companies based on those forecasts. To see the payoff from this investing style, just imagine how much wealth you could have accumulated if you had seen the boom in social media of the last few years and jumped on the bandwagon early. In fact, I would not be surprised if some of the capital flowing into companies like Uber and Airbnb is coming from investors whose narratives are driven by what they see as the explosive growth in the "sharing" market rather than by company-specific stories.

The Steps in a Macro Narrative

The process of building up a macro narrative shares some features with the company narrative process that we described in earlier chapters and deviates from others. It starts with an identification and understanding of the macro variable in question (commodity, cyclicality, or country) and it has to be followed by an assessment of how the company you are trying to value is affected by movements in the macro variable. The final step is a judgment you have to make as to how much you want your valuation to rest on your forecasts of the macro variable and how you plan to build that linkage into your numbers.

The Macro Evaluation

If your company's fortunes are driven primarily by a macro variable or variables, you should start by identifying that variable or variables. Obviously, for an oil company, the macro variable will be oil, but for a mining company, you may have to do a little more digging. With Vale, for instance, a Brazilian mining company that I will value later in this chapter, the key commodity is iron ore, since it accounts for almost three-quarters of Vale's revenues, and the iron ore price for much of the most recent decade had been driven by growth in China. With cyclical companies, while the economy is the obvious choice for the macro variable, you still have to make a judgment on whether it is just the domestic economy, a broader grouping of economies (say, Latin America), or perhaps even the global economy. Once you have the macro variable pinned down, the next step is to collect the historical data for that variable, looking at its movements over time and, if available, the forces that drive the movements. That history is useful not only to get a measure of what constitutes normal for that variable but also to get a sense of the risk in your company.

The Micro Assessment

The second step in the macro storytelling exercise is to turn your attention to the company that you are trying to value. In assessing your company's exposure, you are trying to make a judgment on how movements in the macro variable affect your company's operations. While at first sight this may seem simple, since you would expect oil companies to have higher earnings if oil prices go up, it is critical, because the way an oil company is structured and operates can affect its exposure to oil prices. Thus, an oil company with high-cost reserves may find itself more exposed to oil price variability than one with low-cost reserves, since the company with high-cost reserves will be hurt more by lower oil prices and will benefit more from higher prices. In general, oil companies with high fixed costs will see their earnings respond more violently to oil price changes than oil companies with more flexible cost structures. Finally, oil companies that hedge their output risk, that is, use futures and forward markets to lock in oil prices on future deliveries, will have earnings that are less impacted, at least in the near term, by oil price changes, than companies that do not hedge.

Bringing It Together

In this third step, you will be creating a composite story, in which you bring together your assessments of both the macro variable and the characteristics of the company you are valuing. At this stage, though, you will have to make a decision as to whether you want your valuation to be macro-neutral or to reflect your views on the future direction of the macro variable. Thus, with an oil company, you can value the company based on today's prices (reflected in the current spot price and in futures prices) or on your forecasts of future oil prices.

If you decide to go the macro-neutral route, you will first have to clean up the company's financials for any changes in the macro variable between the period of your financials and today. Consequently, if you are valuing an oil company in March 2015, and your most recent financials are from 2014, recognize that your revenues and earnings are from a period when oil prices averaged $70 a barrel and that the oil price was down to less than $50 a barrel in March of 2015. With those cleaned-up financials, you have then ensured that your forecasts for the future avoid bringing in either your views about oil prices, which may deviate from market views, or the views of market experts.

If you want to forecast oil prices, I would recommend that you start with the macro-neutral valuation first and then revalue the company with your forecasted values for the macro variable. If you are wondering why you need to do two valuations, it will help both you and your valuation audience understand the basis for your conclusions. By separating the two valuations, you are making clear how much of your valuation judgment of the company is driven by your views on the company and how much by your macro forecasts. If your valuation of BHP Billiton is $14 per share in the macro-neutral scenario and $18 per share with your commodity price views, and the stock is trading at $15 per share, and you are buying the stock or asking others to do so, you are pegging your entire recommendation on your macro views. If your recommendations do well consistently, that is a testimonial to your macro forecasting skills, and you should perhaps consider easier pathways to making money (such as buying or selling futures on the macro variable in question). If you just break even or underperform, that should be a signal to you and those who use your valuations that you should not be wasting your time (and money) on macro forecasts.

CASE STUDY 13.1: VALUING ExxonMobil
IN MARCH 2009

I valued ExxonMobil, the world's largest oil company, in March 2009, and my base narrative was that it was a mature oil company and that while oil prices in March 2009 had dropped substantially from prices in prior years, I had no sense of where they would go in the future. ExxonMobil reported pretax operating income in excess of $60 billion in 2008, but that reflected the fact that the average oil price during the year was $86.55 per barrel. By March 2009, the price per barrel of oil had dropped to $ 45, and I knew that the operating income for the coming year would be lower as a consequence.

To estimate what ExxonMobil's operating income would be at the oil price of $45, I drew on a regression in case study 5.2, in which I regressed ExxonMobil's operating income against the average oil price, using data from 1985 to 2008 to arrive at the following:

Operating income = −$6,395 million + $911.32 million (Average oil price)
$$R^2 = 90.2 \text{ percent}$$

Plugging the $45 oil price into this regression, I obtained an estimate for the expected operating income for ExxonMobil of $34.614 billion, which became the basis for the valuation of ExxonMobil in figure 13.1.

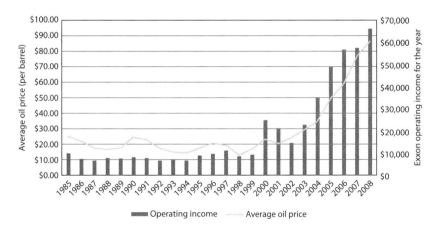

Figure 13.1
An oil price–neutral valuation of ExxonMobil, March 2009.

My story line for ExxonMobil is that it is a mature oil company whose earnings will track oil prices. With its significant competitive advantages, it will earn above-average returns on capital while maintaining its conservative financing policy (of not borrowing too much).

Following through on this story line, I assume a 2% growth rate in perpetuity and use the oil-price correct operating income of $34.6 billion to compute both base year income and a return on capital (of close to 21%). Using a cost of capital of 8.18% (against reflective of a mature oil company) allows me to value Exxon's operating assets at $342.5 billion.

Value the operating assets

$$\text{Value of operating assets} = \frac{34614(1.02)(1-.38)\left[1-\dfrac{2\%}{21\%}\right]}{(.0818-.02)} = \$320{,}472 \text{ million}$$

Adding the cash ($32,007 million) that Exxon had at the time of this valuation and subtracting out debt ($9,400 million) from the operating asset value of $320,472 million yields a value of equity of $ 343,079 million for the company, a value per share of $69.43.

At the prevailing stock price of $64.83, the stock looked slightly undervalued. However, that reflected the assumption that the oil price of $45 was the normalized price. In figure 13.2 I graphed out the value of ExxonMobil as a function of the normalized oil price.

As the oil price changes, the operating income and the return on capital change; I kept the capital invested number fixed and reestimated the return on

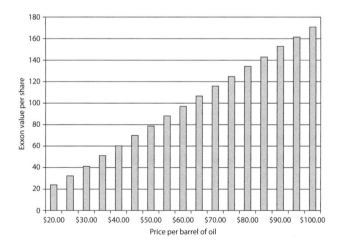

Figure 13.2
ExxonMobil normalized oil price and value per share.

capital with the estimated operating income. If the normalized oil price is $42.52, the value per share is $64.83, equal to the current stock price. Put another way, any investor who believed in March 2009 that the oil price would stabilize above $42.52 would find ExxonMobil to be undervalued.

Since the value per share was so dependent on the oil price, it made more sense to allow the oil price to vary and to value the company as a function of this price. One tool for doing this is a simulation, and it involved the following steps:

Step 1: Determine the probability distribution for the oil prices: I used historical data on oil prices, adjusted for inflation, to both define the distribution and estimate its parameters. Figure 13.3 summarizes the distribution.

Note that oil prices can vary from about $8 a barrel at the minimum to more than $120 a barrel. While I used the current price of $45 as the mean of the distribution, I could have inserted a price view into the distribution by choosing a higher or lower mean value.[1]

Step 2: Link the operating results to commodity price: To link the operating income to commodity prices, I used the regression results from ExxonMobil's history:

Operating income = −$6,395 million + $911.32 million (Average oil price)

This regression equation yields the operating income for ExxonMobil, at any given oil price.

Step 3: Estimate the value as a function of the operating results: As the operating income changed, there were two levels at which the value of the firm was affected. The first was that the changed operating income, other things remaining equal, changed the base free cash flow and the value. The second

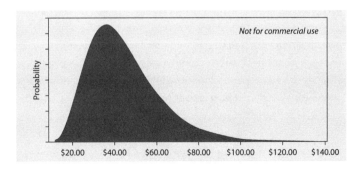

Figure 13.3
Oil price distribution.

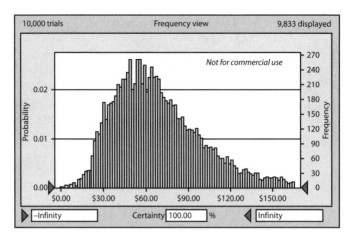

Figure 13.4
ExxonMobil value per share oil price simulation results.

was that the return on capital was recomputed, holding the capital invested fixed, as the operating income changed. As operating income changed, the return on capital changed, and the firm had to reinvest a different amount to sustain the stable growth rate of 2 percent. While I could also have allowed the cost of capital and the growth rate to vary, I felt comfortable with both those numbers and left them fixed.

Step 4: Develop a distribution for the value: I ran 10,000 simulations, letting the oil price vary and valuing the firm and equity value per share in each simulation. The results are summarized in figure 13.4.

The average value per share across the simulations was $69.59, with a minimum value of $2.25 and a maximum value of $324.42; there is, however, a greater than 50 percent chance that the value per share will be less than $64.83 (the current stock price). As an investor, the simulation gave me a much richer set of information on which to base my decision whether to invest in the company by going beyond just the expected value to a distribution of values. I chose not to buy the stock even though it looked mildly undervalued, partly because the distribution of value did not hold enough allure to me.

The Big Stories

The macro variables that you can build corporate stories around are many, but the three that are most used are commodity, cyclicality, and country.

In the first (commodity), you build a story around a commodity-driven company, with the commodity price being the central variable and the company's expected response to commodity price changes determining value. In the second (cyclicality), the valuation is of a company, and the primary driver of operating numbers is the overall health or lack thereof of the economy. Thus, your story starts with the economy, with the company woven into it, and requires that you link your company's prospects to how well or badly the economy does. In the third (country), the driver of value for the company is the country in which it is incorporated and where much of its operations are centered, with your views on the country having a much bigger impact on your value than your views on the company.

The Cycles

Macro variables move in cycles, with some cycles lasting longer than others. With commodity companies, these cycles can last decades and vary in length, thus making it difficult to forecast the next phase. In figure 13.5, for instance, the oil price is graphed from 1946 to 2016 in both nominal and constant dollar terms.

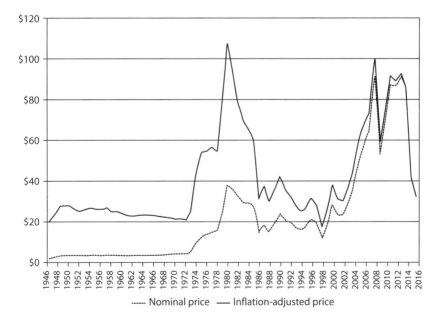

----- Nominal price   —— Inflation-adjusted price

Figure 13.5
Oil price cycles for 1946–2016.

One reason for the long cycles in commodity prices is the time lag between exploration decisions and development of reserves. Thus, oil companies that made the decision to buy reserves or start exploration in 2012 or 2013, when oil prices were still in the triple digits, found themselves starting production in 2014 and 2015, when prices had plummeted. As a consequence, it takes time for commodity companies to adjust their operations to new pricing, making oil prices move in the same direction for extended periods.

With economic cycles, the consensus is that the cycles tend to be shorter than commodity price cycles, but much of the conventional wisdom comes from research done on the U.S. economy, through the twentieth century. These studies concluded that economic cycles are more predictable than commodity price cycles, but that picture may be distorted by the fact that the U.S. economy through the second half of the twentieth century was exceptional in terms of stability and predictability, partly because of prosperity in the decades after the Second World War and partly because of U.S. dominance of the global economy during that period. While it is true that central banks became more adept at managing economic cycles in the last century, it is entirely possible that with globalization, economic cycles will again become more violent and difficult to forecast.

On country risk, the optimistic view is that all countries will converge on a global norm. However, that will take a long time and there will be stragglers, probably in large numbers, that diverge from norm. Even those emerging market economies that move toward normalcy will have setbacks that wipe out years of progress. In 2014 and 2015, for instance, four of the highest-profile emerging markets (Brazil, Russia, India, and China, or BRIC) all went through crises for different reasons. One measure that captures the investor perception of the risk in a country is the sovereign credit default swap (CDS) over time, and in figure 13.6 I report on the CDS spreads for the BRIC countries for the periods that data has been available.

The Predictability

In my experience, there is no aspect of investing that has a worse track record than investment strategies based on macroeconomic forecasting. With commodities, you would be hard-pressed to find a single commodity price reversal (where a commodity on the downside reversed course

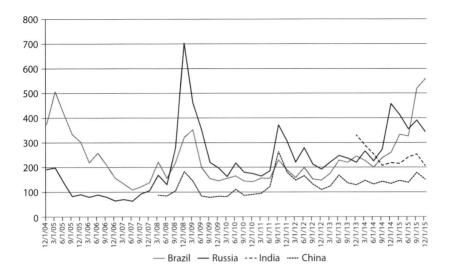

Figure 13.6
CDS spreads for BRIC countries. The Indian CDS has been traded only once since 2013, and China's CDS has been traded only once since 2008.

and starting rising or a rising commodity price started its decline) in the last fifty years that analyst consensus saw coming. With economic cycles, the record is not much better. In fact, if you break down the economic landscape into interest rates, inflation, and economic growth, the forecasts by experts in the field are often no better than forecasts that are made up or based upon purely historical data. With country risk, the herd mentality rules, with emerging market countries heralded as having made the transition to developed market status after a few years of growth and stability, and then just as quickly downgraded to emerging market status after a correction.

This poor track record has not stopped investors—both individuals and institutions—from continuing to make investments based upon their macro views. The reason perhaps lies in the returns that you generate, if you do get it right, and each year, the winners of that year's macro forecasting contest are anointed as the new market gurus. In 2015 there were a few analysts and portfolio managers who forecast the continued drop in oil price and easily beat the market. This may be cynical of me, but I have a feeling their success will be short-lived and the hubris of macro forecasting will come back to hurt them.

The Strategies

There are four broad strategies that you can adopt when dealing with macro stories and they range the spectrum:

1. Cycle forecasting: The first is to attempt to not just forecast direction but the entire cycle for an extended future period. In this approach, you could forecast dropping oil prices for the next three years, followed by five years of increasing prices, and then a decade of flat prices before prices start to decline again; or in the context of the economy, you could predict that the economy will be strong for two years, followed by a recession in year 3 and a recovery in year 4.

2. Level forecasting: The second is to try to make a judgment on direction for the market, and at the risk of oversimplifying this process, there are two substrategies that you can adopt. The first is to *go with momentum*, a strategy in which you assume the direction of price movements in the past will continue into the future. In early 2016, for instance, after two years of precipitous drops in oil prices, this would lead you to forecast continued price decline. The second is to be a *contrarian* and assume that prices are more likely to reverse direction than continue on their existing path; in early 2016 this would yield a prediction of higher oil prices after two years of decline.

3. Normalization: In this approach, rather than forecast cycles or levels, you estimate what you believe is a "normalized" price for that commodity, based either on the historical pricing record or on fundamentals (demand and supply for the commodity). Implicitly, this becomes a forecast of level, since a normal price that is higher than the current price will require the price to climb, and one that is lower will require it go down.

4. The price taker: As a price taker, you concede that you cannot forecast either cycles or normalized prices. Instead, you value the company at today's level, knowing that it will change shortly thereafter.

Which one should you go with? I cannot give you a categorical answer, because it depends on what your strengths are, but I have three suggestions:

1. Be explicit about which path you pick: If you decide to take one of the four paths listed above, you should be careful not to make

midvaluation changes and to be explicit about how that path plays out in your company's story (and value).

2. Tailor your information collection and analysis to your choice of path: The pathway that you pick will determine where you will be spending your time and resources. Thus, a strategy based on normalization will require that you not only look at past data in making this determination but that you consider the factors that may cause this normal to shift over time.

3. Be honest with yourself when assessing results: Your commodity, cyclical, or country views will affect the values you estimate for companies exposed to these factors. As the facts unfold, you will get to see not only whether your judgments on company value are right, but also how your macro strategy holds up to scrutiny. If you build your commodity company valuations on your price views of commodities, and you find that your record on the latter is no better than random (you are right half the time and wrong the rest), you should consider a change of strategy.

CASE STUDY 13.2: VALE, THE 3C COMPANY, NOVEMBER 2014

Vale is one of the largest mining companies in the world, with its primary holdings in iron ore, and is incorporated and headquartered in Brazil. Vale was founded in 1942 and was entirely owned by the Brazilian government until 1997, when it was privatized. Between 2004 and 2014, as Brazilian country risk receded, Vale expanded its reach both in terms of reserves and operations well beyond Brazil, and its market capitalization and operating numbers (revenues, operating income) reflected that expansion. By early 2014 Vale was the largest iron ore producer in the world and one of the five largest mining companies in the world, both in terms of revenues and market capitalization. Notwithstanding this long-term trend line of growth, 2014 had been an especially difficult period for Vale, as iron ore prices dropped and Brazilian country risk increased, leading into a presidential election that was concluded in October 2014. Figure 13.7 captures both effects.

Figure 13.8 shows Vale's stock price between May 2014 and November 2014 and contrasts it with another mining giant, BHP Billiton. While declining commodity prices had affected both companies adversely, note that Vale's stock price, in figure 13.8, dropped more than twice as much as BHP's stock price during this period.

Though there were fundamental reasons for the stock price decline at Vale, the fear factor was clearly also at play, because of Vale's exposure to commodity

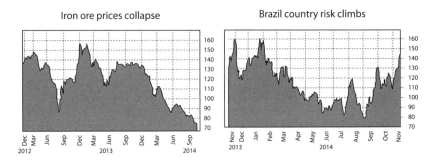

Figure 13.7
Vale's commodity and country risk.

and country risk and significant concerns about corporate governance and currency risk factors.

Focusing specifically on commodity prices, higher iron ore prices over the decade, as shown in figure 13.9, leading into the valuation were a prime factor in Vale's success. It was robust Chinese growth that lifted iron ore prices during this period to highs in 2011.

This history shows why making a judgment about a normal price for iron ore will be difficult. If your historical perspective is restricted to just the last few years, the price of iron ore (about $75/metric ton) in November 2014 looked low, but extending that perspective to cover a longer time period (say twenty to twenty-five years), suggests otherwise.

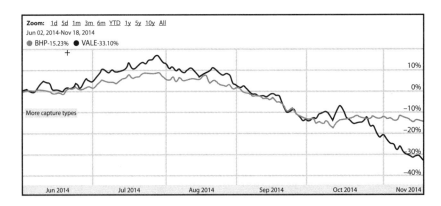

Figure 13.8
Vale's stock price collapse, June to November 2014.

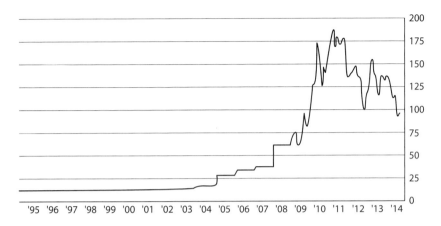

Figure 13.9
Iron ore prices (monthly $US per metric ton), 1995–2015.

In my narrative, I assumed that Vale was a mature commodity company and *that its earnings reflected prevailing iron ore prices ($75/metric
ton)*. Working under the assumption that I could not forecast future iron
ore prices, I valued Vale in U.S. dollar terms and assumed that Vale was a
mature commodity company growing at 2 percent a year in perpetuity. To
estimate the cost of capital, I built off the U.S. 10-year Treasury bond rate as
the risk-free rate and used an equity risk premium of 8.25 percent, reflecting
a weighted average of the equity risk premiums across the countries where
Vale has its reserves (60 percent are in Brazil). I have summarized the valuation in table 13.1.

Note that I attempted to incorporate the effect of commodity price declines
and currency devaluation in the base-year operating income, valuing the company with the depressed income from the last twelve months. The effects of corporate governance were captured in the investment and financing choices made
by the firm, with reinvestment and return on invested capital measuring the
investment policy and the debt mix in the cost of capital reflecting financing
policy. Finally, the country risk was incorporated into the equity risk premium
(in which I used risk premium weighted by the geographic distribution of Vale's
reserves) and the default spread in the cost of debt. The value per share that I got
with this combination of assumptions was $19.40, well above the share price of
$8.53 on November 18, 2014. I did buy the stock at the time, based on my story
and the valuation that came out of it, a decision I came to regret, but more on
that later!

Table 13.1
Vale—The Dark Side Beckons

The story

Vale is a mature iron ore and mining company, whose current earnings are depressed by macro factors (lower commodity price and soaring country risk), but it will stabilize at the levels for the most recent 12 months, as iron ore prices and country risk stabilize.

The history (All currency values in $ millions)

Year	Operating income	Effective tax rate	Book value of debt	Book value of equity	Cash	Invested capital	Return on invested capital
2010	$23,033	18.67%	$23,613	$59,766	$11,040	$72,339	25.90%
2011	$30,206	18.54%	$27,668	$70,076	$9,913	$87,831	28.01%
2012	$13,346	18.96%	$23,116	$78,721	$3,538	$98,299	11.00%
2013	$17,596	15.00%	$30,196	$75,974	$5,818	$100,352	14.90%
2014 (LTM)	$12,475	20.00%	$29,198	$64,393	$5,277	$88,314	11.30%
Average	$19,331	18.23%					18.22%

The cost of capital (in US$)

Business	Unlevered beta	Proportion of value	Debt/equity	Levered beta	Region	Percent of total	Equity risk premium
Metals and mining	0.86	16.65%	66.59%	1.2380	Brazil	68%	8.50%
Iron ore	0.83	76.20%	66.59%	1.1948	Rest of the world	32%	6.45%
Fertilizers	0.99	5.39%	66.59%	1.4251	Vale		7.84%
Logistics	0.75	1.76%	66.59%	1.0796			
Vale	0.84	100%	66.59%	1.2092			

		Cost of equity =	11.98%	
Pretax cost of debt	6.50%	After-tax cost of debt =	4.29%	
Tax rate =	34.00%	Debt-to-capital ratio =	39.97%	
		Cost of capital	8.91%	

The valuation (using trailing 12-month operating income and return on capital)

In keeping with its mature status, the expected growth rate in perpetuity is assumed to be 2% and that Vale will earn the return on capital of 11.30% that it earned in the trailing 12 months. The resulting reinvestment rate and valuation are below:

Reinvestment rate = 2%/11.30%=17.7% $Value\ of\ Operating\ Assets = \dfrac{\$12,475\,(1-.20)(1-.177)}{(.0891-.02)} = \$121,313$

Value of operating assets =	$121,313
+ Cash	$7,873
−Debt	$29,253
Value of equity	$99,933
Number of shares	5150.00
Value per share	$19.40

The stock was trading at $8.53 on November 20, 2013

The Macro Investing Caveat

When a valuation is driven primarily by macro factors, rather than micro ones, there are three consequences for investors that are worth keeping in mind. The first is that the macro cycles that are chronicled, especially with commodities, tend to be long term with upswings and downswings that can last decades. The second is that the macro variables tend to be more difficult to predict using fundamentals than micro variables, because macro variables are interconnected and affected by many forces. Thus, attempts to forecast the price of oil by looking at the production costs and demand for oil have generally not worked very well. The third is that structural shifts in the process can cause breaks from the past that render history moot. As an example, the explosion in shale oil production in the last decade created a supply shock to the oil markets that may have contributed to the oil price collapse in 2014, just as the rise of China as an economic power that was willing to invest unprecedented amounts in infrastructure jolted prices upward in commodity markets in the previous decade.

Let's assume that you are skilled at calling commodity, economic, or country price cycles or at least at estimating what the normalized prices should be. While I have laid out the process you can use to go from this macro view to valuing individual companies, it is worth asking the question "Why bother?," since there is a far simpler and more direct way for you to make money from your macro forecasting skills. You can use the forward, futures, and options market, especially with commodities, to make a killing. There are two reasons for separating your corporate stories into macro and micro parts:

1. It will make clear to you, the narrator of the story, how much of your story comes from each component and will allow you to track your performance on each part. Thus, if you buy Conoco and the stock price drops, you can at least assess whether it was because you got the oil price portion of your story wrong or because your story about Conoco as a company was flawed.

2. Your breakdown of the narrative into macro and micro parts is just as critical for someone hoping to act on your story, first, to aid that person in understanding your story and the valuation that emerges from it, and second, to help your listener judge how much faith he or she should have in your story. After all, if you have a woeful

track record in forecasting oil prices, and the bulk of your story on Conoco is built on your oil price forecasts, I should be skeptical about your final valuation.

CASE STUDY 13.3: THE VALE MELTDOWN, SEPTEMBER 2015

In case study 13.2, I made a judgment that Vale looked significantly undervalued and followed through on that judgment by buying its shares at $8.53/share. I revisited the company in April 2015, with the stock down to $6.15, revalued it, and concluded that while the value had dropped, it looked undervalued at its then prevailing price. The months between April and September 2015 were not good ones for Vale on any of the macro dimensions. The price of iron ore continued to decline, albeit at a slower rate, partially driven by turmoil in China. The political risk in Brazil not only showed no signs of abating but was feeding into concerns about economic growth and the capacity of the country to repay its debt. The run-up in Brazilian sovereign CDS prices continued, with the sovereign CDS spread rising above 4.50 percent in September 2015 (from 2.50 percent a year earlier). The ratings agencies, as always late to the party, had woken up (finally) to reassess the sovereign ratings for Brazil and had downgraded the country, Moody's from Baa2 to Baa3 and S&P from BBB to BB+, on both foreign and local currency bases. While both ratings changes represented only a notch in the ratings scale, the significance was that Brazil had been downgraded from investment-grade status by both agencies. Finally, Vale had updated its earnings yet again, and there seemed to be no bottom in sight, with operating income dropping to $2.9 billion, a drop of more than 50 percent from the prior estimates.

It is undeniable that the earnings effect of the iron ore price effect was much larger than I had estimated it to be in November 2014 or April 2015. Updating my numbers, and using the sovereign CDS spread as my measure of the country default spread (since the ratings were not only in flux but did not seem to reflect the updated assessment of the country), the value per share that I got in September 2015 was $4.29, as shown in table 13.2.

I was taken aback at the changes in value over the previous valuations, which were separated by less than a year, and attempted to look at the drivers of these changes, as shown in figure 13.10.

The biggest reason for the shift in value from November 2014 to April 2015 was the reassessment of earnings (accounting for 81 percent of my value drop), but looking at the difference between my April 2015 and September 2015 valuations, the primary culprit was the uptick in country risk, accounting for almost 61 percent of my loss in value.

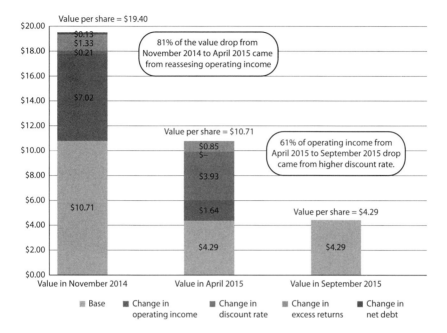

Figure 13.10: Breaking down the meltdown in value
Put simply, my values changed a lot in both sub-periods, but for different reasons. In the November 2014-April 2015 period, the change was from reassessing operating income for iron ore price changes. In the April 2015-September 2015 period, most of the change came from an increase in Brazil country risk.

If I stayed true to my investment philosophy of investing in an asset only if its price is less than its value, the line of no return had been passed with Vale. I sold the stock, but it was not a decision that I made easily or without fighting through my biases. In particular, I was sorely tempted by two impulses:

1. The "if only": My first instinct is to play the blame game and look for excuses for my losses. If only the Brazilian government had behaved more rationally, if only China had not collapsed, if only Vale's earnings had been more resilient to iron ore prices, my thesis would have been right. Not only is this game completely pointless, but it eliminates any lessons that I might be extract from this fiasco.

2. The "what if": As I worked through my valuation, I had to constantly fight the urge to pick numbers that would let me stay with my original thesis and continue to hold the stock. For instance, if I continued to use the sovereign rating to assess default spreads for Brazil, as I did in my first two valuations, the value I would have obtained for the company would have been $6.65. I

Table 13.2
Vale—The Regrets

The story
Vale is a mature iron ore and mining company, whose earnings are depressed because of country risk and commodity price declines, but its normalized earnings are likely to be well below the average income over the recent past.

The history (all currency values in $ millions)

Year	Operating income ($)	Effective tax rate	Book value of debt	Book value of equity	Cash	Invested capital	Return on invested capital
2010	$24,531	18.70%	$27,694	$70,773	$9,942	$88,525	22.53%
2011	$29,109	18.90%	$25,151	$78,320	$3,960	$99,511	23.72%
2012	$14,036	18.96%	$32,978	$75,130	$6,330	$101,778	11.18%
2013	$16,185	15.00%	$32,509	$64,682	$5,472	$91,719	15.00%
2014	$6,538	20.00%	$32,469	$56,526	$4,264	$84,731	6.17%
Last 12 months	$2,927	20.00%	$32,884	$49,754	$3,426	$79,211	2.96%
Average	$18,080	18.59%					15.72%

The cost of capital (in US$)

Business	Unlevered beta	Proportion of value	Debt/ Equity	Levered beta	Region	Percent of total	Equity risk premium
Metals and mining	0.86	16.65%	126.36%	1.5772	Brazil	68%	13.000%
Iron ore	0.83	76.20%	126.36%	1.5222	Rest of the world	32%	7.69%
Fertilizers	0.99	5.39%	126.36%	1.8156	Vale		11.30%
Logistics	0.75	1.76%	126.36%	1.3755			
Vale operations	0.84	100%	126.36%	1.5405			

		Cost of equity =	19.54%
Pretax cost of debt	9.63%	After-tax cost of debt =	6.36%
Tax rate =	34.00%	Debt-to-capital ratio =	55.82%
		Cost of capital	12.18%

The valuation (assuming normalized earnings will be 60% below 5-year average)

Normalized operating income	$7.232
Expected growth rate =	2.00%
Return on capital =	12.18%
Reinvestment rate =	16.42%

$$\text{Value of operating assets} = \frac{7{,}232\,(1.02)(1-.20)(1-.1642)}{(.1642-.02)} = \$48{,}451$$

Value of operating assets =	$48,451
+ Cash	$3,427
+ Equity investments	$4,199
−Debt	$32,884
−Minority interests	$1,068
Value of equity	$22,125
Number of shares	5153.40
Value per share	$4.29

The stock was trading at $5.05 on April 15, 2015

could have then covered up this choice with the argument that CDS markets are notorious for overreacting and that using a normalized value (either a ratings-based approach or an average CDS spread over time) would give me a better estimate.

After wrestling with my own biases for an extended period, I concluded that the assumptions that I would need to make to justify continuing to hold Vale would have to be assumptions about the macro environment: that iron ore prices would stop falling and/or that the market has overreacted to Brazil's risk woes and would correct itself. As a postscript, the stock price fell as low as $2, at which point I did buy shares in Vale. Perhaps, I deserve more punishment before I learn my lesson, but the stock has increased to $5.03, since.

It is said that you can learn more from your losses than from your wins, but the people who like to dish out this advice have either never lost or don't usually follow their own advice. Learning from my mistakes was hard to do, but looking back at my Vale valuations, here is what I see:

1. The dangers of implicit normalization: While I was careful to avoid explicit normalization, that is, assuming that earnings would return to the average level seen over the last five or ten years or that iron ore prices would rebound, I implicitly built in an expectation of normalization by taking the previous twelve-month earnings as reflective of iron ore prices during that period. At least with Vale, there seems to be a lag between the drop in iron ore prices and the earnings effect, perhaps reflecting precontracted prices or accounting lethargy. By the same token, using the default spread based on the sovereign rating provided a false sense of stability, especially when the market's reaction to events on the ground in Brazil has been much more negative.

2. The stickiness of political risk: Political problems need political solutions, and politics does not lend itself easily to either rational solutions or speed in resolution. In fact, the Vale lesson for me should be that when political risk is a big component, it is likely to be persistent and can easily multiply, if politicians are left to their own devices.

3. The debt effect: All of the problems besetting Vale were magnified by its debt load, bloated because of its ambitious growth in the

prior decade and its large dividend payout (Vale had to pay dividends to its nonvoting preferred shareholders). While the threat of default was not imminent, Vale's buffer for debt payments had dropped significantly in the previous year, with its interest coverage ratio dropping from 10.39 in 2013 to 4.18 in 2015.

If I had known in November 2014 what I did in September 2015, I would obviously not have bought Vale, but that is an empty statement.

Conclusion

Macro storytelling is trickier than micro storytelling, but with cyclical companies, commodity companies, or companies in very risky emerging markets, you may have no choice. Even if you have good macro forecasting skills, I would suggest that you first value your company, without bringing those skills into play, and then revalue it with your forecasts. That will allow both you and those using your valuations to see how much of your judgment comes from your views on the company and how much comes from the market.

14

The Corporate Life Cycle

The connection between stories and numbers has been a central theme of this book, but the balance between the two can shift as a company moves through the life cycle from start-up to growth company and into maturity and decline. In this chapter I first introduce the notion of a corporate life cycle with defined stages in corporate evolution and transition points, and then I look at how the connection between narrative and numbers changes as a company ages, with narrative driving numbers early in the life cycle and numbers driving narrative later. In the last part of the chapter, I look at the implications for investors, arguing that the qualities needed for investment success vary across the life cycle and that the valuation and pricing metrics used should be adapted accordingly.

The Aging of a Business

Businesses are born, grow (sometimes), mature, and eventually die, some sooner than others. The corporate life cycle reflects this natural evolution of businesses. In this section I begin by delineating the phases in the corporate life cycle and explain how the demands on storytelling and number crunching change as a company moves through the cycle.

The Life Cycle

The corporate life cycle begins with a business idea, not always original and sometimes not even practical, but designed to meet a perceived unmet need in the market. Most ideas don't make it past that stage, but a few go from idea to a product or service, thus taking the first step toward a viable business. That product or service has to make it through the gauntlet of the marketplace, and if it does, it generates revenues, and at successful companies, those revenues translate into growth. Once that transition is made, successful businesses not only are able to scale up, maintaining growth as they get bigger, but are also able to profit from that growth, fending off competition along the way. Once scaled up and profitable, the mature business goes into defensive mode, building barriers to entry (moats) that allows it to maintain profits. Eventually, those barriers get smaller and fade, setting up the pathway to decline for the business. Figure 14.1 captures the stages in the corporate life cycle.

Note that as businesses transition from stage to stage, there will be changes in how success is measured. The focus for both investors and

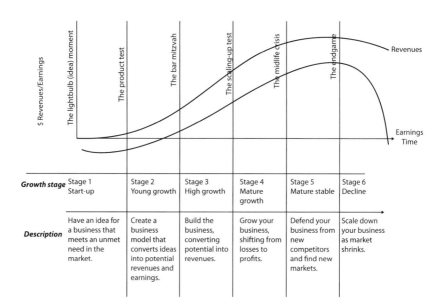

Figure 14.1
The corporate life cycle.

managers will also change with each stage, bringing different challenges and requiring different skills. Early in the life cycle, the transition points test a company's survival skills, since large proportions of firms fail at these stages: converting ideas into products/services and products/services into sustainable businesses. Later in the life cycle, the transitions tests are reality checks, when companies are confronted with a shift from one stage to another (growth to mature, mature to declining), with some accepting the new realities and adjusting to them and others going into denial and trying to fight the aging process, often at substantial cost to themselves and their investors.

Notwithstanding those differences, there are universal themes that cut across the life cycle, and my analysis is built around three broad ones. The first is that as much as we, as investors and managers, dislike uncertainty, aging is a feature, not a bug, in businesses. The second is the oft-repeated theme of this book, that is, while we tend to think of valuation as spreadsheets, models, and data, it is just as much about storytelling as it is about the numbers. The third is that we often use the words "price" and "value" interchangeably, but they are determined by different processes and estimated using different tools and metrics, as I noted in chapter 8.

Determinants of the Life Cycle

While every company goes through a life cycle, the duration and the shape of the cycle can vary across firms. Put differently, some firms seem to grow up faster than others, making the transition from start-up to successful business in years, rather than decades. By the same token, there are firms that stay as mature firms for long periods, while others seem to fade quickly from the limelight. To understand why there are differences in corporate life cycles across firms, I look at three factors:

1. Market entry: Some businesses have substantial barriers to entry, either because of regulatory/licensing requirements or due to capital investments that need to be made. In other businesses, entry is much easier, often requiring little or no regulatory approval or intensive capital investment.
2. Scaling up: Building on the first point, once you enter a business, the ease with which you can scale up will vary across businesses, some requiring time and substantial capital investments to get bigger, and others not.

3. Consumer inertia/stickiness: In some markets, consumers are much more willing to shift from established products to new ones because they have little attachment (emotional or economic) to the products and/or because there are low costs to switching to a new product.

Other things remaining equal, if market entry is easy, scaling up can be done at low cost, and consumer inertia is low, the growth phase of the life cycle will be much more rapid. That good news, though, has to be off-set with the bad news that the same factors will make it difficult to reap the benefits of being a mature business, since new competitors will use the same route to shake it up, setting up the process not only for decline but for rapid decline, as shown in figure 14.2.

This perspective on life cycle can be useful in examining differences in life cycles across sectors and businesses. Take, for instance, the technology companies that have increasingly come to dominate the market in the last three decades. Technology businesses tend to have low barriers to entry, allow for easy scaling up, and have consumers who generally are much more willing to experiment with innovation and new products. Not surprisingly, therefore, tech companies have been able to grow faster than non-tech companies, but

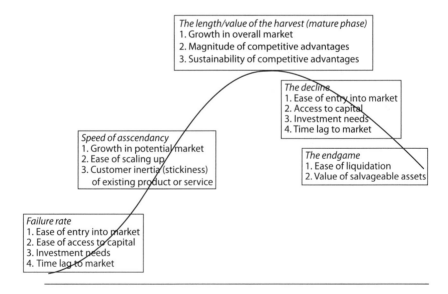

Figure 14.2
The corporate life cycle: drivers and determinants.

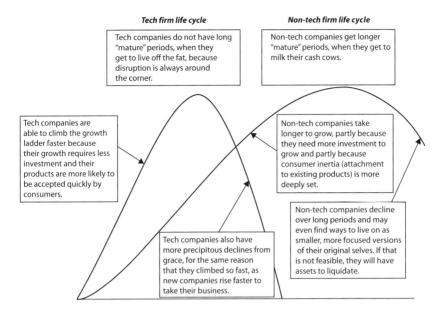

Figure 14.3
A comparison of corporate life cycles in tech and non-tech companies.

just as predictably, barring a few exceptions, they have been quicker to age, as shown in Figure 14.3, and many (Yahoo, Blackberry, and Dell, among others) have transitioned from high growth to decline in a few years.

In the next section we will build on this foundation of a corporate life cycle to talk about how the emphasis shifts from stories to numbers as companies age, and how it is important to be realistic about where you are in the life cycle when telling your story about a business.

Narrative and Numbers Across the Corporate Life Cycle

While it is true that every valuation is a combination of narrative and numbers, the importance of each component changes as you move through the life cycle. Early in the life cycle, when the company has posted few historical numbers and its business model is still in flux, it is almost entirely narrative that drives the value. As the company's business model takes form and it starts delivering results, the numbers start to play a bigger role in driving value, though the narrative still has the upper hand. In maturity, the narrative starts to take a secondary role and the numbers come to the fore.

Narrative Drivers Across the Life Cycle

The components of a compelling narrative shift as you move through the life cycle. In the start-up phase, investors are attracted to *expansive narratives* that can lead to big markets and are often willing to reward companies with high value for big stories. As companies try to convert ideas into products and services, the questions center around plausibility, and it is at this stage that narratives either become narrower, as businesses struggle with resource constraints and market constraints, or break down. Once the product or service is introduced, the narrative focus turns to *costs and profitability*, which in turn requires grappling with competitors in the product market. If you pass the profitability test, the emphasis in storytelling becomes *scalability*, that is, the capacity of the company to make itself bigger, testing the limits of productive, managerial, and financial capacities. Assuming that you make it through all these tests to become a profitable, mature company, the attention in the narratives shifts to *barriers to entry* and *competitive advantages* that allow the mature company to harvest markets for earnings and cash flows. In decline, the story turns to *the endgame*, when the company maps out a plan to shrink and perhaps disappear while generating as much as it can for investors on its way out. Figure 14.4 summarizes the narrative drivers across the life cycle.

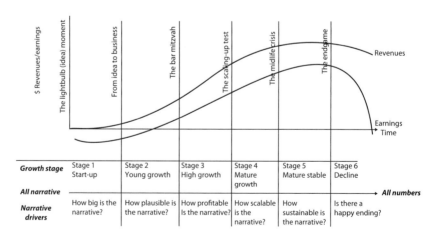

Figure 14.4
Narrative drivers across the corporate life cycle.

There is nothing more disconcerting in business than watching a narrator (who can be a founder, a top manager, or an equity research analyst) tell a story about a company that does not fit where the company falls in the life cycle: an expansive growth story for a company in decline or a story about sustainability for a young start-up.

The Constraints and Story Types

The best way to describe how your narrative gets more constrained as a company ages is to think like a writer who has been asked to come in and complete a book whose author is deceased. Early in the life cycle, the company is like a book just beginning to be written; the story is unformed and you will be able to create your own characters and mold it to your tastes. Later in the life cycle, think of the company as a book that has mostly been written; you have less freedom to change characters or to introduce new story lines.

It follows then that the type of stories that you will tell will also vary depending on where in the life cycle you are. Early in the life cycle, your stories will be big market and disruption stories of a young start-up entering a business filled with giants and vanquishing them in the market. As the company's business model gets more established, your stories will tend to get less ambitious, partly because they have to be consistent with the numbers you are delivering. Telling a story of expansive growth and high profit margins will become more and more unsustainable if your revenue growth lags and you are having a difficult time making money. Once a company becomes mature, your story can either become one about preserving the status quo (and the profits that come with it) or about reinvention and exploring the possibilities of rediscovering growth (perhaps through acquisitions or by entering new markets). In decline, the story may be tinged with nostalgia for glory days past, but to be realistic, it should reflect the company's charged circumstances.

You are also more likely to see big differences in narratives earlier in the life cycle, as observers of a company have more room to create their own pathways for the company. As a company ages, its history begins to restrict the potential narratives that different investors can derive for it. Investors looking at a company like Uber, for instance, will diverge on everything from what business Uber is in to what type of networking effects it will have to how much risk it is exposed to, and that will create a greater spread in the values investors attach to the company. In contrast, investors looking at Coca-Cola or JCPenney are likely to agree on most parts of the story and deviate only on small pieces.

CASE STUDY 14.1: VALUING A YOUNG COMPANY—GoPro IN OCTOBER 2014

On June 26, 2014, GoPro, a company that makes action cameras you can use to record yourself doing a sports activity (running, swimming, hiking), went public, with its stock price jumping 30 percent on its offering date (from $24 to $31.44) and then continuing its rise to $94 on October 7, 2014, before falling back to $70 on October 15, 2014, at the time of this valuation. The stock had accumulated a large number of vocal short-sellers who were convinced that this was a highflier destined for a fall, and many of them were burnt in the price run-up.

At the time of the valuation, the company produced three models of its camera (the Hero, the Hero 3, and the Hero 4), multiple accessories, and two free software products (the GoPro App and GoPro Studio) to convert the recordings into viewable videos. The company's cameras had found a ready market, with revenues hitting $986 million in 2013 and increasing to $1,033 million in the twelve months ending in June 2014. In spite of large investments in R&D ($108 million in the trailing twelve months), the company still managed to be profitable, with operating income of $70 million in that period. Capitalizing R&D increased their pretax operating margin to 13.43 percent, impressive for a young company. Figure 14.5 looks at the evolution of revenues and units sold over the history of the company through the time of this valuation.

In valuing GoPro, I faced all of the typical challenges associated with valuing a company early in its life cycle: determining the business it was in, the market potential, and imminent competition. GoPro was nominally a camera company, but in my narrative, I argued that the action-camera market was *a subset of the smartphone market* and its customers would be *physically active people who also happen to be active on social media (overactive oversharers)*. I estimated the market for action cameras to be $31 billion in 2013, and applying a 5 percent growth rate on this market yielded a potential market of $51 billion in 2023. Figure 14.6 captures the sequence of assumptions that yielded this number.

GoPro was the first mover in the market, and to gauge the expected market share that GoPro could get of this market, it was necessary to take into account that competition was starting to form—upstarts, established camera makers, and some smartphone manufacturers. I did not see any potential networking

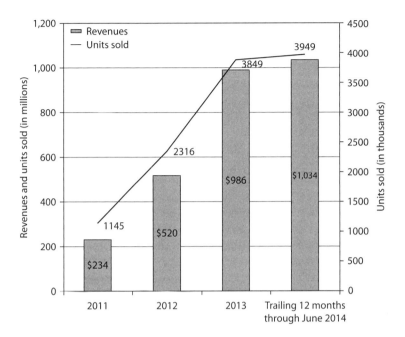

Figure 14.5
The history of GoPro.

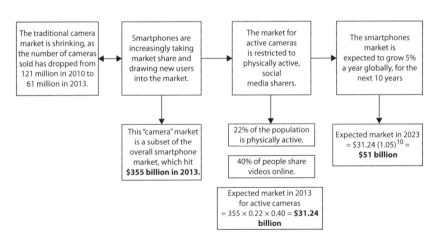

Figure 14.6
Estimating the potential market for GoPro cameras.

Table 14.1

GoPro—Profit Margins Over Its Lifetime

	2011	2012	2013	Trailing 12 months (ending June 2014)
Gross margin	52.35%	43.75%	36.70%	40.13%
EBITDA margin	18.74%	12.73%	12.60%	9.82%
Adjusted EBITDA margin	22.59%	14.50%	13.71%	14.14%
R&D adjusted operating margin	20.24%	16.70%	15.98%	13.43%
Operating margin	16.57%	10.31%	10.01%	6.75%
Net margin	10.50%	6.21%	6.15%	3.27%

advantages that GoPro could bring to this process that would allow it, even if successful, to control a dominant share of this market as the market grew. Drawing from the established camera-business market shares, I assigned a market share of 20 percent (resulting in revenues of about $10 billion for GoPro in 2023, i.e., 20 percent of $51 billion), roughly similar to the 20 percent share of the camera market in 2013 held by Nikon, the leading camera maker. On the profit margin, GoPro's first-mover advantage had given it a head start in this market, allowing it to charge premium prices, and I assumed it would earn a pretax operating margin of 12.5 percent in the future, slightly lower than the margin (13.43 percent) posted by the company in the most recent twelve months but reflecting the trend lines over the life of the company (as seen in table 14.1).

This estimate of the pretax operating margin (12.5 percent) was significantly higher than the 6–7.5 percent margin reported by camera companies and similar to the 10–15 percent margin reported by smartphone companies. I was, in effect, assuming that GoPro would preserve its premium pricing, even in the face of competition. To estimate the reinvestment needs, I made the assumption that the company would have to invest $1 for every $2 in additional revenues generated in years 1–10. This, in turn, would move the return on capital for the company from its current levels to about 16 percent in year 10.

GoPro had a social media focus for its user-generated videos, but in October 2014 the company generated all of its revenues from selling cameras and accessories. GoPro's focus on creating partnerships with Xbox and Pinterest suggested that it saw the possibility of generating revenues from becoming a media company, with the videos created by its customers as content. In October 2014, though, this was more in the realm of the possible than the plausible or the probable, and I assumed that GoPro's video generation capability would continue to generate no revenues but would help it sell more cameras. To estimate a cost of

The Inputs

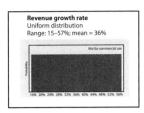

Revenue growth rate
Uniform distribution
Range: 15–57%; mean = 36%

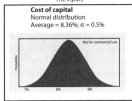

Cost of capital
Normal distribution
Average = 8.36%; σ = 0.5%

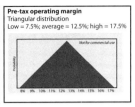

Pre-tax operating margin
Triangular distribution
Low = 7.5%; average = 12.5%; high = 17.5%

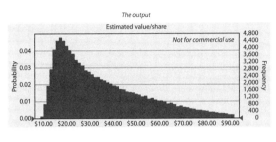

The output

Percentiles	Forecast values
0%	$8.63
10%	$15.58
20%	$18.56
30%	$21.84
40%	$25.75
50%	$30.53
60%	$36.33
70%	$43.31
80%	$52.50
90%	$65.39
100%	$123.27

Statistics:	Forecast values
Trials	100,000
Base case	$31.73
Mean	$36.02
Median	$30.53

Figure 14.7
A simulated GoPro valuation, October 2014.

capital for GoPro, I considered its prevailing mix of debt and equity (2.2 percent debt, 97.8 percent equity) as my starting point, and estimated a cost of capital of 8.36 percent for the company, declining to 8 percent by year 10.

With this spectrum of choices on the inputs (revenue growth derived from the total market/market share assumptions, operating margin, sales-to-capital ratio, and cost of capital), I assessed the value of GoPro as a distribution rather than as a single estimate of value. Figure 14.7 summarizes my assumptions and results.

Reading this distribution, you can see that while the expected value across the simulations was only $32/share, well below the market price of $70, there were outcomes that delivered values higher than the market price. It would have been difficult, but not impossible, to justify buying GoPro on an intrinsic value basis at its $70 price per share. To get to that price, GoPro would have to attract new users (physically active oversharers) into the market and fend off competition with innovative features that create networking benefits. That was a narrow path, and while it was plausible, it did not meet the probability tests that would have convinced me to buy GoPro.

CASE STUDY 14.2: VALUING A DECLINING COMPANY— JCPENNEY IN JANUARY 2016

JCPenney has been a longtime player in the U.S. retail market, tracing its history back to 1902. Started in Wyoming, the company initially grew in the Rocky Mountain states before moving its headquarters to New York in 1914. The company opened its first department store in 1961 and started selling through its catalogs in 1963. When Sears closed it catalog business in 1993, JCPenney became the largest catalog retailer in the country.

In January 2016 the company was facing bleak times, whipsawed by the growth of online retailing in general, and Amazon in particular, and changing consumer tastes. Figure 14.8 summarizes revenues and operating margins for the company by year, from 2000 to 2015.

Over this period, the company saw its revenues drop by more than 50 percent, and it reported operating losses from 2012 to 2015.

Given this history and the nature of the competition, my narrative for JCPenney is one of *continued decline*, in which I see revenues continue to drop 3 percent a year as the company shuts down unprofitable stores. I did have a slightly optimistic ending to the story, in which the company managed to find its place in

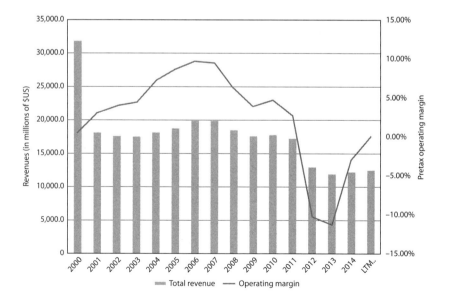

Figure 14.8
JCPenney revenues and operating margins.

Table 14.2

JCPenney case study

	Base year	1	2	3	4	5	6	7	8	9	10
Revenue growth rate[a]		–3.00%	–3.00%	–3.00%	–3.00%	–3.00%	–2.00%	–1.00%	0.00%	1.00%	2.00%
Revenues	$12,522	$12,146	$11,782	$11,428	$11,086	$10,753	$10,538	$10,433	$10,433	$10,537	$10,478
EBIT (operating) margin[b]	1.32%	1.82%	2.31%	2.80%	3.29%	3.79%	4.28%	4.77%	5.26%	5.76%	6.25%
EBIT (operating income)	$166	$221	$272	$320	$365	$407	$451	$498	$549	$607	$672
Tax rate	35.00%	35.00%	35.00%	35.00%	35.00%	35.00%	36.00%	37.00%	38.00%	39.00%	40.00%
EBIT (1–t)	$108	$143	$177	$208	$237	$265	$289	$314	$341	$370	$403
– Reinvestment[c] \		$(188)	$(182)	$(177)	$(171)	$(166)	$(108)	$(53)	$—	$52	$105
FCFF		$331	$359	$385	$409	$431	$396	$366	$341	$318	$298
Cost of capital[d]		9.00%	9.00%	9.00%	9.00%	9.00%	8.80%	8.60%	8.40%	8.20%	8.00%
PV (FCFF)		$304	$302	$297	$290	$280	$237	$201	$173	$149	$129
Terminal value	$5,710										
PV (terminal value)	$2,479										
PV (CF over the next 10 years)	$2,362										
Sum of PV	$4,841										
Probability of failure[e] =	20.00%										
Proceeds if firm fails =	$2,421										
Value of operating assets =	$4,357										

[a]Declining business: Revenues expected to drop by 3% a year for the next 5 years.

[b]Margins improve gradually to median for U.S. retail sector (6.25%).

[c]As stores shut down, cash released from real estate.

[d]The cost of capital is at 9%, higher because of high cost of debt.

[e]High debt load and poor earnings put survival at risk. Based on bond rating, 20% chance of failure, and liquidation will bring in 50% of book value.

the retailing business, albeit as a smaller player, and improved operating margins to reach the median for the retail business of 6.25 percent over the next decade. Given the high debt load, there was a significant chance that the company would not make it through the next decade, but if it did, it would be able to survive as a smaller, stable-growth company. I valued JCPenney, using the valuation inputs from my narrative, and Table 14.2 summarizes the numbers.

The revenues I projected for JCPenney ten years in the future were about 15 percent lower than prevailing revenues, and the value that I obtained for the operating assets of the company was $4.36 billion. That value was well below the outstanding debt (inclusive of leases), reflecting the tenuous state of the company and the very real possibility that this story could have a bad ending.

CASE STUDY 14.3: NARRATIVE DIFFERENCES— UBER IN DECEMBER 2014

In chapter 9 I valued Uber, based on my narrative for the company in June 2014, as an urban car service company with local networking benefits, and I arrived at an estimate value of $6 billion for its equity. In chapter 10 I valued Bill Gurley's counternarrative for the firm, as a logistics company with global networking benefits, and arrived at a value of $29 billion for equity. These are only two of many stories that you can tell about Uber as a company. To understand how narratives drive values for young companies, and how narrative differences can result in divergent values, I broke down the narrative process for Uber into steps and looked at the choices investors looking at the company could make at each step:

1. Business and potential market: The business that you see Uber in sets the limits of growth for the company, and the more broadly defined the market, the larger the potential growth (and the higher the value). Your choices are listed in table 14.3, with the consequences that I see for Uber's total market next to each one.

Table 14.3
Uber's Business and Potential Market

Uber's business is	Market size (in millions)	Description
A1. Urban car service	$100,000	Taxi cabs, limos, and car services (urban)
A2. All car service	$150,000	+ Rental cars + non-urban car service
A3. Logistics	$205,000	+ Moving + local delivery
A4. Mobility services	$285,000	+ Mass transit + car sharing

2. Effect on total market: In my valuations of Uber in chapters 9 and 10, I pointed to the possibility that it could attract new users to the car service market, thus increasing the size of the market over time. In table 14.4 I outline four possibilities for this growth effect.

Table 14.4
Uber's Effect on Total Market

Uber's effect on total market	Annual growth rate	Overall effect over next decade
B1. None	3.00%	No change in market size
B2. Increase market by 25%	5.32%	Increase market size by 25% over 10 years
B3. Increase market by 50%	7.26%	Increase market size by 50% over 10 years
B4. Double market size	10.39%	Double market size over 10 years

3. Networking benefits: In my valuation of Uber, I assumed that it would have local networking benefits, allowing it to capture a 10 percent market share of the total market, but in an alternative narrative in chapter 10, I pointed to the possibility of global networking benefits, giving it a much larger market share. Table 14.5 lists the possible choices.

Table 14.5
Uber's Networking Benefits

In its business, Uber will have	Market share	Description of networking effect
C1. No network effects	5%	Open competition in every market
C2. Weak local network effects	10%	Dominance in a few local markets
C3. Strong local network effects	15%	Dominance in multiple local markets
C4. Weak global network effects	25%	Weak spillover benefits in new markets
C5. Strong global network effects	40%	Strong spillover benefits in new markets

4. Competitive advantages: The competitive advantages that Uber creates as it builds up its business will affect whether it can keep its slice of driver revenues at 20 percent and preserve strong operating margins or see slimmer profits even if it is able to generate large revenues. Table 14.6 lists the choices on Uber's competitive advantages.

Table 14.6
Uber's Competitive Advantages

Uber's competitive advantages	Slice of ride receipts	Description of competitive effect
D1. None	5%	Unrestricted entry + no pricing power
D2. Weak	10%	Unrestricted entry + some pricing power
D3. Semistrong	15%	Unrestricted entry + pricing power
D4. Strong and sustainable	20%	Restricted entry + pricing power

5. Capital intensity: While my initial valuation of Uber assumed that it would be able to continue to grow with its prevailing business model (of not owning the cars or hiring the drivers), there is the possibility that as the company grows, it will have to adopt a model that requires more investments (in cars, technology, or infrastructure). Table 14.7 outlines some of the possibilities.

Table 14.7
Uber's Capital Investment Model

Uber's capital model	Sales-to-capital ratio	Description of model
E1. Unchanged	5.00	No investment in cars or infrastructure
E2. Moderate	3.50	Some investments in cars or infrastructure
E3. High	1.50	Large investments in driverless cars and or technology

Table 14.8
Uber—Narrative and Valuations, December 2014

Total market	Growth effect	Network effect	Competitive advantages	Value of Uber in $ millions
A4. Mobility services	B4. Double market size	C5. Strong global network effects	D4. Strong and sustainable	$90,457
A3. Logistics	B4. Double market size	C5. Strong global network effects	D4. Strong and sustainable	$65, 158
A4. Mobility services	B3. Increase market by 50%	C3. Strong local network effects	D3. Semistrong	$52, 346
A2. All car service	B4. Double market size	C5. Strong global network effects	D4. Strong and sustainable	$47,764
A1. Urban car service	B4. Double market size	C5. Strong global network effects	D4. Strong and sustainable	$31,952
A3. Logistics	B3. Increase market by 50%	C3. Strong local network effects	D3. Semistrong	$14,321
A1. Urban car service	B3. Increase market by 50%	C3. Strong local network effects	D3. Semistrong	$7,127
A2. All car service	B3. Increase market by 50%	C3. Strong local network effects	D3. Semistrong	$4, 764
A4. Mobility services	B1. None	C1. No network effects	D1. None	$1,888
A3. Logistics	B1. None	C1. No network effects	D1. None	$1,417
A2. All car service	B1. None	C1. No network effects	D1. None	$1,094
A1. Urban car service	B1. None	C1. No network effects	D1. None	$799

Depending on the choices—total market, growth in that market, Uber's market share, and revenue slice—the valuation results vary. While the number of combinations of assumptions is prohibitively high to show value estimates under each one, I summarized the value estimates in Table 14.8 for at least a subset of plausible choices.

Looking at the range of values ($799 million to $90.5 billion) that I obtain for Uber in case study 14.3, you may find your worst fears about valuation models vindicated, that is, that they can be used to deliver whatever number you want, but that is not the way I see it. Instead, here are four lessons that I draw from this table:

1. Soaring narratives, soaring values: I know that some people view DCF models as inherently conservative and thus unsuited to valuing young companies with lots of potential. As you can see in table 14.8, if you have a soaring narrative about a huge market, a dominant market share, and hefty profit margins, the model will deliver a value to match. It also stands to reason that when you have big differences in value estimates, it is almost always because you have different narratives for a company, not because you have a disagreement on an input number.

2. Not all narratives are created equal: While I have listed multiple narratives, some of which deliver huge values and some of which do not, not all are equal. Looking to the future as investors, some narratives are more plausible than others and thus have better odds of succeeding.

3. Narratives need reshaping: The narrative for Uber that you develop is based on what you know today. As events unfold, it is critical that you check your narrative against the facts and tweak, change, or even replace the narrative if the facts require those adjustments, which was the point that I made in chapter 11.

4. Narratives matter: Success when investing in young companies comes from getting the narrative right, not the numbers. That may explain why some successful venture capitalists can get away being surprisingly sloppy with their numbers. After all, if your skill set includes finding start-ups with strong narratives and picking founders/entrepreneurs who can deliver on those narratives, the fact that you cannot tell the difference between EBITDA and free cash flow or compute the cost of capital will be of little consequence.

Implications for Investors

The interplay between corporate life cycles, narratives, and numbers provides a template for understanding differences between investment philosophies and what it may take to succeed with each one.

Investor Skill Sets

As I argued in the last section, venture capitalists, who focus on companies early in the life cycle, will succeed or fail based more on their skills in assessing stories (that founders tell them about companies) than on their number crunching. In contrast, old-time value investors whose attention is on mature companies will be able to make money with mostly number crunching driving their choices, even if their narrative skills are weak or narrow (focused on assessing moats and competitive advantages).

If you are an investor trying to determine where the payoff from investing will be greatest for you, in addition to gauging your storytelling and number-crunching capabilities, I would suggest that you look at how well you deal with uncertainty and being wrong. If you are easily thrown off your game or rendered off balance by results that are different from your expectations, you should steer away from young businesses, in which narratives (and values) are more likely to change over time. In contrast, if it is big shifts in value that attract you to investments, you will not find many opportunities among mature companies.

Investor Tool Kits

As your investment focus shifts from young businesses to mature ones, the tools you use to examine investments also need to change. If you make investments based on value, that is, you buy only if price is less than your estimated value, the valuation models you use should draw on the same fundamentals but the way you build them will change over the life cycle. For young companies, your valuation models will have to start from the total market and work down, just as my Uber valuation did, and they also will have to be much more flexible to allow you to bring narratives into value. For more mature companies, you can build models that build upon the historical data for the company, and as long as the base narrative does not shift dramatically, you can get a reasonable estimate of value. Since this is effectively what many large spreadsheet financial models do, it should come as no surprise that while they deliver reasonable estimates of value for stable firms, they fall flat with younger or transitioning businesses.

If your investments are not based on value but are based on pricing judgments, you will have to make relative judgments, that is, ask whether the company is cheap or expensive relative to other priced companies in the business. That almost always will require you to choose a pricing multiple, where you scale the price paid to a common variable. Early in a company's life cycle, when there is little tangible data on operations, that variable may be something that you believe will eventually lead to revenues and profits, say number of users, downloads, or subscribers, but as the company moves through the cycle, you will scale value to operating metrics, starting with revenues (for growth companies that are still building up profitability), moving on to earnings (for mature companies), and ending with book value (as a proxy for liquidation value for declining companies). Figure 14.9 captures these shifts in investor skill sets and tool kits over the corporate life cycle, illustrating why there is often a divide between growth investors and value investors and between venture capitalists and public market investors.

Using its own metrics and tools, each group will find the other's investment judgments to be almost incomprehensible. Just as old-time value investors ask, "Who would buy a stock that trades at a thousand times earnings?" about investors who buy growth stocks, growth investors just as frequently wonder why anyone would buy a company whose revenues are expected to decline.

Conclusion

I started this chapter with a description of the corporate life cycle, in which companies move from the start-up phase to maturity and eventual decline, and I used it to examine how the balance between narrative and numbers changes over the life cycle. Early on, not only is it your story that drives your valuation of a business, but you are also likely to see wide variations across investors in story lines and valuations. As a company ages, the numbers start to play a greater role in determining value, and it is possible that

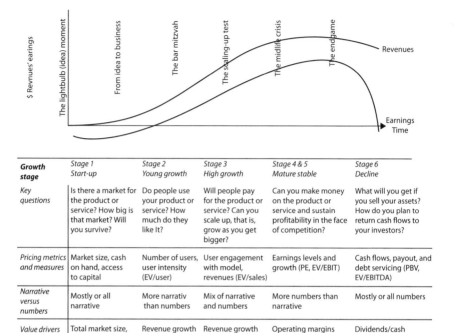

Figure 14.9
Investor Challenges across Life Cycle

you can attach a value for a company based purely on its numbers, perhaps by extrapolating historical data.

If you accept this argument, it follows that your investment philosophy and focus should match your skills and mental makeup. If you enjoy telling corporate stories, are good at connecting these stories to value, and are comfortable with being terribly wrong, you will be drawn to investing in young companies, as a venture capitalist or as an investor in young, growth companies in the public marketplace. If your preference is to work with numbers and you like rigid rules on investing, you will be more comfortable working with mature companies. To each, his (or her) own!

15

The Managerial Challenge

While much of this book has been written from the perspective of investors in companies and how they can combine storytelling and number-crunching skills in investing, there are lessons for managers and founders of businesses as well. In this chapter I go back to the corporate life cycle that I introduced in chapter 14, but I look at the connection between narrative and numbers from the perspective of managers, owners, or founders rather than investors. As with investors, I argue that the qualities needed to be a successful top manager will change as a company moves from start-up to decline, perhaps explaining why the founders of many successful start-ups are unable to transition to becoming CEOs of more established businesses and why CEOs of established businesses do badly at start-ups. I also look at why it is critical that top managers at companies not only have clear, compelling, and credible stories to tell about their businesses at every stage in the life cycle but take actions consistent with these stories.

A Life Cycle Perspective on Managerial Imperatives

In the last chapter I introduced the corporate life cycle structure to explain how the balance between narrative and numbers shifts as a company transitions from a start-up to a growth firm and then moves to being a mature business before slipping into decline. Not surprisingly, the challenges faced by those who manage these businesses also change as they move through the life cycle.

The Managerial Imperative

In keeping with the narrative/number mix over the corporate life cycle, the challenges faced by managers/founders shifts as a company ages. Early in the life cycle, founders need to be compelling storytellers, capable of convincing investors of the viability and potential of a business, even when there are no results (or even products) to point to. As the firm transitions from the idea to the business stage, the promoters of the business need to bring business-building skills into the equation to convert promise to numbers. When the firm starts to grow, the test for managers is whether they can start delivering results that back up the story. In maturity, managers need to frame their narratives to match up to the numbers that are being delivered; continuing to tell a growth story when a company's revenues are flat will lead to a loss of credibility. In the final stages, managers will be tested on their ability to get past denial, accept that the business is in decline, and act accordingly. Figure 15.1 illustrates these shifts.

Early in the life cycle, having the right person at the head of the company is key to whether it succeeds or fails, but as a company matures, there will be a point in its life cycle, especially if it has found a formula that works and is in a settled business, when it may not matter much who its top managers are. ExxonMobil's value is unlikely to change much with a different top management team, and that may well explain why you could be an investor in ExxonMobil and not know who its CEO is, or even care. In contrast, it would be foolhardy on your part to invest in a GoPro or Uber without finding out more about who runs these companies and without being comfortable with their styles and philosophies.

If you buy into this notion that the managerial challenge shifts as companies move through the life cycle, it stands to reason that the qualities you look for in a CEO are different at each stage. Early in the process, it is the *visionary CEO* who is best suited to telling the company's story and convincing others that a business idea has potential. As you move from idea to product, while vision is still critical, it has to be supplemented by the *capacity to build a business*. As the business takes hold and you seek to

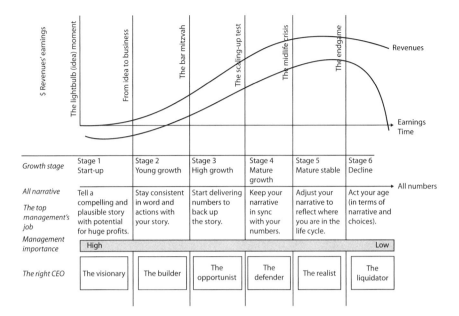

Figure 15.1
The corporate life cycle and managerial challenges.

scale up, it is the *opportunistic CEO* who finds new markets and businesses that the company can enter to grow efficiently. Once the company is established as a successful business, the CEO has to learn how to *play defense*, as competitors are drawn by success to imitate and improve on the company's offerings. As the business moves into its mature phase, the CEO has to be a *realist* about growth and its costs, recognizing that going for more growth, at any cost, can be value destructive. In the decline phase, the CEO has to be comfortable with the conclusion that the best course for the company may be to shrink, *liquidating* assets that others are willing to pay higher prices for or that have outlived their usefulness.

Narrative and Numbers: Management Lessons Across the Life Cycle

While the challenges that management faces can vary across the life cycle, there are some constants that emerge from looking at successful businesses and their leaders over time.

1. Control the story: Managing is not just about delivering numbers and meeting analyst expectations. It is about telling a story about the business that allows investors to understand not only its history but where you (as the leader) plan to take it in the future. If top managers do not craft a credible story about the company, investors and analysts will step into the vacuum and craft their own stories, leaving the company playing a game that is not of its own choosing.

2. Stay consistent with that story: Managers are also judged on whether their story stays consistent over time. That does not mean that you can never change your story, as you often must in response to events, but it does mean that if your story changes, you have to explain why and how. If your narrative changes from period to period, with no explanation and perhaps to be in sync with whatever investors and customers are most enamored with in that period, your story will lose credibility and risk being displaced by alternate ones.

3. Act in accordance with the story: As managers make decisions on where to invest, how to fund those investments, and how much cash to return to investors, they will be watched closely to see whether their actions match up to the story they have told about the business. A CEO who frames a narrative about his or her business being a global player but never invests or seeks out opportunities in foreign markets will find that investors stop believing that story.

4. Deliver results that back up the story: As a CEO, you can tell a great story and stay consistent with it over time and with your actions, but if the results don't measure up, you will still be found wanting. If your numbers consistently tell a different story than the one that you have been offering to markets, the numbers will win out. Thus, a CEO who pushes a high-growth story to investors while delivering flat revenues will have to either change his or her story or risk being ignored.

Here again, there is a tie to where the company is in the life cycle. Early in the life of a business, managers have to decide whether to push for a soaring narrative, in which they promise the moon, or be more restrained and settle for a smaller narrative. The trade-off is simple. A soaring narrative is more exciting and is likely to attract more investor attention and yield a higher valuation or pricing for the company than a smaller, more constrained one. However, a soaring narrative will also require more resources to convert into reality and is more likely to result in disappointments down the road.

CASE STUDY 15.1: CONSISTENT NARRATIVE—THE AMAZON LESSON

There is no company that better illustrates the value of having a CEO who crafts a narrative, stays consistent with that narrative, and then delivers results that match the narrative than Amazon. In the period during which I have followed Amazon, which is almost since inception, Jeff Bezos has told the same story about Amazon, framing it as an innovative company that would fearlessly go after new businesses, with no concerns for profits, but with every intent of growing its revenues.[1] Amazon started in retailing but has since expanded into the entertainment, technology, and cloud computing businesses. Along the way, the company has done exactly what Bezos promised: gone after revenue growth with no concern for profits in the near term but with a promise that it would find a way to make profits in the future. It is for this reason that I described Amazon as the *Field of Dreams* company in an earlier chapter.

While markets generally are not forgiving of companies that do not convert revenues to profits for long periods, Amazon is clearly an exception. Almost twenty years after its founding, it was still struggling to show a profit in 2015, but investors seemed to be willing to overlook that shortcoming. Jeff Bezos seemed not only to have won investors over with his Amazon story but to have changed the metrics the market uses to measure success, at least for his company, from profitability to revenue growth.

Even Jeff Bezos will eventually be called upon to deliver on the other half of his promise, which is that he will find a way to generate healthy profits on immense revenues, but markets have been patient for far longer with Amazon than for other companies, precisely because of the trust they have in its CEO.

CASE STUDY 15.2: BIG VERSUS SMALL NARRATIVES—LYFT VERSUS UBER IN SEPTEMBER 2015

In chapter 11 I valued Uber in September 2015 and generated a value of more than $23 billion, largely because of its ambitious push into other countries and new businesses. At the time of the valuation, Uber's primary competitor in the

United States was Lyft, but Uber was viewed as the hands-down winner of the ride-sharing battle. The contrast between the two companies in September 2015 can be seen in table 15.1.

Looking at table 15.1, there are three points to be made. First, Uber was clearly going after the global market, uninterested in forming alliances or partnerships with local ride-sharing companies. In September 2015 Lyft had made explicit its intention to operate in the United States, at least for the moment, and seemed intent on partnering with large ride-sharing companies in other markets. Within the United States, Uber operated in more than twice as many cities as Lyft. Second, both companies were growing, though Uber was growing at a faster rate than Lyft, as captured in both the number of rides and gross billings at the companies. Third, both companies were losing money, and significant amounts at that, as they went for higher revenue growth.

The business models of the two companies, at least when it comes to ride sharing, were very similar. Neither owned the cars that were driven under their names and both claimed that the drivers are independent contractors. Both companies used the 80/20 split for ride receipts, with 80 percent staying with the driver and 20 percent going to the company, but that surface agreement hid the cutthroat competition under the surface. Both companies offered incentives (think of them as sign-up bonuses) for drivers to start driving for them or, better still, to switch from the other company. They also offered riders discounts, free rides, or other incentives to try them or to switch from the other ride-sharing company. At times, both companies had been accused of stepping out of bounds in trying to get ahead in this game, and Uber's higher

Table 15.1
Lyft Versus Uber, September 2015

	Uber	Lyft
Number of cities served in the United States	150	65
Number of cities served globally	>300	65
Number of countries	60	1
Number of rides (in millions) in 2014	140	NA
Number of rides (in millions) in 2015 (estimated)	NA	90
Number of rides (in millions) in 2016 (estimated)	NA	205
Gross billings (in millions of US$) in 2014	$2,000	$500
Gross billings (in millions of US$) in 2015 (estimated)	$10,840	$1,200
Gross billings (in millions of US$) in 2016 (estimated)	$26,000	$2,700
Estimated growth for 2015	442%	140%
Estimated growth for 2016	140%	125%
Operating loss in 2014 (in millions of US$)	−$470	−$50

profile and reputation for ruthlessness had made it the more commonly named culprit. The other big operating difference was that unlike Uber, which was attempting to expand its sharing model into the delivery and moving markets, Lyft, at least in September 2015, had stayed much more focused on the ride-sharing business, and within that business, it had also been less ambitious in expanding its offerings to new cities and new types of car services than Uber. Table 15.2 captures the narrative differences between Uber and Lyft, at least in September 2015.

In short, my Lyft narrative was narrower and more focused (on ride sharing and in the United States) than my Uber narrative. That put Lyft at a disadvantage in terms of both value and pricing in September 2015, but it could work in its favor as the game unfolds. The adjustments to the Lyft valuation, relative to my Uber valuation, were primarily in the total market numbers, but I did make minor adjustments to the other inputs as well.

1. Smaller total market: Rather than use the total global market, as I did for Uber, I focused on just the U.S. portion of these markets. That reduced the total market size substantially. In addition, I assumed, given Lyft's focus on ride sharing, that its market was constrained to the car service market. Notwithstanding these changes in my assumption, the potential market still remained a large one, with my estimate about $150 billion in 2025.

Table 15.2
Uber Versus Lyft—Narrative Differences

	Lyft	Uber
Potential market	U.S.-centric ride-sharing company	Global logistics company
Growth effect	Double ride-sharing market in the United States in the next 10 years	Double logistics market globally in the next 10 years
Market share	Weak national networking benefits	Weak global networking benefits
Competitive advantage	Semistrong competitive advantages	Semistrong competitive advantages
Expense profile	Drivers as partial employees	Drivers as partial employees
Capital intensity	Low capital intensity	Low capital intensity, with potential for shift to more capital-intense model
Management culture	Aggressive within ride-sharing business; milder with regulators and media	Aggressive with all players (competitors, regulators, media)

2. National networking benefits: Within the U.S. market, I assumed that the increased cost of entry into the business would restrict new competitors and that Lyft would enjoy networking benefits across the country, enabling it to claim a 25 percent market share of the U.S. market.

3. Drivers become partial employees: My assumptions on drivers becoming partial employees and competition driving down the ride-sharing company slice of revenues parallel the ones that I made for Uber in September 2015, resulting in lower operating margins (25 percent in steady state) and a smaller slice of revenues (15 percent).

4. Lyft is riskier than Uber: Finally, I assumed that Lyft was riskier than Uber, given its smaller size and lower cash reserves, and I set its cost of capital at 12 percent, in the 90th percentile of U.S. companies, and allowed for a 10 percent chance that the company would not make it.

The value I derived for Lyft with these assumptions is captured in Table 15.3. My value for Lyft in September 2015 was $3.1 billion, less than one-seventh of the value that I estimated for Uber ($23.4 billion) at that time.

If narrative drives numbers and value, the contrast between Uber and Lyft was in their narratives. Uber is a big narrative company, presenting itself as a sharing company that can succeed in different markets and across countries. Giving credit where it is due, Travis Kalanick, Uber's CEO, had been disciplined in staying true to this narrative and acting consistently. Lyft, on the other hand, seemed to have consciously chosen a smaller, more focused narrative, staying with the story that it was a car service company and further narrowing its react by restricting itself to the United States.

The advantage of a big narrative is that if you can convince investors that it is feasible and reachable, it will deliver a higher value for the company, as is evidenced by the $23.4 billion value I estimated for Uber. It is even more important in the pricing game, especially when investors have very few concrete metrics to attach to the price. Thus, it is the two biggest market companies, Uber and Didi Kuaidi, that commanded the highest prices toward the end of 2015. Big narratives do come with costs, and those costs may dissuade companies from going for the "big story."

With Uber, you see the pluses and minuses of a big narrative. It is possible that UberEats (Uber's food-delivery service), UberCargo (moving), and UberRush (delivery) are all investments that Uber had to make to back its narrative as an on-demand company, but it is also possible that these are distractions at a moment when the ride-sharing market, which remains Uber's heart and soul, is heating up. It is undoubtedly true that Uber, while growing revenues at exponential rates, is also spending money at those same rates to keep its big growth going, and it is not only likely, but a certainty, that Uber will disappoint its investors at some time, simply because expectations have been set so high. It is perhaps to avoid these

Table 15.3

			The Story		

Lyft is a U.S. car service company, enjoying weak networking benefits across the country while seeing its slice of revenues slip (85/15), higher costs (with drivers as partial employees), and low capital intensity.

The Assumptions

	Base year	Years 1–5	Years 6–10	After year 10	Story link
Total market	$55 billion	Grow 10.39% a year		Grow 2.25%	U.S. Car Service + New users
Gross market share	2.18%	2.18%>25%		25%	Weak global networking
Revenue share	20.00%	20% -> 15%		15.00%	Lower revenue share
Pretax operating margin	−66.67%	−66.67% ->25%		25.00%	Semi-strong competitive position
Reinvestment	NA	Sales to capital ratio of 5.00		Reinvestment rate = 9%	Low capital intensity model
Cost of capital	NA	12.00%	12%-> 8%	8%	At 90th percentile of U.S. firms
Risk of failure	10% chance of failure (with equity worth zero)				The Uber threat

The Cash Flows (in $ millions)

	Total market	Market share	Revenues	EBIT $(1-t)$	Reinvestment	FCFF
1	$60,715	4.46%	$650	$(258)	$70	$(328)
2	$67,023	6.75%	$1,040	$(342)	$78	$(420)
3	$73,986	9.03%	$1,469	$(385)	$86	$(472)
4	$81,674	11.31%	$1,940	$(384)	$94	$(478)
5	$90,159	13.59%	$2,451	$(332)	$102	$(434)
6	$99,527	15.87%	$3,002	$(224)	$110	$(334)
7	$109,867	18.16%	$3,590	$(57)	$118	$(174)
8	$121,283	20.44%	$4,214	$174	$125	$50
9	$133,885	22.72%	$4,967	$470	$131	$339
10	$147,795	25.00%	$5,542	$831	$135	$696
Terminal year	$151,120	25.00%	$5,667	$850	$320	$774

The Value

Terminal value	$13,453	
PV(terminal value)	$4,828	
PV (CF over next 10 years)	($1,362)	
Value of operating assets =	$3,466	
Probability of failure	10%	
Value in case of failure	$-	
Adjusted value for operating assets	$3,120	VCs priced Lyft at about $2.5 billion at the time of the valuation.

risks that Lyft consciously pushed a smaller narrative to investors, focused on one business (ride sharing) and one market (the United States). Lyft is avoiding the distractions, the costs, and the disappointments of the big-narrative companies, but at a cost. Not only will it cede the limelight and excitement to Uber, but that will lead it to be both valued and priced less than Uber. In fact, Uber used its large value and access to capital as a bludgeon to go after Lyft in its strongest markets.

As an investor, there is nothing inherently good or bad about either big or small narratives, and a company cannot become a good investment just because of its narrative choice. Thus, Uber, as a big-narrative company, commanded a higher valuation ($23.4 billion) but was priced even more highly ($51 billion) in September 2015. Lyft, as a small-narrative company, had a much lower value ($3.1 billion) but was priced at a lower number ($2.5 billion). At these prices, as I valued them, Lyft was a better investment than Uber.

Transitional Tectonics

If the qualities that make for a good CEO are different as you move through the life cycle, it stands to reason that transitions from one phase of the life cycle to the next will be fraught with danger for companies and their top managers. In this section I will start with the easy transitions, in which a company is able to navigate its way painlessly through, either because it has a long life cycle or because it has an adaptable CEO with multiple skills. I will then look at the more common problem of CEOs who are successful in one phase of the life cycle but become misfits in a different phase.

Easy Transitions

Given the different demands put on managers at each stage of the life cycle, can you ever have transitions happen seamlessly? It is unlikely, but there are three scenarios in which it can happen:

1. A company may be lucky enough to have *a versatile CEO who is adaptable enough to change his or her management style* as the company changes. Thomas Watson served as CEO of IBM from 1914 to 1956, presiding over its growth into a technology giant over that period and changing as the company changed. Drawing on a more recent example, Bill Gates proved to be adept at making the

transition from the founder of a technology start-up to running one of the largest companies in the world during his tenure as CEO of Microsoft from 1975 to 2000. While it is early to pass judgment at Facebook, Mark Zuckerberg seems to be showing the same type of versatility while navigating Facebook from the start-up phase to high growth over the course of a few years.

2. *If the life cycle for a company is a long one*, the passage of time may allow for easier transitions, since CEOs will age with the company. By the time that key transitions occur, the CEO may be at a point where he or she is considering moving on. Henry Ford was CEO of Ford Motors from 1906 to 1945, presiding over its growth from a small, struggling start-up to the second-largest automobile company in the world, but the extended life cycle of automobile companies allowed for a transition at Ford to others better suited to running the mature automobile company it had become by the 1950s.

3. With some *multibusiness family companies*, the problem of transitions is managed within the family, with different family members (often from different generations) being given responsibility for businesses that best fit their skill sets. That will, of course, work only if the family in question is not dysfunctional, with family patriarchs or matriarchs who insist on sticking with what worked for them in decades past and younger family members put in charge of businesses they are unsuited to run.

Misfit CEOs

While easy transitions are ideal, it is much more common to see friction at transition points, as CEOs find it difficult to adjust to the new demands as their companies change. To the extent that those at the top of an organization find it difficult to let go, the stage is set for battles that can be bloody and often leave no winners. Here are a few examples of mismatches between businesses and CEOs:

1. The visionary who cannot build: Noam Wasserman, in a study of 212 start-ups in the 1990s and the first part of the 2000s, found that by the time these ventures were three years old, half of all founders were no longer CEOs and fewer than 25 percent stayed in place until

these firms made their public offerings.[2] Most of the CEOs who left did not do so voluntarily, with 80 percent of them being forced to step down. In many cases, the push for change came from investors (usually venture capitalists) who saw more potential value if the company was run by someone other than the founder. This has led to some pushback, with at least one prominent venture capitalist firm (Kleiner, Perkins, Caufield & Byers) arguing that investors are too eager to push out founders and replace them with "professional" managers (with no vision) and presenting evidence, based upon looking at more than a thousand financing transactions, that firms where founders stayed on as top managers are more successful at raising capital and creating value than those where founders were replaced.[3]

2. The builder who cannot scale: The second transition is to take a business that has succeeded in its initial try (by creating a product or service that is a commercial success) and to scale it up. The corporate landscape is littered with companies that emerged out of nowhere with dazzling growth but faded almost as fast, partly because they were managed by individuals who thought that scaling up just meant replicating what worked the first time around. Crocs, a shoe manufacturer, captured the world with its modified version of a nursing shoe, tripling sales between 2006 and 2007. Seven years later, faced with declining revenues and operating losses, the company announced a restructuring plan to streamline operations and become a smaller company.

3. The scaler who cannot defend: There are CEOs who are adept at going for growth but find it much more difficult to defend their turf. This is the challenge that growth companies face, and especially if the growth has been lucrative, when they become the status quo. Mike Lazaridis, along with co-CEO Jim Balsillie, grew Blackberry (Research in Motion) into one of the most innovative and valuable technology companies in the world but was unable to defend its smartphone franchise against the iPhone and Android assaults. By the time the duo stood down in 2012, the damage had already been done at Blackberry.

4. The defender who cannot liquidate: Growing old is hard to do, whether you are a person or a company. In perhaps the most difficult transition of all, a CEO of a mature company with a history of profitability will find it challenging to make the adjustment to

a phase in which the objective is to shrink the company rather than to grow it. Empire builders are not well suited to dismantling them, a point that Winston Churchill was making in 1942, when he said that he "had not become the King's First Minister in order to preside over the liquidation of the British Empire." Well, history stops for no man, even one as great as Churchill, and it was Clement Atlee, who defeated Churchill at the polls in 1945, who oversaw the dismantling of the colonial empire.

Corporate Governance and Investor Activism

The corporate life cycle transitions, which test management skills and create the possibility of mismatched CEOs, also create the conditions that give rise to activist investing, that is, investing with the intent of getting companies to change the way they are run. With young companies, as I noted earlier, the activism comes from venture capitalists pushing for changes in management, but at later stages in the life cycle, it is private equity and activist investors that are the primary catalysts of change.

This should also provide some perspective on how investors should view the importance of corporate governance at companies. When companies are successful, investors tend to be casual about governance questions, arguing that since the company is well managed, there is little need for change. Consequently, they are too quick to accept shares with different voting rights, stacked and captive boards of directors, and opaque corporate structures at these companies. They will come to regret these concessions at transition points, when managers at these companies may need to be held accountable and perhaps constrained. This is perhaps the worst legacy of the Google story. While few will contest Google's success at delivering growth and profitability in the last decade, the company has been structured and run as a corporate dictatorship. When Sergey Brin and Larry Page, Google's cofounders, decided to go public with two classes of shares with different voting rights, they were breaking with a decades-long tradition in the United States of offering equal voting rights on all shares. The rapturous reception accorded to the offering by investors, and Google's subsequent rise, laid the platform for a generation of newer tech companies that have followed the Google model of shares with different voting rights. Thus, Mark Zuckerberg controls more than 50 percent of Facebook's voting rights, while holding less than 20 percent of its shares. It is possible that Google's and Facebook's stockholders will not pay a price for failing to protect their voting rights and that both the Brin and Page team and Zuckerberg will adapt well to corporate transitions. It is more likely, though, that at some stage in each of these companies' lives, investors and managers will diverge on the best path forward, and that is when investors will come to regret their lack of power.

CASE STUDY 15.3: THE CHALLENGES OF MANAGING AGING
COMPANIES—YAHOO AND MARISSA MAYER

Yahoo characterized the dot-com boom of the 1990s, going from start-up to large market capitalization company in the space of a few years. Its core business, built around a search engine, dominated online search in the early part of the online revolution, but Google's rise cast a shadow over the company. After repeated attempts by different management teams to turn it around, the company hired Marissa Mayer, an up-and-coming executive at Google, to be its CEO in 2012.

By the time Marissa Mayer became CEO, Yahoo's glory days were well in its past, as you can see in figure 15.2, which traces its history from young, start-up to its standing in 2012.

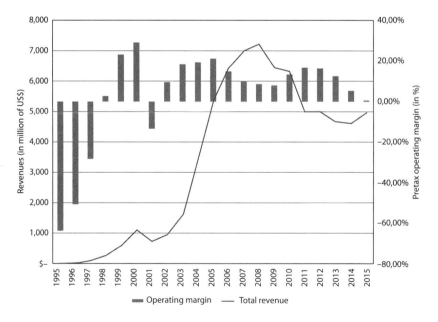

Figure 15.2
Yahoo's operating history.

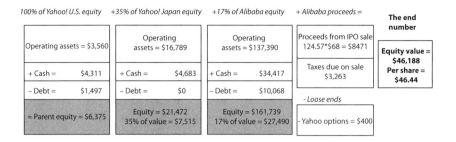

Figure 15.3
The intrinsic value of Yahoo—a sum of the parts.

Not only had Yahoo decisively and permanently lost the search engine fight to Google, but it was a company in search of a mission, with no clear sense of where its future lay.

Ironically, the two best investments that Yahoo made during the years immediately leading up to 2012 were not in its own operations but in other companies, an early one in Yahoo Japan, which prospered even as its U.S. counterpart stumbled, and the other in Alibaba in 2005, a prescient bet on a then-private company. In earlier parts of the book, I argued that Alibaba was a legitimate symbol of the China story and valued it at almost $161 billion, just before its IPO. At the time of that IPO in September 2014, I valued Yahoo as a company, first by breaking it into its parts (its operations, Yahoo Japan, and Alibaba). Figure 15.3 provides a breakdown of my estimates of intrinsic value for each of the three pieces. Note that of my total estimated value of $46.2 billion for the equity in the company in September 2014, less than 10 percent (about $3.6 billion) comes from Yahoo's operating assets.

The challenge that Mayer took on was to turn around not only a company that had lost its way in terms of its core business, but one that derived most of its value from holdings in two companies over which she had no control. Her history of success at Google and the fact that she was young, attractive, and female, all played a role in some choosing her as the anointed one, the savior of Yahoo. The odds of Mayer succeeding at Yahoo, at least in the ways that many of her strongest supporters defined success, were low right from the beginning, for two reasons:

1.   It is hard enough to turn a company around, but it becomes even harder when you are given control of only the rump of the company. The reality is that on any given day, the value of Yahoo as a company was more influenced by what Jack Ma did that day at Alibaba than what Marissa Mayer did at Yahoo.

2. In chapter 14 I argued that tech companies face compressed life cycles, growing faster than non-tech companies but also aging much faster, and that a twenty-year-old tech company like Yahoo is closer to being geriatric than middle-aged. I give long odds to any aging technology company that tries to rediscover its youth. Lest I sound fatalistic, it is true that there are counterexamples, aging tech companies that have rediscovered their youth, as evidenced by IBM's rebirth in 1992 and Apple's new start under Steve Jobs. Much as I would like to give Lou Gerstner and Steve Jobs all the credit for pulling off these miraculous feats, I believe that it was a confluence of events (many of them out of the control of either man) that allowed both miracles to happen. The Lou Gerstner turnaround at IBM was aided and abetted by the tech boom in the 1990s, and as for Steve Jobs, the myth of the visionary CEO who could do no wrong has long since overtaken the reality. By promoting both turnarounds as purely CEO triumphs, you set yourself up for the Yahoo scenario, where a new CEO (Marissa Meyer) is assumed to have the power to turn a company around, but we are then disappointed in her failure to do so. I was less disappointed in Mayer than were many others, since my expectations on what she could do at Yahoo were much lower right from the start.

In December 2015 Yahoo's problems bubbled up to the surface as the board considered whether to sell its Internet business, leaving it effectively as a holding company, with Yahoo Japan and Alibaba as its investments. When the board delayed its decision, Starboard Value, an activist investor, pushed for more urgency and a plan for liquidation of the company. The corporate life cycle, in a sense, had caught up with both Yahoo and Marissa Mayer.

Conclusion

What are the qualities that make for a good top manager? The answer depends on where a company is in its life cycle. Early in a company's life, you want a visionary top manager, adept at packaging and telling a compelling story. As the company grows, the skill set you look for will shift to include more business-building skills, and those will be displaced by more administrative capabilities with mature companies. Finally, in decline, you want a realist running the business, someone who has no qualms about shrinking its size. Given these shifting demands, it is not surprising that as companies transition from one phase of the life cycle to the next, the chances of a managerial mismatch also go up, creating the potential for conflict and change.

16

The Endgame

I started this book with the argument that stories without numbers are just fairy tales and numbers without stories to back them up are exercises in financial modeling. In the intervening chapters, I hope that I have filled in the gap between the storytellers and number crunchers and perhaps offered each side a guide on how to build a bridge to the other side. Along the way, I hope (though I may not always have succeeded) that I kept the conversation going with investors, managers, entrepreneurs, and even interested onlookers.

Storytellers and Number Crunchers

At the very beginning, I made a confession that I was more of a number cruncher at heart and that storytelling was hard for me, at least when I started. The good news that I have for those of you who are number crunchers is not only that it gets easier but that it even gets to be fun. I find myself looking at everything from news stories to duty-free magazines on planes in an entirely new light, as I have discovered how quickly a corporate story can be changed by small revelations.

If you are a storyteller, I know that parts of this book may have been tough sledding for you, and I apologize. I continue to believe that anyone can value companies and that the accounting and mathematical skills you need for valuation are basic. That may reflect my biases, but if you were able to get even a small measure of the steps of getting from stories to numbers in chapters 8, 9, and 10, I will consider my mission accomplished. In fact, I would be delighted if you feel empowered enough to challenge a banker or an analyst on a valuation and confident enough to stand your ground.

Finally, I hope that there will be more forums in the future where storytellers and number crunchers get to interact. I know that each side speaks its own language and is often convinced of its own rightness, but there is much that we can learn from each other, as long as we are willing to listen to those who think differently.

Lessons for Investors

If you are an investor reading this book, you are probably disappointed if you were expecting to find a magic bullet or a formula that will help you find stock market winners. In fact, my message is that rigid rules that claim to find market winners may work in a very small subset of mature businesses but not in the larger marketplace. As I see it, the future of investing belongs to those who are flexible in their thinking and capable of moving easily from one segment of the market to another.

One of the first books that I read on valuation was Ben Graham's *Security Analysis*, a bible for many value investors. Unlike some of those investors, I have learned to take what I want from the book and leave the rest behind, because it reflects the time when it was written and the audience for whom it was written. I don't find much use for Graham's screens and formulas, but I find great value in his philosophy, which is that your investments should be based on your judgments of the value of a business rather than driven by the perceptions of others or by investor mood. If I apply Graham's tools to assess growth companies or start-ups, I will always find them wanting, but applying his philosophy allows me to keep the door open to the possibility that they can be good investments.

Through much of this book, I have danced around the difference between value and price, but I think it is a choice as to which you base your decisions on and that you and I have to make that choice sooner rather than later. I believe in value, and I have faith that price will eventually move to value, and my investing reflects that faith. I am willing to buy any business, young or old, if I can get it at a price that is less than value, but I also realize that my faith will not only be tested by the market but that there is no guarantee of rewards for being right on value.

Finally, uncertainty about the future has been part of every story that I have told in this book, and it will continue to be a part of every investing story that I will tell in the future. One by-product of my increased willingness to tell stories is that I have not only become more comfortable with being uncertain but that I am more accepting of disagreement, that is, I recognize that others may have different stories to tell about a company I have valued. Storytelling has also made me more serene about being wrong, especially when my story has a substantial macro component, as was the case with my investment in Vale in 2013 and 2014.

Lessons for Entrepreneurs, Business Owners, and Managers

If you are the founder of a business or a business owner, I hope that the lesson you take away from this book is not that it is all about storytelling. Don't get me wrong! The story you tell about your business is critical and has to be credible, not only to attract investors, employees, and customers but also for your business to have staying power and succeed. Harking back to chapter 7, and my suggestion that stories be tested on whether they are possible, plausible, or probable, it is important that you not only reality-test your story but that you adjust the story to reflect the shifting facts on the ground. No story is forever and no valuation is timeless!

I also noted the trade-offs for founders in going for soaring stories in which the sky is the limit and more restrained stories in chapter 15. Tempting though it is to go for the former, as you seek out investors and capital, you are also more likely to find yourself stretched for resources and punished for disappointing results. Thus, if your desire is to build a viable business for the long term, choosing the less ambitious story line upfront may be the better option.

Finally, if you are a top manager at a business, it is your job to frame the narrative for that business rather than have it framed for you by investors, equity research analysts, or journalists. That narrative will be more likely to hold up if it aligns with where your business is in the life cycle and if you can deliver results that back it up. Your greatest personal peril is at transition points in the corporate life cycle, where unless you adapt, you will be challenged and perhaps displaced.

Conclusion

I have enjoyed writing this book immensely, and I hope that my joy shows through, at least in some places. If you have enjoyed reading the book, I consider it a success, but I will be even happier if you take a look at the biggest investment in your portfolio tomorrow and not only think about the story that led you to make the investment but convert that story into numbers and value.

NOTES

1. A Tale of Two Tribes

1. Michael Lewis, *Moneyball: The Art of Winning an Unfair Game* (New York: Norton, 2004).

2. Tell Me a Story

1. Paul Zak, "Why Your Brain Loves Good Storytelling," *Harvard Business Review*, October 28, 2014.

2. Greg Stephens, Lauren Silbert, and Uri Hasson, "Speaker-Listener Neuro Coupling Underlies Successful Communication," *Proceedings of the National Academy of Scientists USA* 107, no. 32 (2010): 14425–14430.

3. Peter Guber, *Tell to Win* (New York: Crown Business, 2011).

4. Melanie Green and Tim Brock, *Persuasion: Psychological Insights and Perspectives*, 2nd ed. (Thousand Oaks, Calif.: Sage, 2005).

5. Arthur C. Graesser, Murray Singer, and Tom Trabasso, "Constructing Inferences During Narrative Text Comprehension," *Psychological Review* 101 (1994): 371–395.

6. D. M. Wegner and A. F. Ward, "The Internet Has Become the External Hard Drive for Our Memories," *Scientific American* 309, no. 6 (2013), 58–61.

7. John Huth, "Losing Our Way in the World," *New York Times*, July 20, 2013.

8. Daniel Kahnemann, *Thinking, Fast and Slow* (New York: Farrar, Straus and Giroux, 2011).

9. Tyler Cowen, "Be Suspicious of Stories," TEDxMidAtlantic, 16:32, November 2009, www.ted.com/talks/tyler_cowen_be_suspicious_of_stories.

10. Jonathan Gotschall, "Why Storytelling Is the Ultimate Weapon," Fast Company, 2012. http://www.fastcocreate.com/1680581/why-storytelling-is-the-ultimate-weapon.

11. J. Shaw and S. Porter, "Constructing Rich False Memories of Committing Crime," *Psychological Science* 26 (March 2015): 291–301.

12. Elizabeth F. Loftus and Jacqueline E. Pickrell, "The Formation of False Memories," *Psychiatric Annals* 25, no. 12 (December 1995): 720–725.

13. Charles Mackay, *Extraordinary Delusions and the Madness of Crowds* (reprint edition; CreateSpace October 22, 2013).

14. John Carreyrou, "Hot Startup Theranos Has Struggled with Its Blood-Test Technology," *Wall Street Journal*, October 16, 2015, www.wsj.com/articles/theranos-has-struggled-with-blood-tests-1444881901.

15. Caitlin Roper, "This Woman Invented a Way to Run 30 Lab Tests on Only One Drop of Blood," *Wired*, February 18, 2014, www.wired.com/2014/02/elizabeth-holmes-theranos.

3. The Elements of Storytelling

1. Aristotle's *Poetics* is the earliest surviving work of dramatic theory and dates back to before 300 B.C.E.

2. Freytag explained his dramatic structure in *Die Technik des Dramas* (Leipzig: S. Herzel, 1863). That structure was renamed "Freytag's pyramid."

3. Joseph Campbell, *The Hero with a Thousand Faces* (Novato, Calif.: New World Library, 1949).

4. The original version of the story has seventeen phases to it. The simplified version, which was created by Christopher Vogler for Disney Studios, has only twelve, but the core of the story is retained.

5. C. Booker, *The Seven Basic Plots: Why We Tell Stories* (London: Bloomsbury Academic, 2006).

4. The Power of Numbers

1. Michael Lewis, *Moneyball: The Art of Winning an Unfair Game* (New York: Norton, 2004).

2. Ibid., xiv.

3. I am using two standard errors to get an interval that I feel confident captures the outcome 95 percent of the time. With a 67 percent confidence interval, the

mistake could be 2.30 percent in either direction, yielding a range of 3.88 percent to 8.48 percent.

5. Number-Crunching Tools

1. See Nassim Taleb's work, either in his books and articles or on his website, fooledbyrandomness.com, for his trenchant critique of the use and abuse of the normal distribution in financial modeling.

6. Building a Narrative

1. Sergio Marchionne's presentation can be found at www.autonews.com/Assets /pdf/presentations/SM_Fire_investor_presentation.pdf.
2. Aswath Damodaran, *The Dark Side of Valuation* (Upper Saddle River, N.J.: Prentice Hall/FT Press, 2009).

7. Test-Driving a Narrative

1. Benjamin Graham and David L. Dodd, *Security Analysis*, 6th edition (New York: McGraw-Hill, 2009).

10. Improving and Modifying Your Narrative—The Feedback Loop

1. Bill Gurley, "How to Miss By a Mile: An Alternative Look at Uber's Potential Market Size," *Above the Crowd* (blog), July 11, 2014, http://abovethecrowd.com/2014/07/11 /how-to-miss-by-a-mile-an-alternative-look-at-ubers-potential-market-size.
2. Daniel Kahneman, *Thinking, Fast and Slow* (New York: Farrar, Straus and Giroux, 2011).

13. Go Big—The Macro Story

1. I used thirty years of historical data on oil prices, adjusted for inflation, to create an empirical distribution. I then chose the statistical distribution that seemed to provide the closest fit (lognormal) and parameter values that yielded numbers closest to the historical data.

15. The Managerial Challenge

1. You can read Bezos's 1997 letter to Amazon shareholders on the SEC website at: www.sec.gov/Archives/edgar/data/1018724/000119312513151836/d511111dex991.htm. After almost two decades, the Amazon story remains almost unchanged at its core.

2. Noam Wasserman, "The Founder's Dilemma," *Harvard Business Review* 86, no. 2 (February 2008): 102–109.

3. Kleiner, Perkins, Caufield & Byers looked at 895 young companies that had IPOs or were acquired between 1994 and 2014 and classified them based on whether one of the founders was a CEO at the time of the exit or not.

INDEX

Churchill, Winston, 259
Coats, Emma, 35
Coca-Cola, 234
commodity price, 205–6, 213–14, 215;
    declines, 221, 224; operating results
    link to, 212
company history, 71, 72
competition, 73
competitive advantages, 174
competitive analysis, *74*
competitive landscape, 74
composite story, 208
Confessions of a Capital Junkie
    (Marchionne), 75
con game storytelling with a subversive
    edge case study, 20–21
connections story, 29
consistent narrative, 251
constant change, 7–8
consumption inertia, 230
continuum of skepticism, *95*
control illusion, 46–47
corporate finance, equity risk premium
    input, 42
corporate governance, 259
corporate governance stories, 200–204
corporate life cycle, *8,* 8–9, 266; aging of a
    business, 228–31; business idea, begins
    with, 228; determinants for, 229–331,
    230; drivers for, *230, 232*–33; growth
    phase of, 230; for management culture,
    249; narrative and numbers across,
    231–46, *246*; for non-tech and tech
    companies, *231*; number crunching
    in, 227; problems, 233; start-up phase
    of, 232; stories of, *9,* 233; storytelling
    in, 227; for tech companies, *231*;
    transitions of, 229, 256; Yahoo, 261
corporate new stories, 191; AB InBev, and
    SABMiller consolidation story case
    study, 193–96, *194, 195, 196*; investment
    news, 191–93, *192, 193*
corporate scandal and misconduct:
    of American Express, 15; stories

damaged by, 200; Valeant drug
    business model case study, 201–3, *202*;
    Volkswagen, 75, 200–201
corporate story. *See* business narrative
corporate story, micro and macro factors,
    222
correlation coefficient, 58
cost structure, 75, 82; ride-sharing, 175–76
counternarrative, 151; Alibaba, 146;
    Amazon, *119, 142*; against Gurley
    Uber narrative, 163; Uber, 162;
    uncertainty with, 161. *See also*
    alternative narrative
country risk, 214–16; Brazilian, 218; Vale,
    217–21, *218, 220,* 223, *224*
covariance, 58
Cowen, Tyler, 18
credit default swap (CDS), 215, 223
Crocs, 258
cross holdings, 132–33
crowdvaluing, 161
currency invariance, 134
cycle forecasting, 216

damage control, 200
Damodaran narrative *versus* Gurley
    narrative, *165*
dangers of numbers, 40; fall of
    quant investing case study, 50–51;
    illusion of control, 46–47; illusion
    of objectivity, 44–45; illusion of
    precision, *41,* 41–42, *42*; intimidation
    factor, 48; intimidation problem,
    48–49; lemming problem, 49; noisy
    historical equity risk premium case
    study, 42–44, *43, 44*; numbers and
    bias with equity risk premium case
    study, 45; sad (but true) story of
    long-term capital management case
    study, 47; storytelling as antidote,
    49–51
dangers of storytelling, 17; con game
    storytelling with a subversive
    edge case study, 20–21; emotional

qualitative factors: number cruncher
problems with, 123; quantitative
factors connection with, 124;
storyteller problems with, 123; value
affected by, 123
qualitative meets quantitative, 123–24
qualitative news, 168
quant hedge fund, 49
quant investing: case study, 39–40; fall of,
case study, 50–51
quantitative factors, 124
quantitative news, 168
quants, 4, 9; investor importance of,
37; power of, 39; strategy biases
in, 50–51; strategy storytelling
connection with, 51

R&D. See research and development
reference tables, 62
regression: advantage of, 60; of
ExxonMobil, 67, 212
regulatory commission, 46
reinvestment rate, 130
religion, 11
research and development (R&D), 65;
revenue growth in, 66
restricted shares, 133
return on invested capital, and cost of
capital, 78
revenue: of JCPenney, 238, 240; for online
advertising, 106
revenue, operating income and price
reaction, 181
revenue growth: of Alibaba, 120; for
Amazon, 144; auto companies of, 76
rev it up strategy, 107; for Ferrari, 117,
139–41; plausibility of, 117
ride-sharing companies: competition
for, 175; cost structure of, 175;
landscape case study, 79–80; Uber,
79; Uber versus Lyft case study,
251–56
risk value of money, 136
runaway story, 20

SABMiller, 193, 195
sad (but true) story of long-term capital
management case study, 47
scaling up, 229
scenario analysis: for Alibaba, 155; for
uncertainty, 153
Scholes, Myron, 47
scientific method, 38
Sears, 238
Security Analysis (Graham), 264
selection bias, 55
sensitivity analysis, 46
share expectations, 187
show, don't tell, 33
Silbert, Lauren, 12
Silver, Nate, 38
simple regression, 59
simple test, 1–2
simulations: for Alibaba, 156; for
ExxonMobil, 212; for investors, 213;
mean in, 157; median in, 157; for
uncertainty, 154
skewness, 57
small narratives, 252, 256
S&P. See Standard and Poor's
speculators, 126
Standard and Poor's (S&P), 55;
bond ratings for U.S. companies
by, 58
standard deviation, 57
standard error, 41
start-up phase, 232
statistics: estimation process of, 41;
importance of, 4, 57; mean in, 57;
median in, 57; mode in, 57; standard
deviation in, 57; standard error
in, 41
status quo, 174, 176
Stephens, Greg, 12
steps for storytellers, 32–34
Steve Jobs master storyteller case study,
15–16
Stewart, Martha, 30
stock-based compensation, 133

valuation (*continued*)
of, 149, *150*; divergences in,
157; equity risk premium input
of, 42; expectations of, 159; of
ExxonMobil, 67, 210; for Facebook,
191; fears about, 243; feedback loop
transparent for, 160; of Ferrari, 75;
for GoPro, 234; information of, 135;
of JCPenney, 238–40; lessons for,
243; macro factors driven of, 221;
of macro-neutral, 208; net debt in,
131–32; numbers bridge as, 5; of
plausibility, 93; of possibility, 93;
pretax operating margin of, 112;
pricing difference of, 124; pricing
divergence of, 158; of probability,
93; process for, 131; refinements
of, 134–35; sensitivity analysis
addendum for, 46; steps in, *129*;
stock-based compensation in, 133;
into stories, 149; stories bridge as, 5;
of Uber, 84–85, 179; uncertainty in,
153; U.S. tax codes in, 132; of Vale,
220; valuation inputs for, 128; of
Volkswagen, 75; with subsidiaries,
134; for young companies, 234
valuation as a bridge, *5, 5–7, 6*
valuation inputs, 127; for Amazon, *142*;
connecting stories to, *113*; of Ferrari,
116, 139; Field of Dreams story line
as, *118*; interconnectedness of, 129;
narrative changes relate to, 173–74; for
Uber, 114, 137; for valuation, 128
valuation simulations: of Alibaba, *156*; for
GoPro, *237*

value: assessment of, 6; breaking down
of, 110–12, 149; DCF use in, 125;
deconstruction of, *150*; drivers of, 110,
128; estimation of, 125, 212; growth of,
111; inputs of, 6; qualitative factors of,
123; synergy of, *195*
value at risk (VAR), 46–47, 48
value investing, 40, 95
value investors, 126
VAR. *See* value at risk
venture capitalists (VC): against DCF, 135;
entrepreneur connection with, 100;
overconfidence of, 100
venture capital valuation, *126*
volatile stock returns, *43*
Volkswagen, 75; corporate scandal of,
200–201

Wasserman, Noam, 257
Wosniak, Steve, 27

Xbox, 236

Yahoo: case study challenges of managing
aging company, and Marissa Mayer,
260, 260–62, *261*; intrinsic value of, *261*;
management culture of, 260; operating
history of, *260*; transitions for, 261
young companies: analysis of, 73;
assessment of, 73; business narrative
for, 72; failure risk of, 112; valuation
for, 234

Zak, Paul, 12, 14
Zuckerberg, Mark, 259